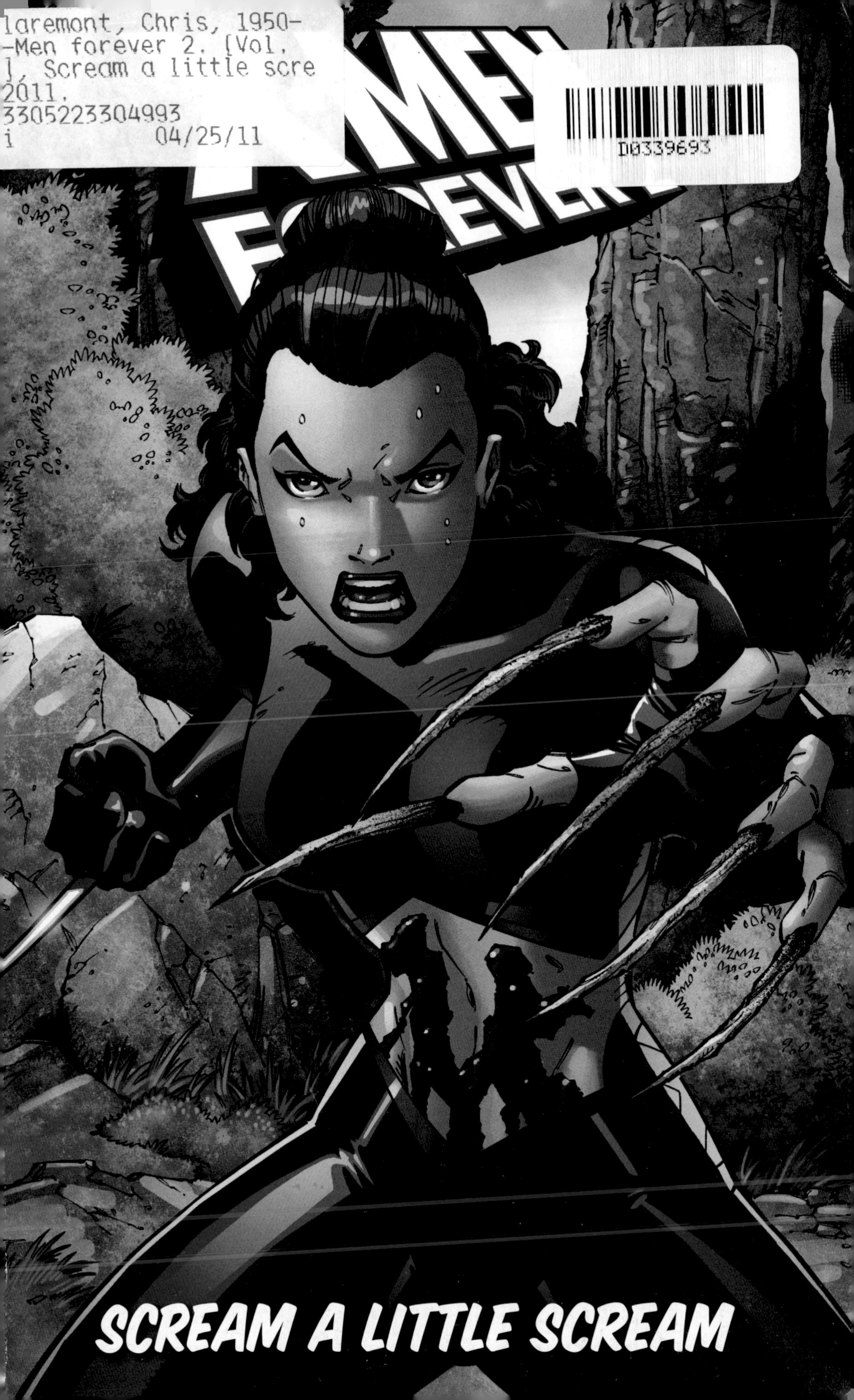

SCREAM A LITTLE SCREAM

X-MEN FOREVER

Writer
CHRIS CLAREMONT

Pencilers
TOM GRUMMETT (ISSUE #6),
RON LIM (ISSUES #7-8)
& MIKE GRELL (ISSUES #9-10)

Inkers
**CORY HAMSCHER (ISSUES #6-8)
& NELSON (ISSUES #9-10)
WITH ANDREW HENNESSY (ISSUES #6 & 10)**

Colorists
**WIL QUINTANA (ISSUES #6-8) &
VERONICA GANDINI (ISSUES #9-10)**

Letterers
**DAVE SHARPE (ISSUE #6) &
TOM ORZECHOWSKI (ISSUES #7-10)**

Cover Art
**TOM GRUMMETT, CORY HAMSCHER,
WIL QUINTANA & VERONICA GANDINI**

Assistant Editor
JOHN DENNING

Editor
MICHAEL HORWITZ

Consulting Editor
MARC SUMERAK

Senior Editor
MARK PANICCIA

Collection Editor: **JENNIFER GRÜNWALD** • Editorial Assistants: **JAMES EMMETT & JOE HOCHSTEIN**
Assistant Editors: **ALEX STARBUCK & NELSON RIBEIRO**
Editor, Special Projects: **MARK D. BEAZLEY** • Senior Editor, Special Projects: **JEFF YOUNGQUIST**
Senior Vice President of Sales: **DAVID GABRIEL**

Editor in Chief: **AXEL ALONSO** • Chief Creative Officer: **JOE QUESADA**
Publisher: **DAN BUCKLEY** • Executive Producer: **ALAN FINE**

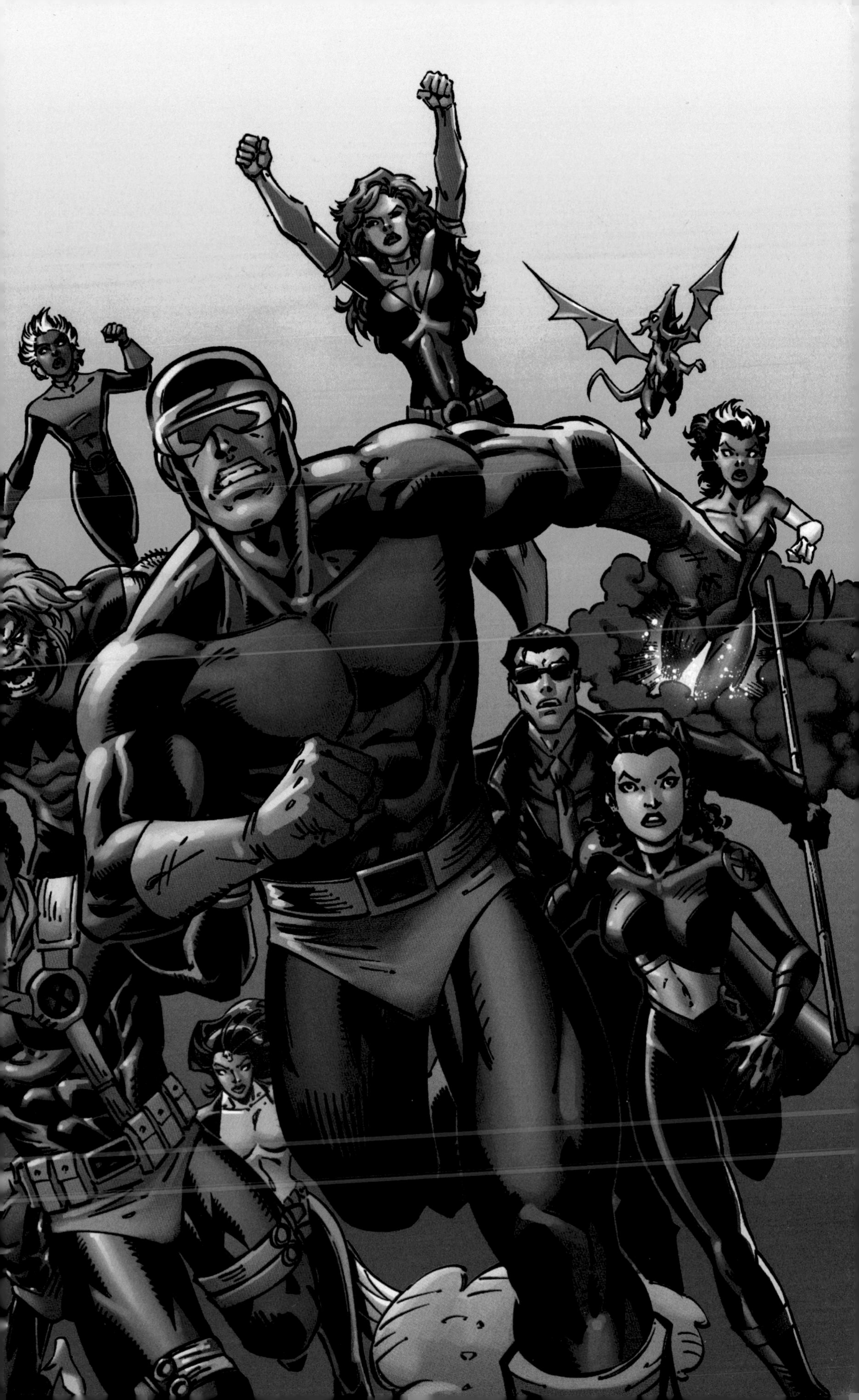

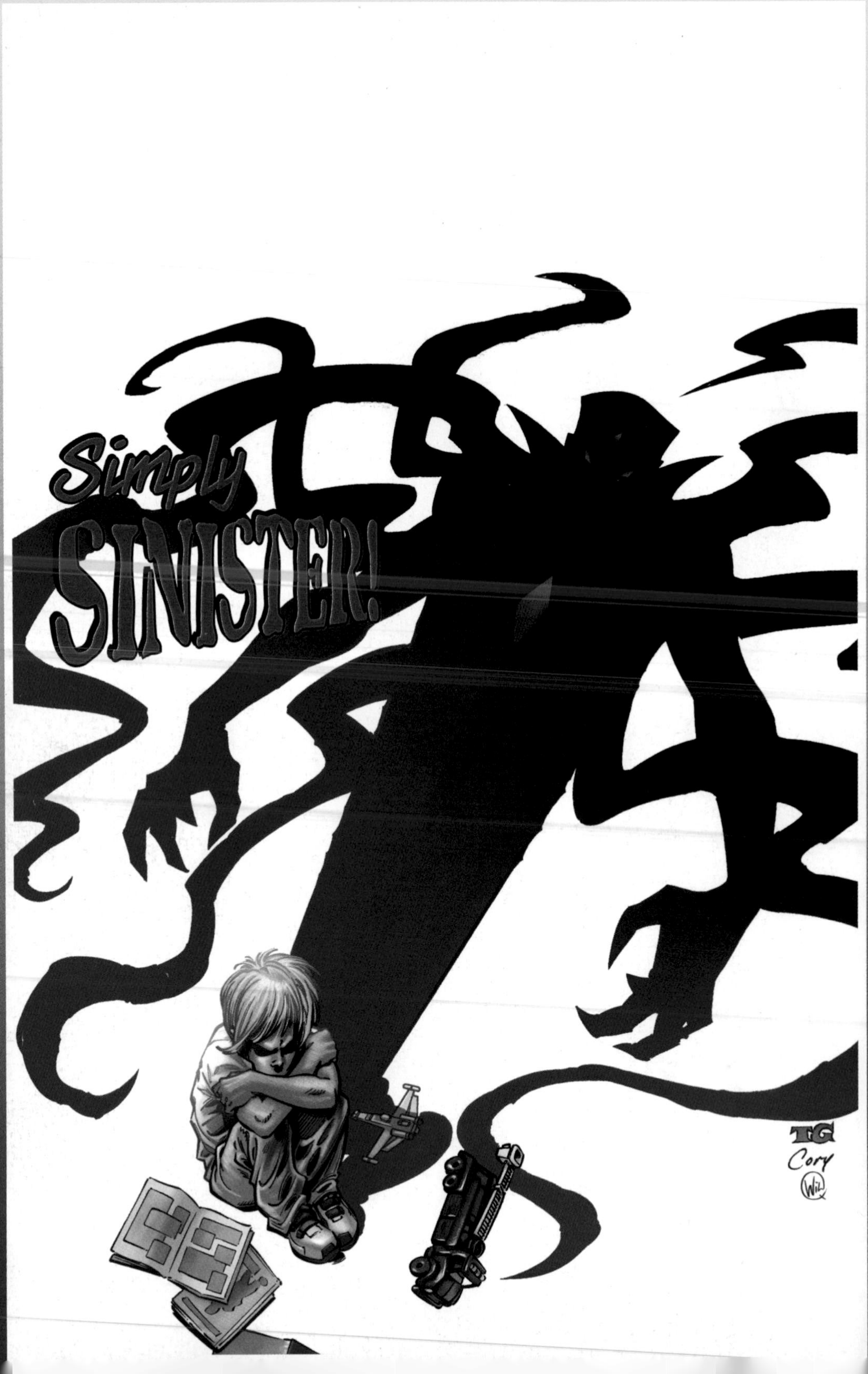
Simply
SINISTER!
TG
Cory
Wil

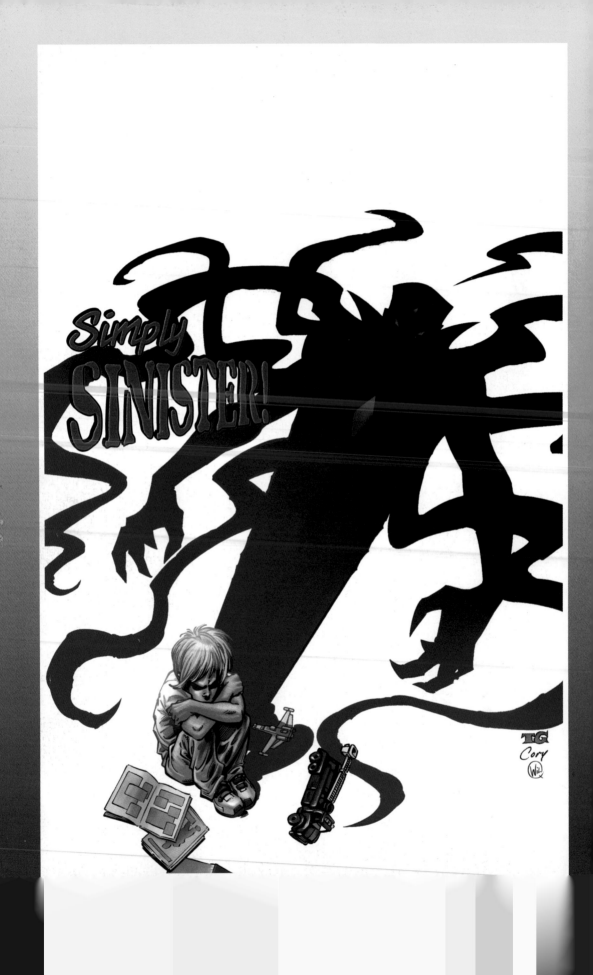

*Comics legend Chris Claremont had an epic 16-year run on **X-MEN**, which concluded with **X-MEN: MUTANT GENESIS** #1-3 in 1991. Now, in an unprecedented comics event, Claremont returns to his iconic run on the **X-MEN**.*

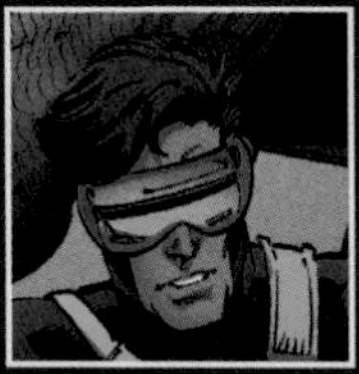

CYCLOPS
Scott Summers

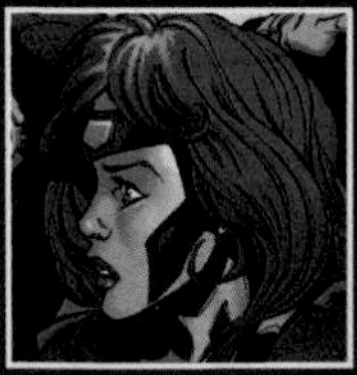

JEAN GREY

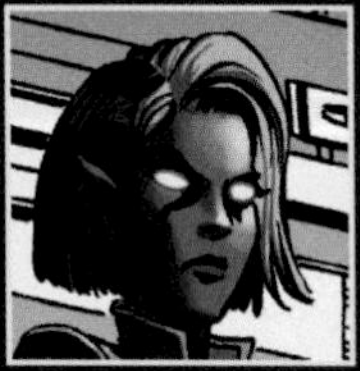

ROGUE
Anna Marie Raven

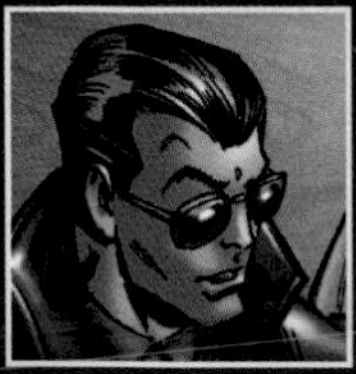

GAMBIT
Remy Picard

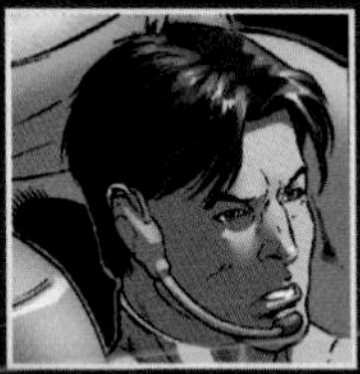

NIGHTCRAWLER
Kurt Wagner

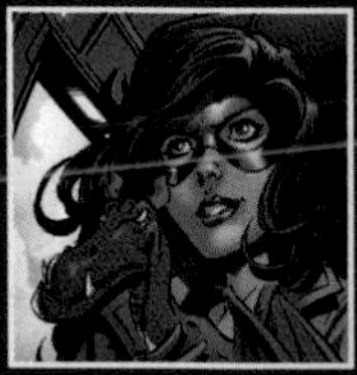

SHADOWCAT
Kitty Pryde

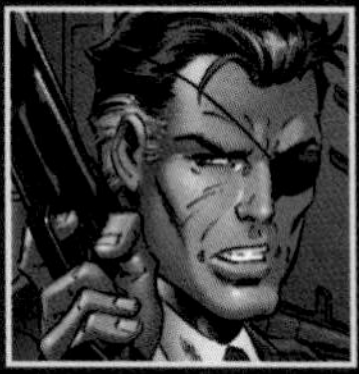

NICK FURY
Director of S.H.I.E.L.D.

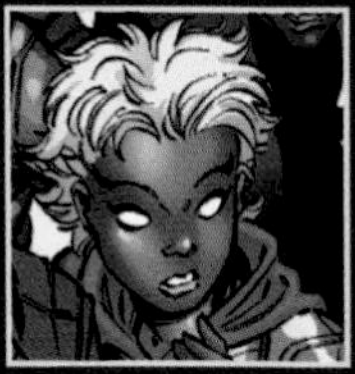

LIL' 'RO
Ororo Munroe?

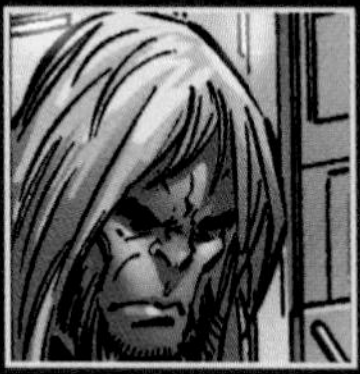

SABRETOOTH
'Nuff Said

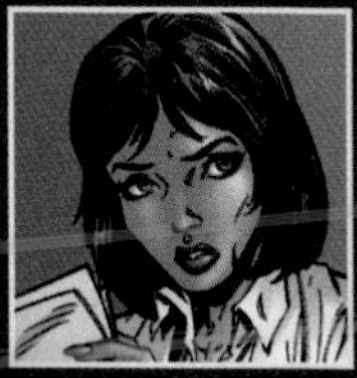

MOIRA MACTAGGERT
Top Geneticist

Previously, in X-MEN FOREVER

The X-Men's desperate efforts to cure Mutant Burnout—a condition that sentences mutants to an early death—put them in the crosshairs of the anti-mutant cabal known as the Consortium. Not only have the X-Men been unable to halt Burnout, but they've suffered heavy casualties at the Consortium's hand, including Wolverine and Beast. It's clear that these are desperate times for the world's most hated heroes…

When the Morlocks kidnapped Moira MacTaggert and Sabretooth, the X-Men delved into the tunnels to recover their teammates. The rescue mission quickly turned into a free-for-all when the government agency S.H.I.E.L.D. arrived on the scene. The X-Men escaped and the Morlocks were taken into custody, but the agents are taken off-guard by former Morlock queen Callisto, who frees her brothers under orders of the mysterious Ghost Panther.

With this minor victory and the new truce between Mystique and her estranged children, Rogue and Nightcrawler, one would assume the X-Men's notorious bad luck has changed. One would be very, very wrong…

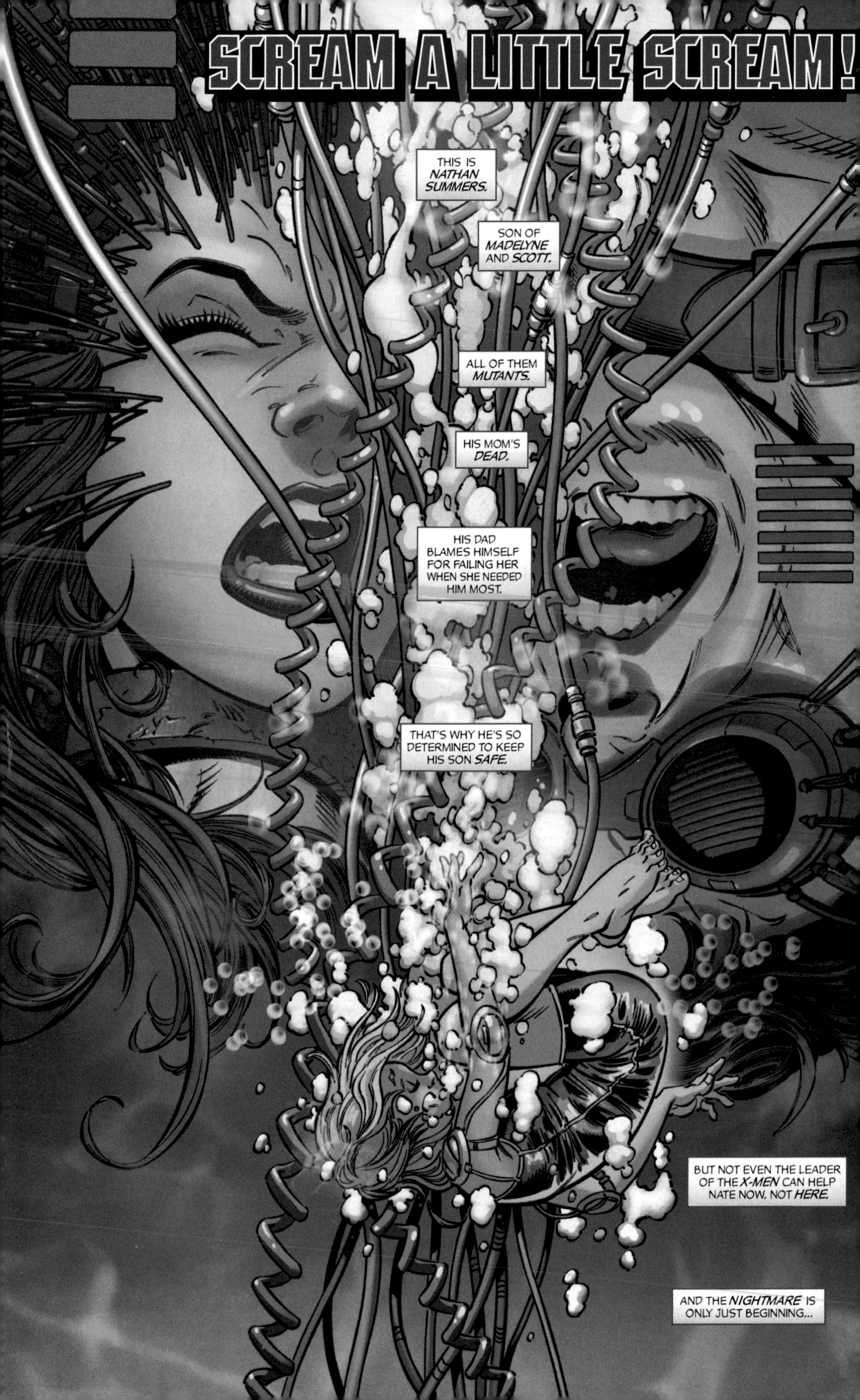
SCREAM A LITTLE SCREAM!
THIS IS NATHAN SUMMERS.
SON OF MADELYNE AND SCOTT.
ALL OF THEM MUTANTS.
HIS MOM'S DEAD.
HIS DAD BLAMES HIMSELF FOR FAILING HER WHEN SHE NEEDED HIM MOST.
THAT'S WHY HE'S SO DETERMINED TO KEEP HIS SON SAFE.
BUT NOT EVEN THE LEADER OF THE X-MEN CAN HELP NATE NOW. NOT HERE.
AND THE NIGHTMARE IS ONLY JUST BEGINNING...

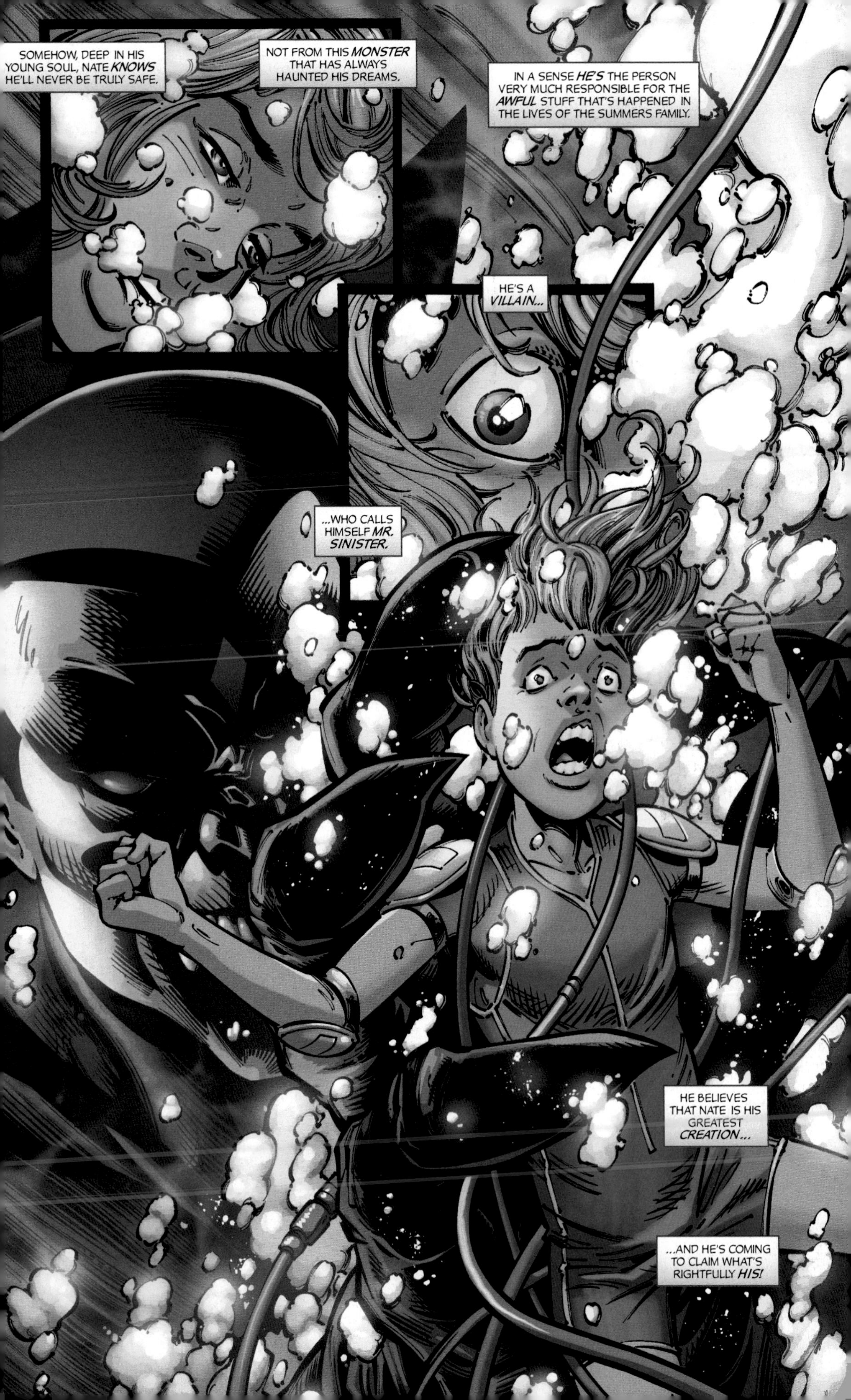
SOMEHOW, DEEP IN HIS YOUNG SOUL, NATE KNOWS HE'LL NEVER BE TRULY SAFE.
NOT FROM THIS MONSTER THAT HAS ALWAYS HAUNTED HIS DREAMS.
IN A SENSE HE'S THE PERSON VERY MUCH RESPONSIBLE FOR THE AWFUL STUFF THAT'S HAPPENED IN THE LIVES OF THE SUMMERS FAMILY.
HE'S A VILLAIN...
...WHO CALLS HIMSELF MR. SINISTER.
HE BELIEVES THAT NATE IS HIS GREATEST CREATION...
...AND HE'S COMING TO CLAIM WHAT'S RIGHTFULLY HIS!

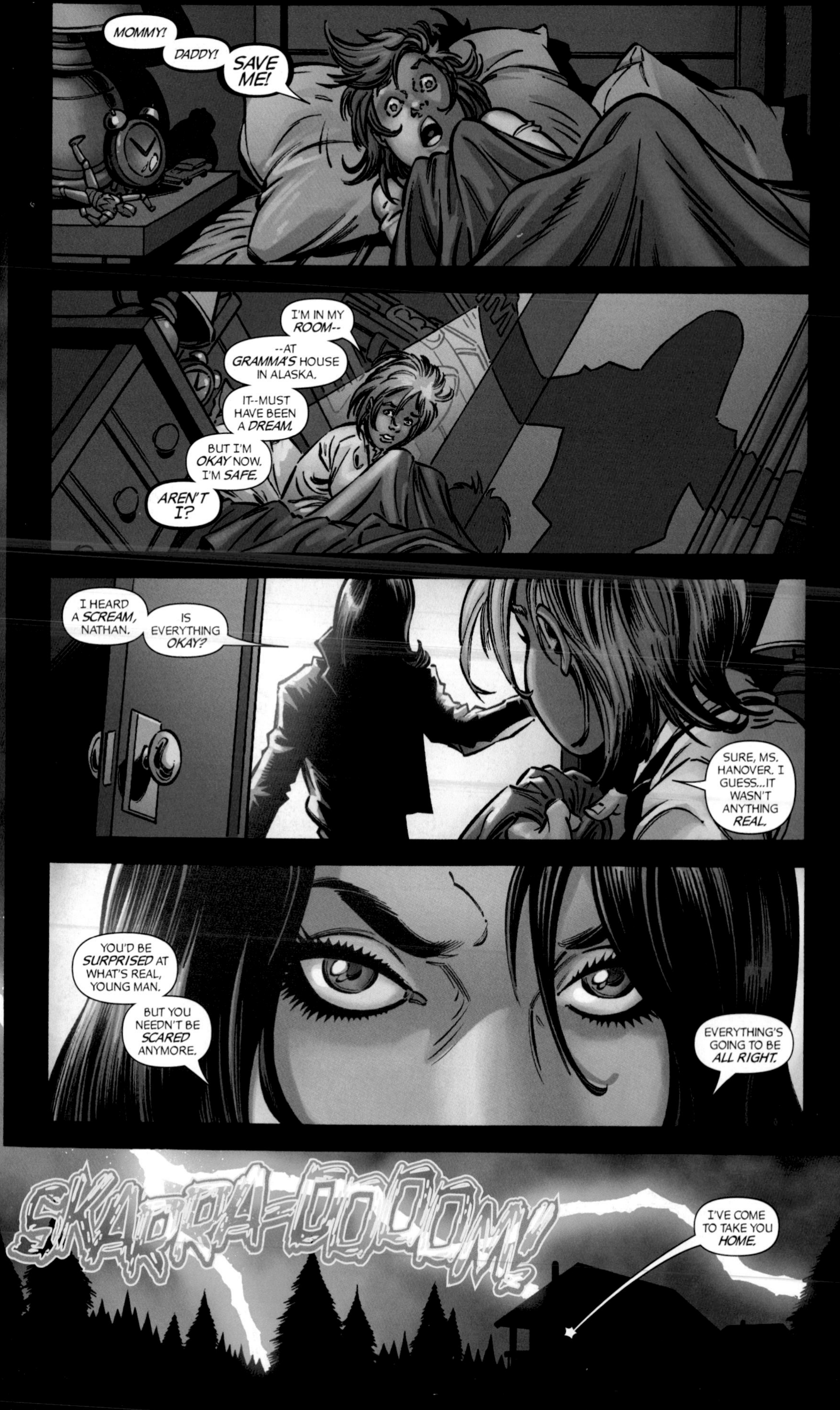
MOMMY!
DADDY!
SAVE ME!
I'M IN MY ROOM--
--AT GRAMMA'S HOUSE IN ALASKA.
IT--MUST HAVE BEEN A DREAM.
BUT I'M OKAY NOW. I'M SAFE.
AREN'T I?
I HEARD A SCREAM, NATHAN.
IS EVERYTHING OKAY?
SURE, MS. HANOVER. I GUESS...IT WASN'T ANYTHING REAL.
YOU'D BE SURPRISED AT WHAT'S REAL, YOUNG MAN.
BUT YOU NEEDN'T BE SCARED ANYMORE.
EVERYTHING'S GOING TO BE ALL RIGHT.
SKABRA-DOOOM!
I'VE COME TO TAKE YOU HOME.

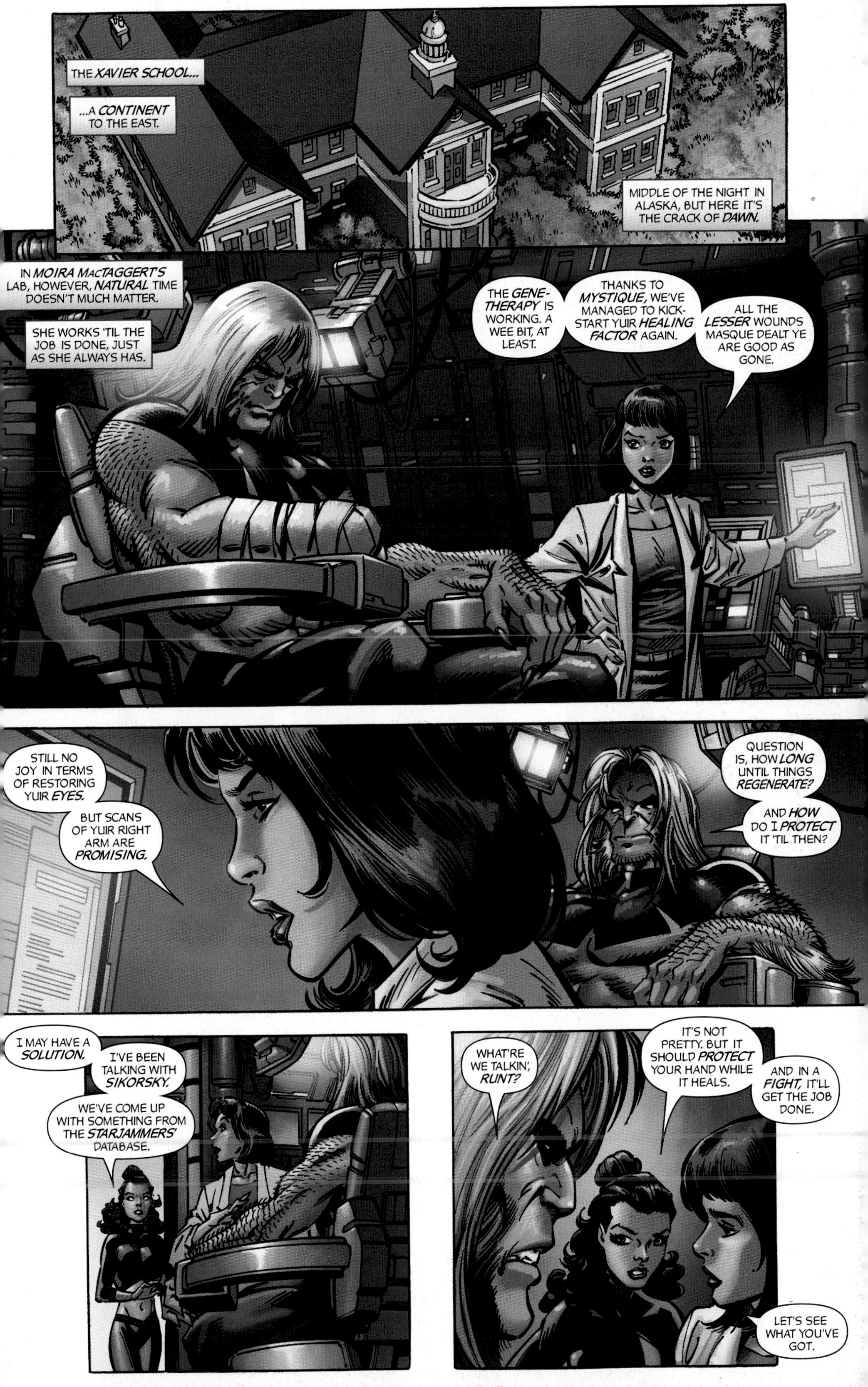
THE XAVIER SCHOOL...
...A CONTINENT TO THE EAST.
MIDDLE OF THE NIGHT IN ALASKA, BUT HERE IT'S THE CRACK OF DAWN.
IN MOIRA MacTAGGERT'S LAB, HOWEVER, NATURAL TIME DOESN'T MUCH MATTER.
SHE WORKS 'TIL THE JOB IS DONE, JUST AS SHE ALWAYS HAS.
THE GENE-THERAPY IS WORKING. A WEE BIT, AT LEAST.
THANKS TO MYSTIQUE, WE'VE MANAGED TO KICK-START YUIR HEALING FACTOR AGAIN.
ALL THE LESSER WOUNDS MASQUE DEALT YE ARE GOOD AS GONE.
STILL NO JOY IN TERMS OF RESTORING YUIR EYES.
BUT SCANS OF YUIR RIGHT ARM ARE PROMISING.
QUESTION IS, HOW LONG UNTIL THINGS REGENERATE?
AND HOW DO I PROTECT IT 'TIL THEN?
I MAY HAVE A SOLUTION.
I'VE BEEN TALKING WITH SIKORSKY.
WE'VE COME UP WITH SOMETHING FROM THE STARJAMMERS' DATABASE.
WHAT'RE WE TALKIN', RUNT?
IT'S NOT PRETTY. BUT IT SHOULD PROTECT YOUR HAND WHILE IT HEALS.
AND IN A FIGHT, IT'LL GET THE JOB DONE.
LET'S SEE WHAT YOU'VE GOT.

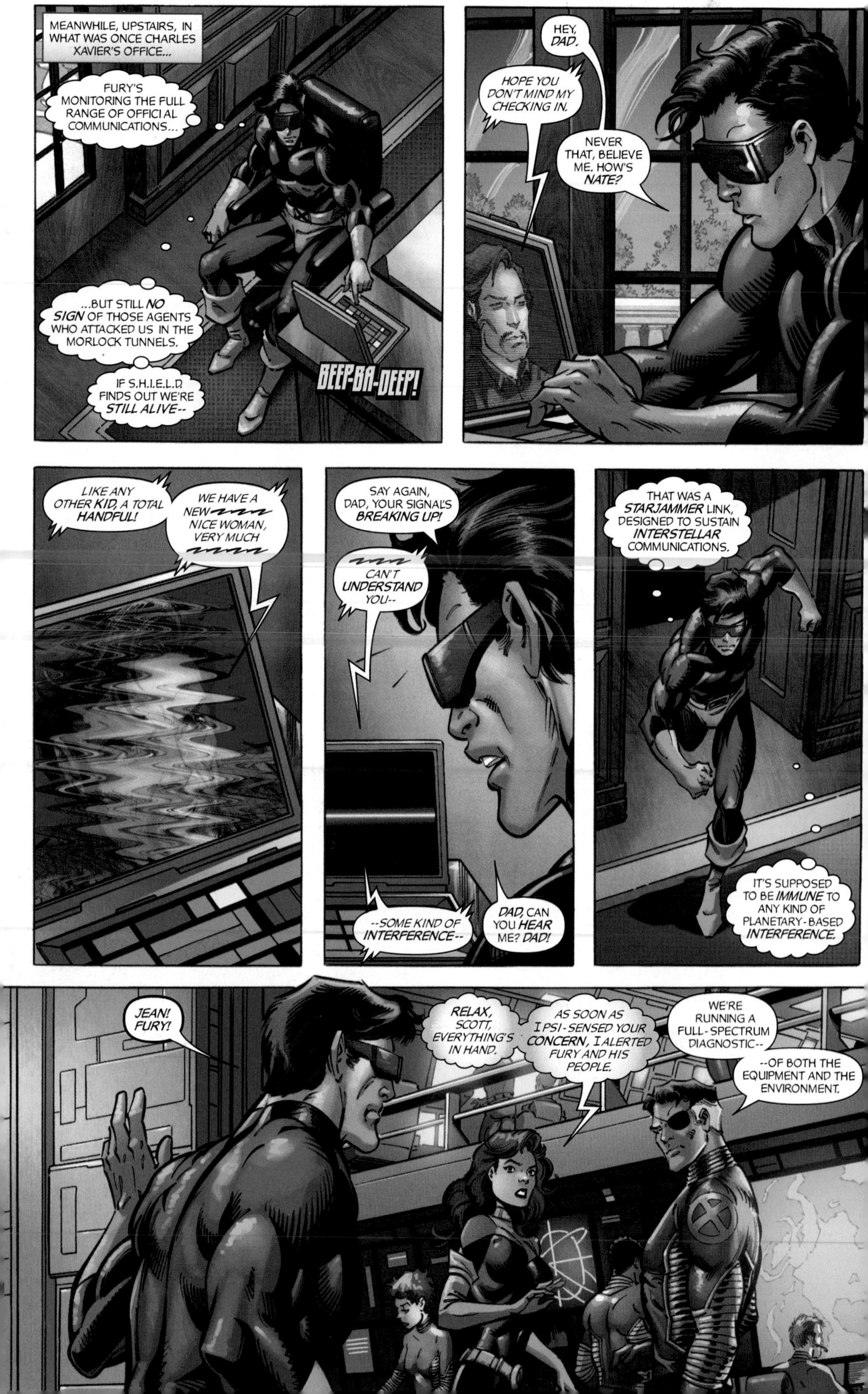

MEANWHILE, UPSTAIRS, IN WHAT WAS ONCE CHARLES XAVIER'S OFFICE...
FURY'S MONITORING THE FULL RANGE OF OFFICIAL COMMUNICATIONS...
...BUT STILL NO SIGN OF THOSE AGENTS WHO ATTACKED US IN THE MORLOCK TUNNELS.
IF S.H.I.E.L.D. FINDS OUT WE'RE STILL ALIVE--
BEEP-BA-DEEP!
HEY, DAD.
HOPE YOU DON'T MIND MY CHECKING IN.
NEVER THAT, BELIEVE ME. HOW'S NATE?
LIKE ANY OTHER KID, A TOTAL HANDFUL!
WE HAVE A NEW NICE WOMAN, VERY MUCH
SAY AGAIN, DAD, YOUR SIGNAL'S BREAKING UP!
CAN'T UNDERSTAND YOU--
--SOME KIND OF INTERFERENCE--
DAD, CAN YOU HEAR ME? DAD!
THAT WAS A STARJAMMER LINK, DESIGNED TO SUSTAIN INTERSTELLAR COMMUNICATIONS.
IT'S SUPPOSED TO BE IMMUNE TO ANY KIND OF PLANETARY-BASED INTERFERENCE.
JEAN! FURY!
RELAX, SCOTT, EVERYTHING'S IN HAND.
AS SOON AS I PSI-SENSED YOUR CONCERN, I ALERTED FURY AND HIS PEOPLE.
WE'RE RUNNING A FULL-SPECTRUM DIAGNOSTIC--
--OF BOTH THE EQUIPMENT AND THE ENVIRONMENT.

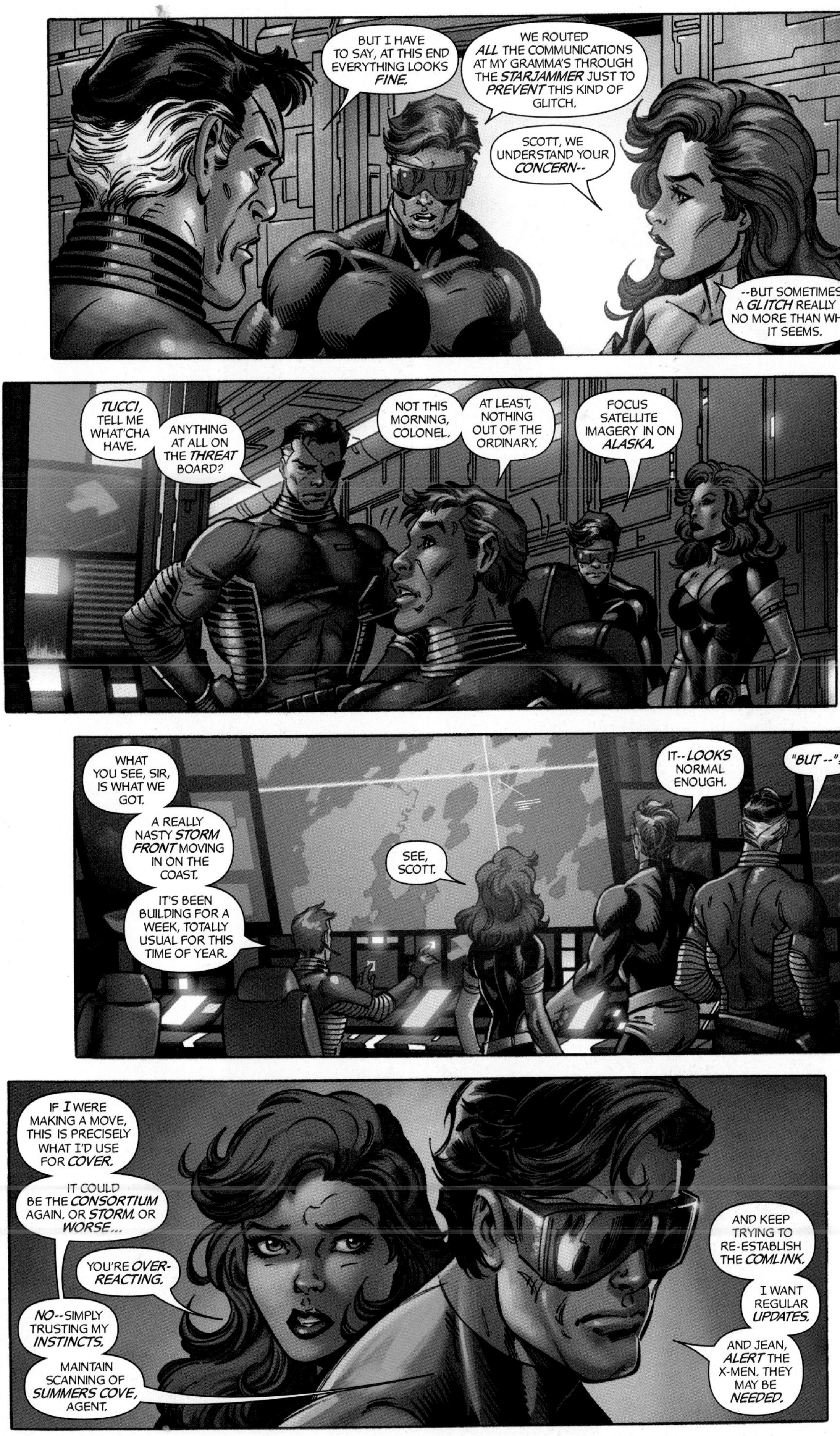
BUT I HAVE TO SAY, AT THIS END EVERYTHING LOOKS FINE.
WE ROUTED ALL THE COMMUNICATIONS AT MY GRAMMA'S THROUGH THE STARJAMMER JUST TO PREVENT THIS KIND OF GLITCH.
SCOTT, WE UNDERSTAND YOUR CONCERN--
--BUT SOMETIMES A GLITCH REALLY IS NO MORE THAN WHAT IT SEEMS.
TUCCI, TELL ME WHAT'CHA HAVE.
ANYTHING AT ALL ON THE THREAT BOARD?
NOT THIS MORNING, COLONEL.
AT LEAST, NOTHING OUT OF THE ORDINARY.
FOCUS SATELLITE IMAGERY IN ON ALASKA.
WHAT YOU SEE, SIR, IS WHAT WE GOT.
A REALLY NASTY STORM FRONT MOVING IN ON THE COAST.
IT'S BEEN BUILDING FOR A WEEK, TOTALLY USUAL FOR THIS TIME OF YEAR.
SEE, SCOTT.
IT--LOOKS NORMAL ENOUGH.
"BUT --"?
IF I WERE MAKING A MOVE, THIS IS PRECISELY WHAT I'D USE FOR COVER.
IT COULD BE THE CONSORTIUM AGAIN, OR STORM, OR WORSE...
YOU'RE OVER-REACTING.
NO--SIMPLY TRUSTING MY INSTINCTS.
MAINTAIN SCANNING OF SUMMERS COVE, AGENT.
AND KEEP TRYING TO RE-ESTABLISH THE COMLINK.
I WANT REGULAR UPDATES.
AND JEAN, ALERT THE X-MEN. THEY MAY BE NEEDED.

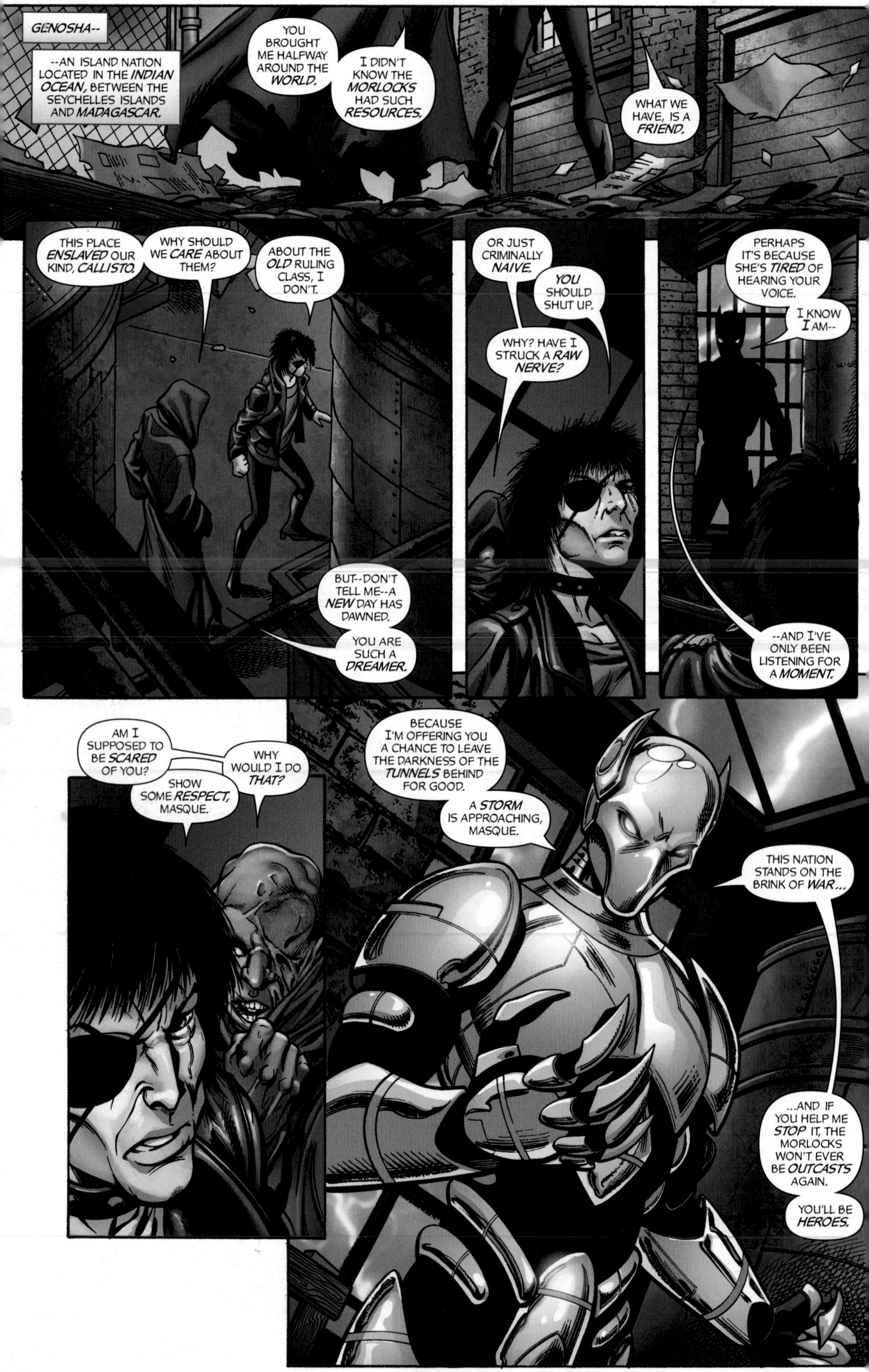
GENOSHA--
--AN ISLAND NATION LOCATED IN THE INDIAN OCEAN, BETWEEN THE SEYCHELLES ISLANDS AND MADAGASCAR.
YOU BROUGHT ME HALFWAY AROUND THE WORLD.
I DIDN'T KNOW THE MORLOCKS HAD SUCH RESOURCES.
WHAT WE HAVE, IS A FRIEND.
THIS PLACE ENSLAVED OUR KIND, CALLISTO.
WHY SHOULD WE CARE ABOUT THEM?
ABOUT THE OLD RULING CLASS, I DON'T.
BUT--DON'T TELL ME--A NEW DAY HAS DAWNED.
YOU ARE SUCH A DREAMER.
OR JUST CRIMINALLY NAIVE.
YOU SHOULD SHUT UP.
WHY? HAVE I STRUCK A RAW NERVE?
PERHAPS IT'S BECAUSE SHE'S TIRED OF HEARING YOUR VOICE.
I KNOW I AM--
--AND I'VE ONLY BEEN LISTENING FOR A MOMENT.
AM I SUPPOSED TO BE SCARED OF YOU?
WHY WOULD I DO THAT?
SHOW SOME RESPECT, MASQUE.
BECAUSE I'M OFFERING YOU A CHANCE TO LEAVE THE DARKNESS OF THE TUNNELS BEHIND FOR GOOD.
A STORM IS APPROACHING, MASQUE.
THIS NATION STANDS ON THE BRINK OF WAR...
...AND IF YOU HELP ME STOP IT, THE MORLOCKS WON'T EVER BE OUTCASTS AGAIN.
YOU'LL BE HEROES.

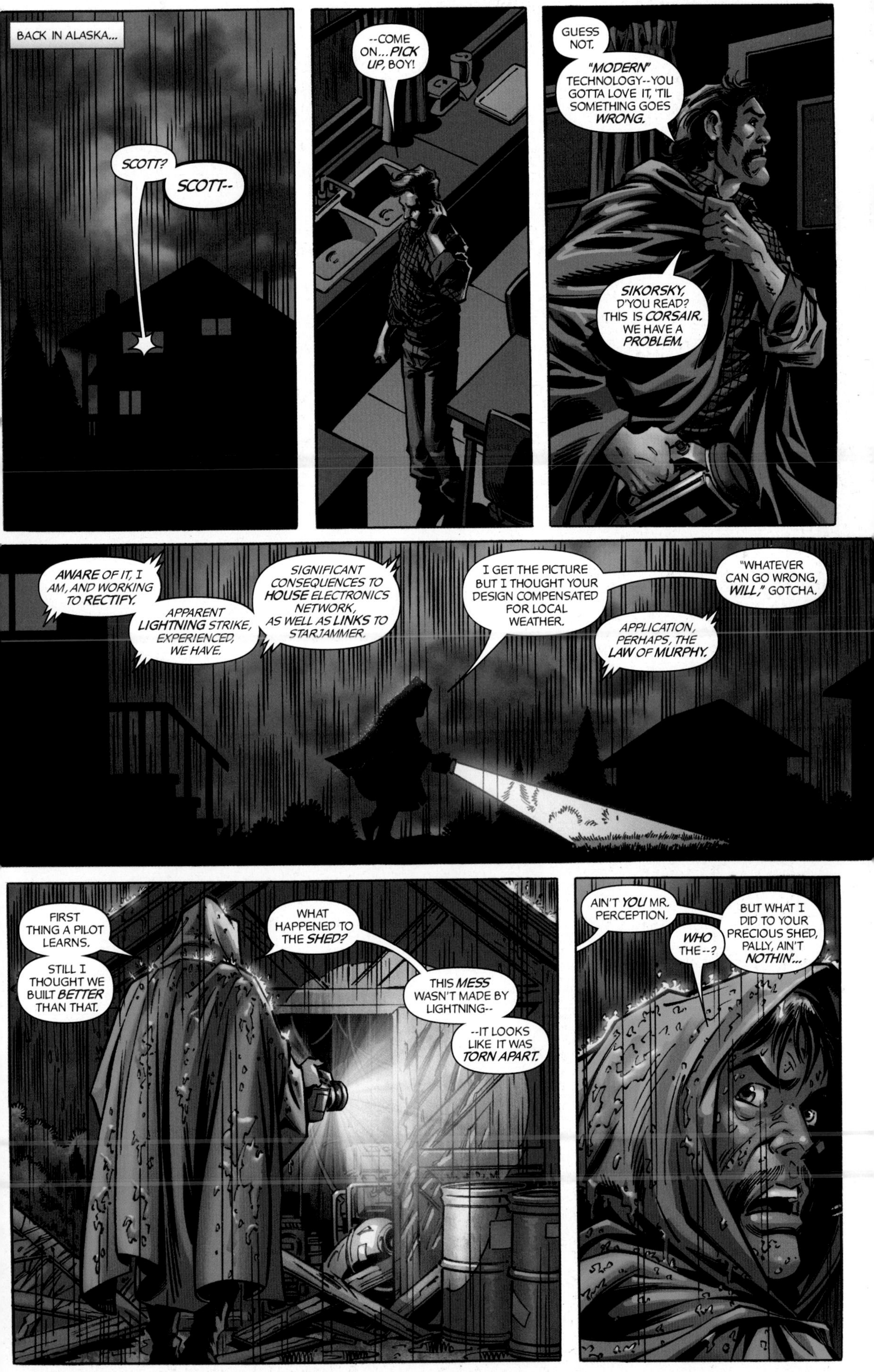
BACK IN ALASKA...
SCOTT?
SCOTT--
--COME ON... PICK UP, BOY!
GUESS NOT.
"MODERN" TECHNOLOGY--YOU GOTTA LOVE IT, 'TIL SOMETHING GOES WRONG.
SIKORSKY, D'YOU READ? THIS IS CORSAIR. WE HAVE A PROBLEM.
AWARE OF IT, I AM, AND WORKING TO RECTIFY.
APPARENT LIGHTNING STRIKE, EXPERIENCED, WE HAVE.
SIGNIFICANT CONSEQUENCES TO HOUSE ELECTRONICS NETWORK, AS WELL AS LINKS TO STARJAMMER.
I GET THE PICTURE BUT I THOUGHT YOUR DESIGN COMPENSATED FOR LOCAL WEATHER.
APPLICATION, PERHAPS, THE LAW OF MURPHY.
"WHATEVER CAN GO WRONG, WILL," GOTCHA.
FIRST THING A PILOT LEARNS.
STILL I THOUGHT WE BUILT BETTER THAN THAT.
WHAT HAPPENED TO THE SHED?
THIS MESS WASN'T MADE BY LIGHTNING--
--IT LOOKS LIKE IT WAS TORN APART.
AIN'T YOU MR. PERCEPTION.
BUT WHAT I DID TO YOUR PRECIOUS SHED, PALLY, AIN'T NOTHIN'...
WHO THE--?

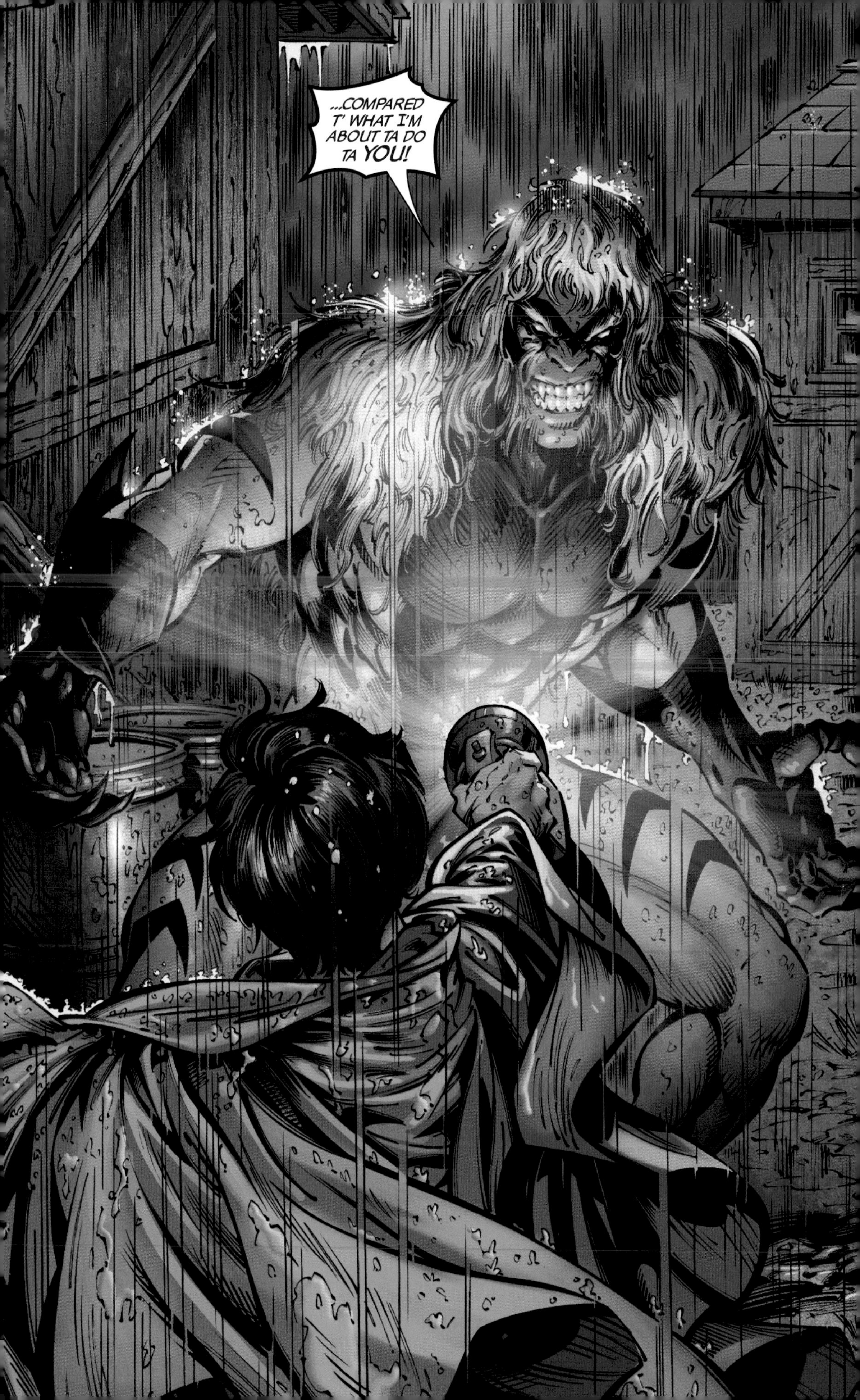
...COMPARED T' WHAT I'M ABOUT TA DO TA YOU!

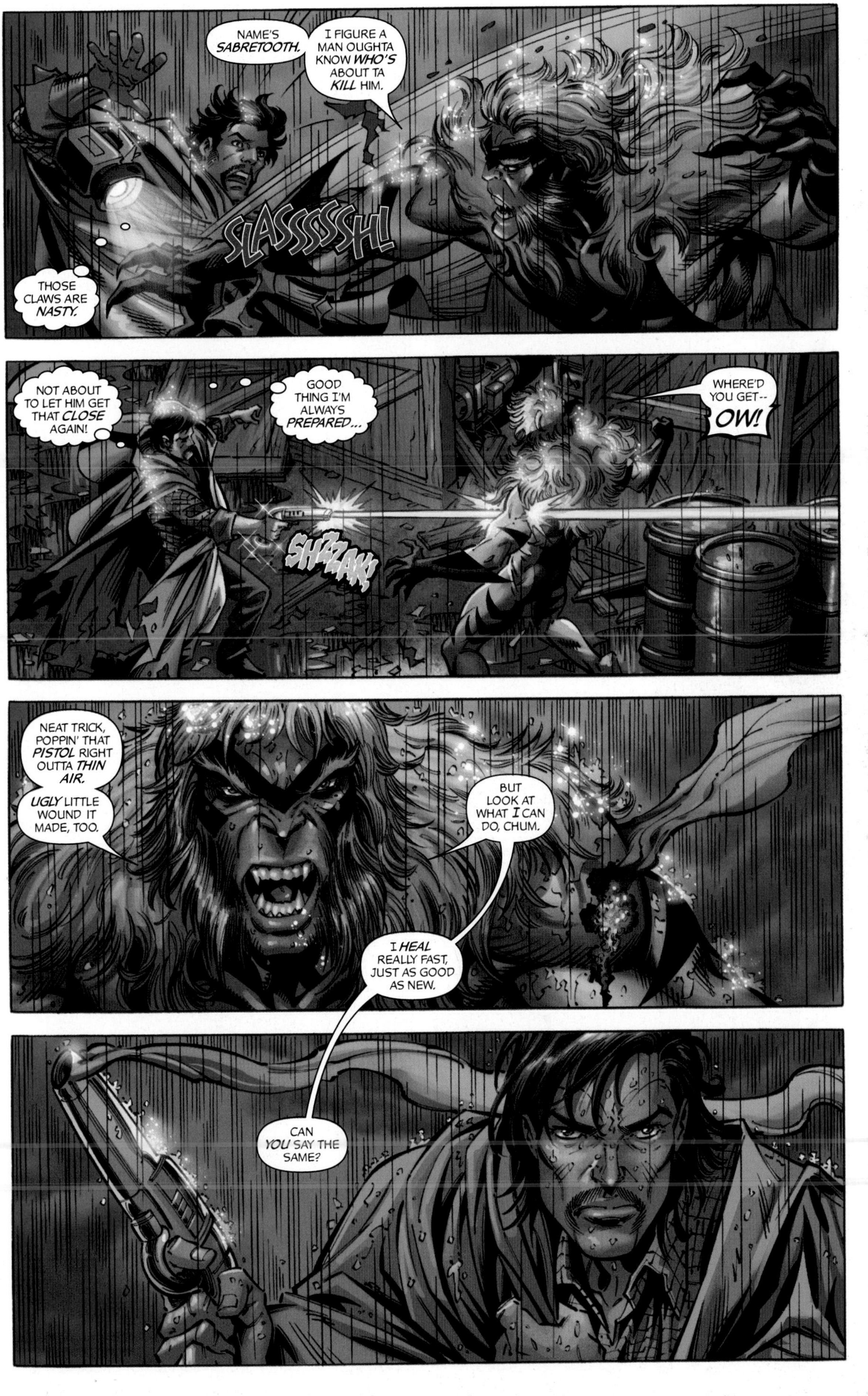
NAME'S SABRETOOTH.
I FIGURE A MAN OUGHTA KNOW WHO'S ABOUT TA KILL HIM.
SLASSSSSSH!
THOSE CLAWS ARE NASTY.
NOT ABOUT TO LET HIM GET THAT CLOSE AGAIN!
GOOD THING I'M ALWAYS PREPARED...
WHERE'D YOU GET-- OW!
SHZZAK!
NEAT TRICK, POPPIN' THAT PISTOL RIGHT OUTTA THIN AIR.
UGLY LITTLE WOUND IT MADE, TOO.
BUT LOOK AT WHAT I CAN DO, CHUM.
I HEAL REALLY FAST, JUST AS GOOD AS NEW.
CAN YOU SAY THE SAME?

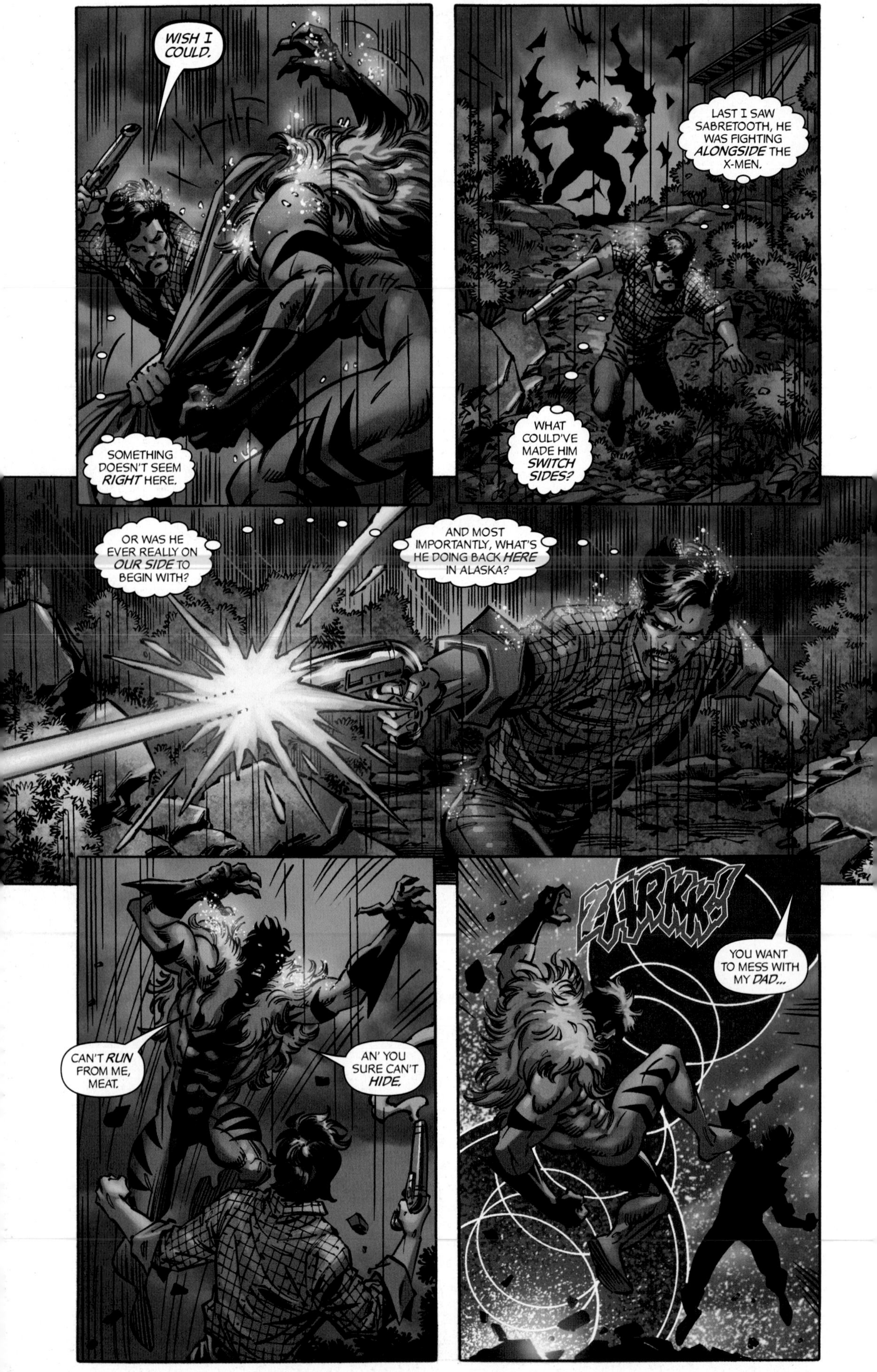
WISH I COULD.
SOMETHING DOESN'T SEEM RIGHT HERE.
LAST I SAW SABRETOOTH, HE WAS FIGHTING ALONGSIDE THE X-MEN.
WHAT COULD'VE MADE HIM SWITCH SIDES?
OR WAS HE EVER REALLY ON OUR SIDE TO BEGIN WITH?
AND MOST IMPORTANTLY, WHAT'S HE DOING BACK HERE IN ALASKA?
CAN'T RUN FROM ME, MEAT.
AN' YOU SURE CAN'T HIDE.
ZARKK!
YOU WANT TO MESS WITH MY DAD...

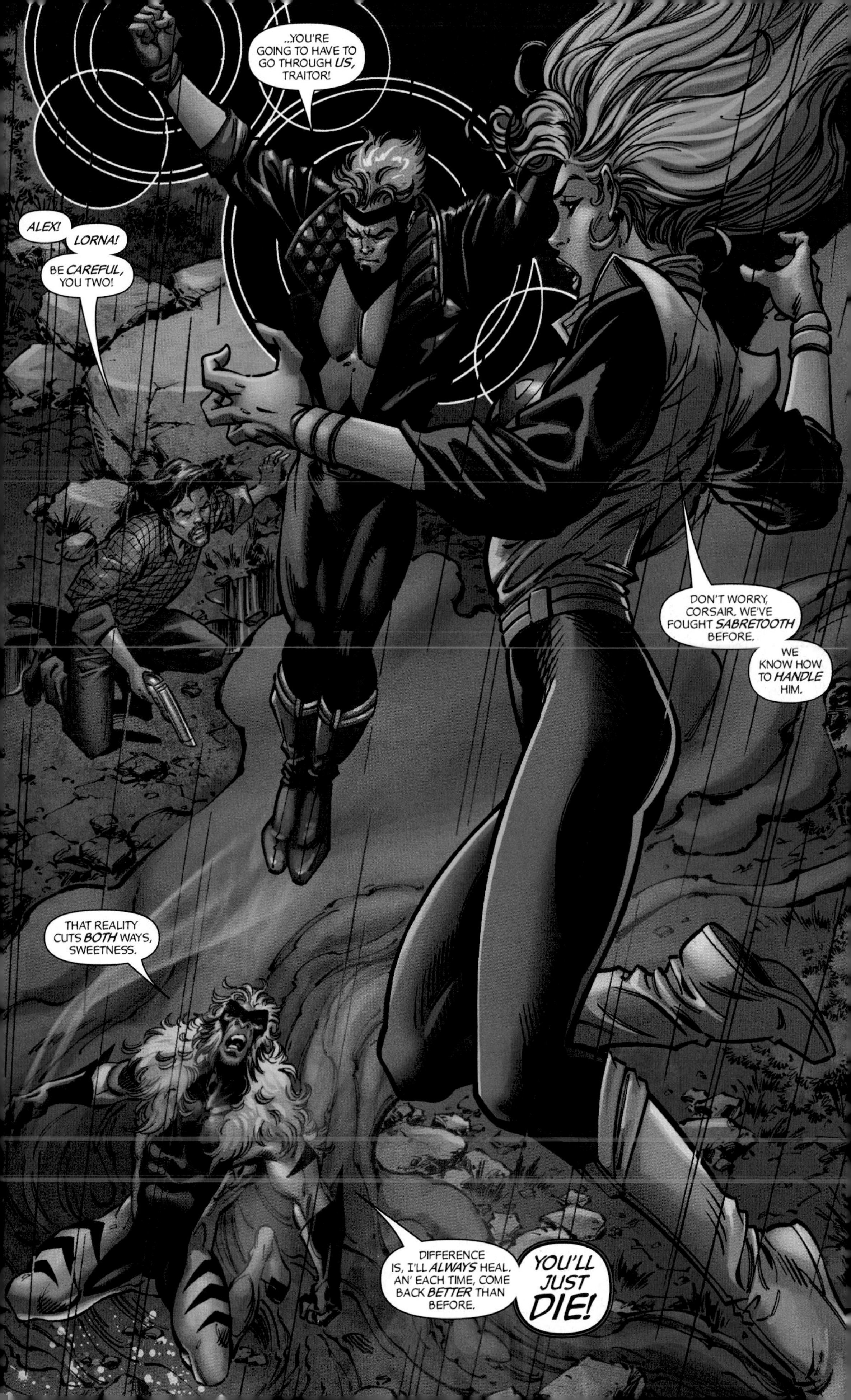
...YOU'RE GOING TO HAVE TO GO THROUGH *US,* TRAITOR!
ALEX!
LORNA!
BE *CAREFUL,* YOU TWO!
DON'T WORRY, CORSAIR. WE'VE FOUGHT *SABRETOOTH* BEFORE.
WE KNOW HOW TO *HANDLE* HIM.
THAT REALITY CUTS *BOTH* WAYS, SWEETNESS.
DIFFERENCE IS, I'LL *ALWAYS* HEAL. AN' EACH TIME, COME BACK *BETTER* THAN BEFORE.
YOU'LL JUST DIE!

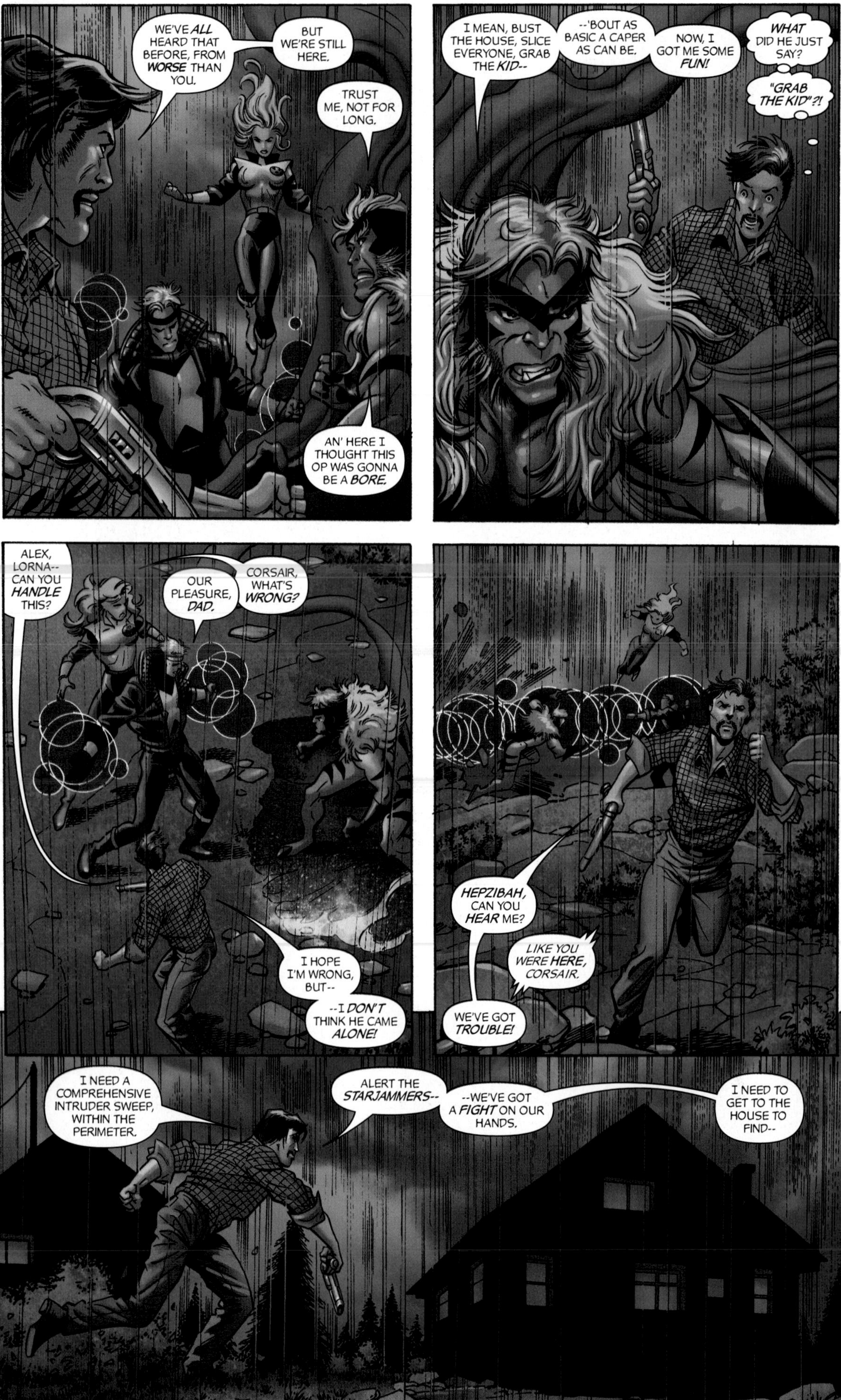

WE'VE ALL HEARD THAT BEFORE, FROM WORSE THAN YOU.
BUT WE'RE STILL HERE.
TRUST ME, NOT FOR LONG.
AN' HERE I THOUGHT THIS OP WAS GONNA BE A BORE.
I MEAN, BUST THE HOUSE, SLICE EVERYONE, GRAB THE KID--
--'BOUT AS BASIC A CAPER AS CAN BE.
NOW, I GOT ME SOME FUN!
WHAT DID HE JUST SAY?
"GRAB THE KID"?!
ALEX, LORNA-- CAN YOU HANDLE THIS?
OUR PLEASURE, DAD.
CORSAIR, WHAT'S WRONG?
I HOPE I'M WRONG, BUT--
--I DON'T THINK HE CAME ALONE!
HEPZIBAH, CAN YOU HEAR ME?
LIKE YOU WERE HERE, CORSAIR.
WE'VE GOT TROUBLE!
I NEED A COMPREHENSIVE INTRUDER SWEEP, WITHIN THE PERIMETER.
ALERT THE STARJAMMERS--
--WE'VE GOT A FIGHT ON OUR HANDS.
I NEED TO GET TO THE HOUSE TO FIND--

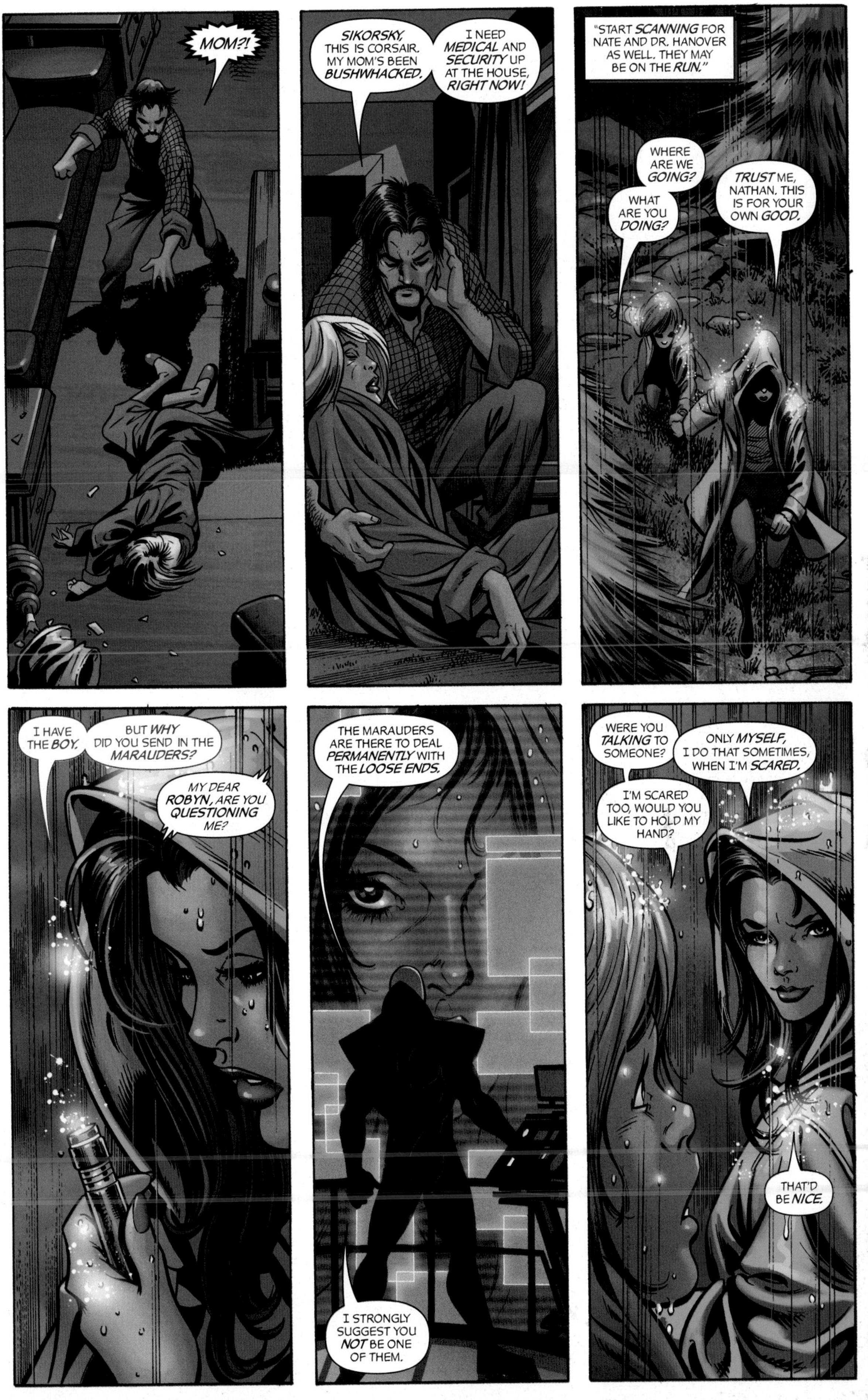
MOM?!
SIKORSKY, THIS IS CORSAIR. MY MOM'S BEEN BUSHWHACKED.
I NEED MEDICAL AND SECURITY UP AT THE HOUSE, RIGHT NOW!
"START SCANNING FOR NATE AND DR. HANOVER AS WELL. THEY MAY BE ON THE RUN."
WHERE ARE WE GOING?
WHAT ARE YOU DOING?
TRUST ME, NATHAN. THIS IS FOR YOUR OWN GOOD.
I HAVE THE BOY.
BUT WHY DID YOU SEND IN THE MARAUDERS?
MY DEAR ROBYN, ARE YOU QUESTIONING ME?
THE MARAUDERS ARE THERE TO DEAL PERMANENTLY WITH THE LOOSE ENDS.
I STRONGLY SUGGEST YOU NOT BE ONE OF THEM.
WERE YOU TALKING TO SOMEONE?
ONLY MYSELF, I DO THAT SOMETIMES, WHEN I'M SCARED.
I'M SCARED TOO, WOULD YOU LIKE TO HOLD MY HAND?
THAT'D BE NICE.

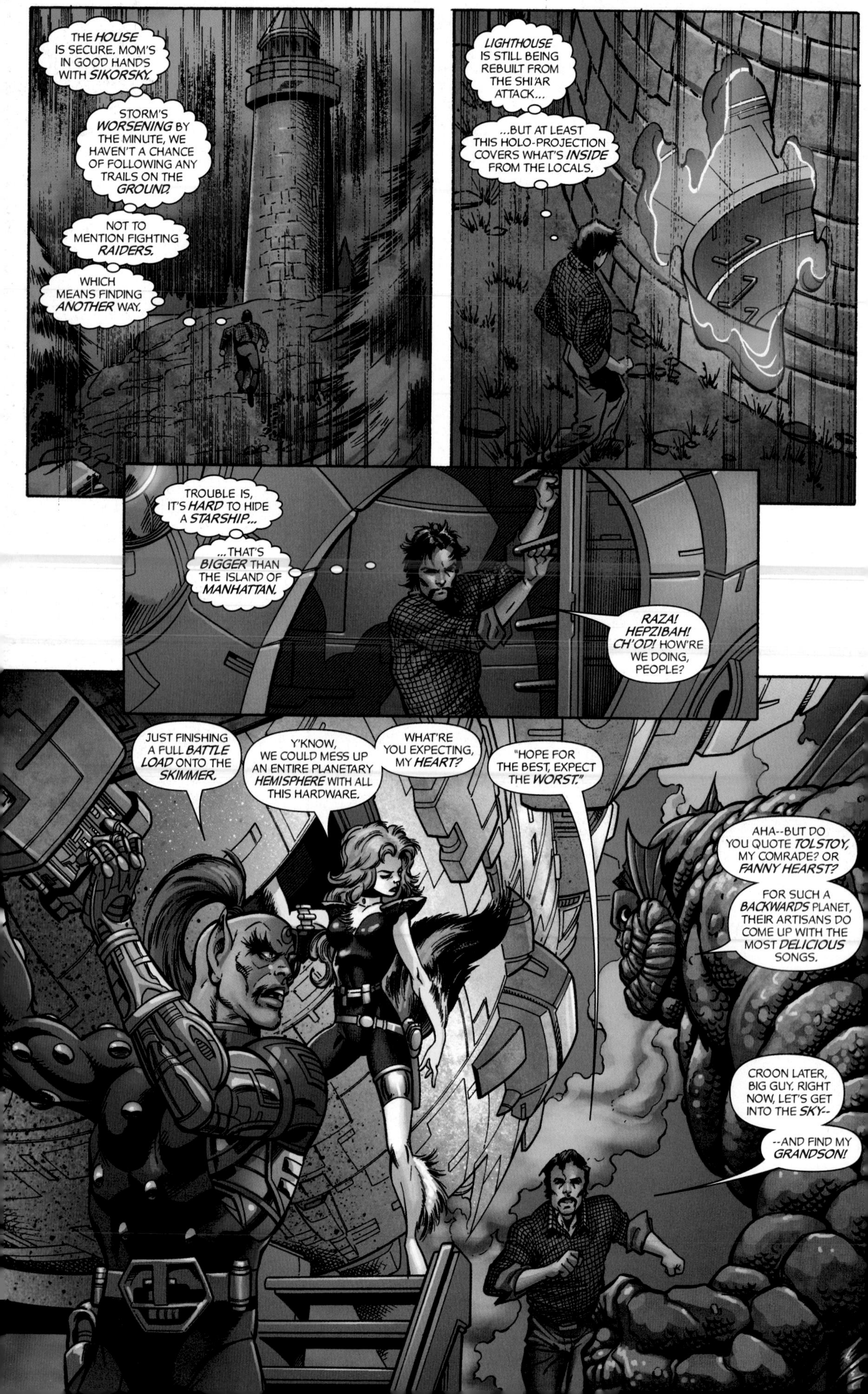
THE HOUSE IS SECURE. MOM'S IN GOOD HANDS WITH SIKORSKY.
STORM'S WORSENING BY THE MINUTE. WE HAVEN'T A CHANCE OF FOLLOWING ANY TRAILS ON THE GROUND.
NOT TO MENTION FIGHTING RAIDERS.
WHICH MEANS FINDING ANOTHER WAY.
LIGHTHOUSE IS STILL BEING REBUILT FROM THE SHI'AR ATTACK...
...BUT AT LEAST THIS HOLO-PROJECTION COVERS WHAT'S INSIDE FROM THE LOCALS.
TROUBLE IS, IT'S HARD TO HIDE A STARSHIP...
...THAT'S BIGGER THAN THE ISLAND OF MANHATTAN.
RAZA! HEPZIBAH! CH'OD! HOW'RE WE DOING, PEOPLE?
JUST FINISHING A FULL BATTLE LOAD ONTO THE SKIMMER.
Y'KNOW, WE COULD MESS UP AN ENTIRE PLANETARY HEMISPHERE WITH ALL THIS HARDWARE.
WHAT'RE YOU EXPECTING, MY HEART?
"HOPE FOR THE BEST, EXPECT THE WORST."
AHA--BUT DO YOU QUOTE TOLSTOY, MY COMRADE? OR FANNY HEARST?
FOR SUCH A BACKWARDS PLANET, THEIR ARTISANS DO COME UP WITH THE MOST DELICIOUS SONGS.
CROON LATER, BIG GUY. RIGHT NOW, LET'S GET INTO THE SKY--
--AND FIND MY GRANDSON!

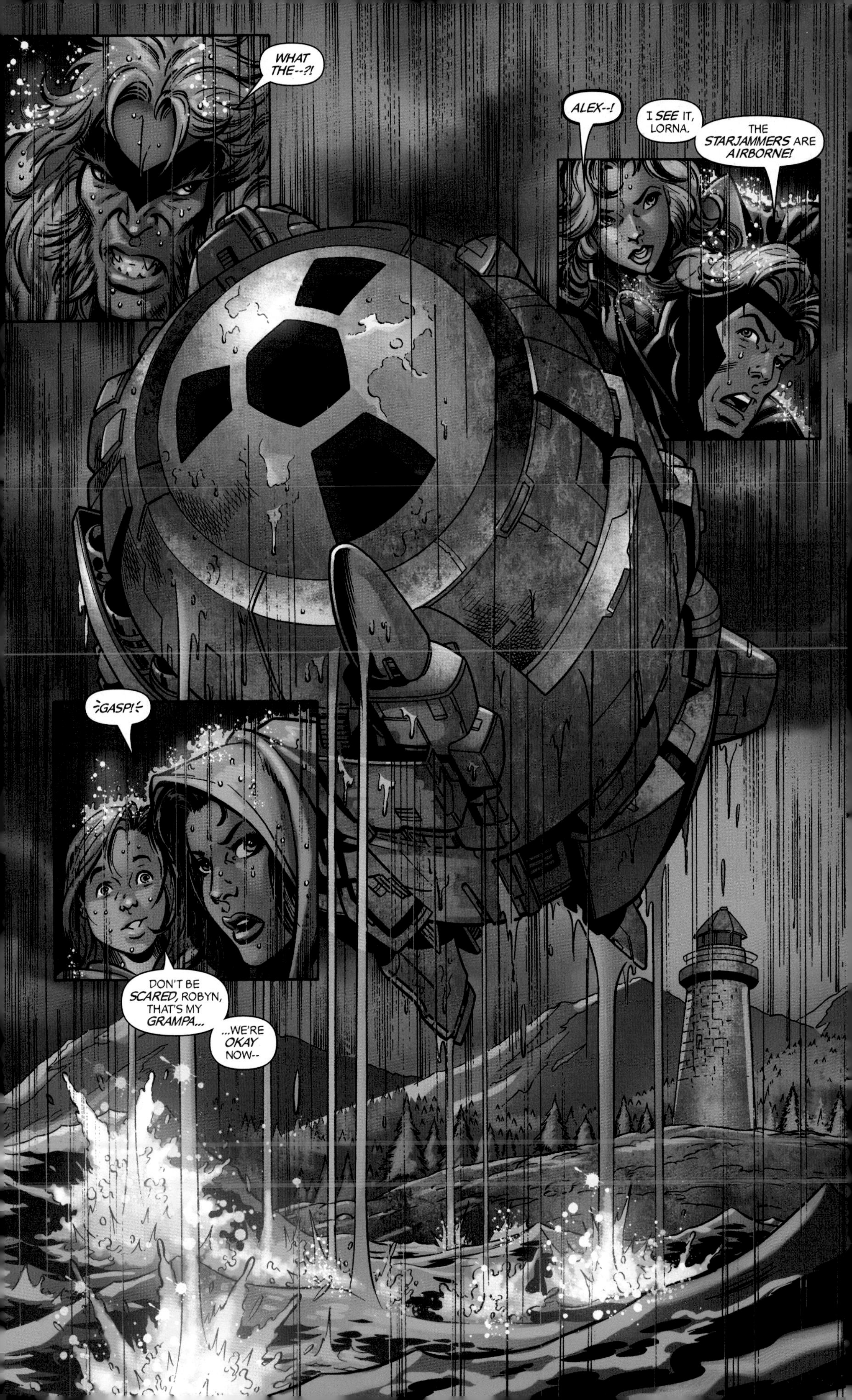
WHAT THE--?!
ALEX--!
I SEE IT, LORNA.
THE STARJAMMERS ARE AIRBORNE!
-GASP!-
DON'T BE SCARED, ROBYN, THAT'S MY GRAMPA...
...WE'RE OKAY NOW--

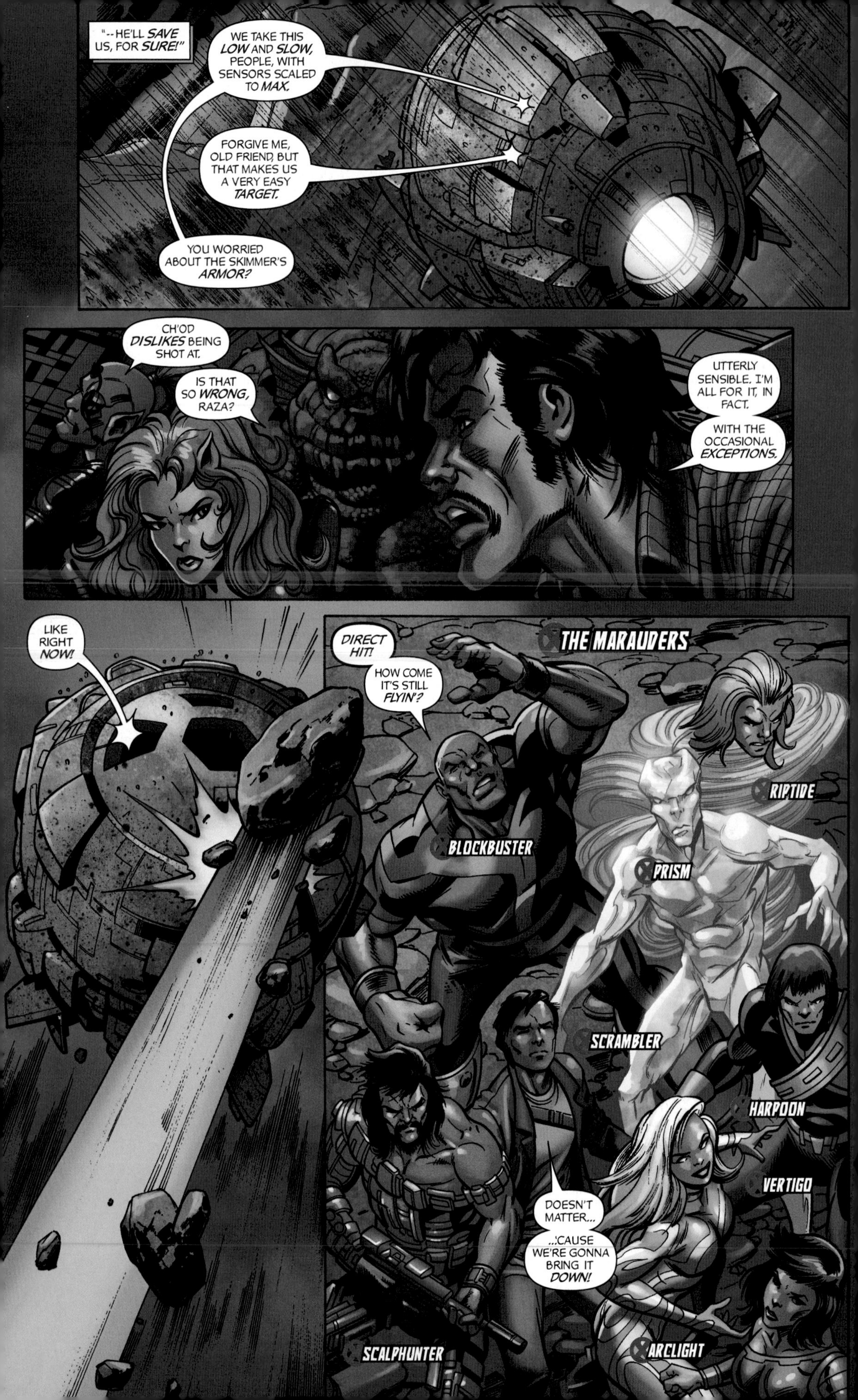
"--HE'LL SAVE US, FOR SURE!"
WE TAKE THIS LOW AND SLOW, PEOPLE, WITH SENSORS SCALED TO MAX.
FORGIVE ME, OLD FRIEND, BUT THAT MAKES US A VERY EASY TARGET.
YOU WORRIED ABOUT THE SKIMMER'S ARMOR?
CH'OD DISLIKES BEING SHOT AT.
IS THAT SO WRONG, RAZA?
UTTERLY SENSIBLE. I'M ALL FOR IT, IN FACT.
WITH THE OCCASIONAL EXCEPTIONS.
LIKE RIGHT NOW!
THE MARAUDERS
DIRECT HIT!
HOW COME IT'S STILL FLYIN'?
RIPTIDE
BLOCKBUSTER
PRISM
SCRAMBLER
HARPOON
VERTIGO
DOESN'T MATTER...
...'CAUSE WE'RE GONNA BRING IT DOWN!
SCALPHUNTER
ARCLIGHT

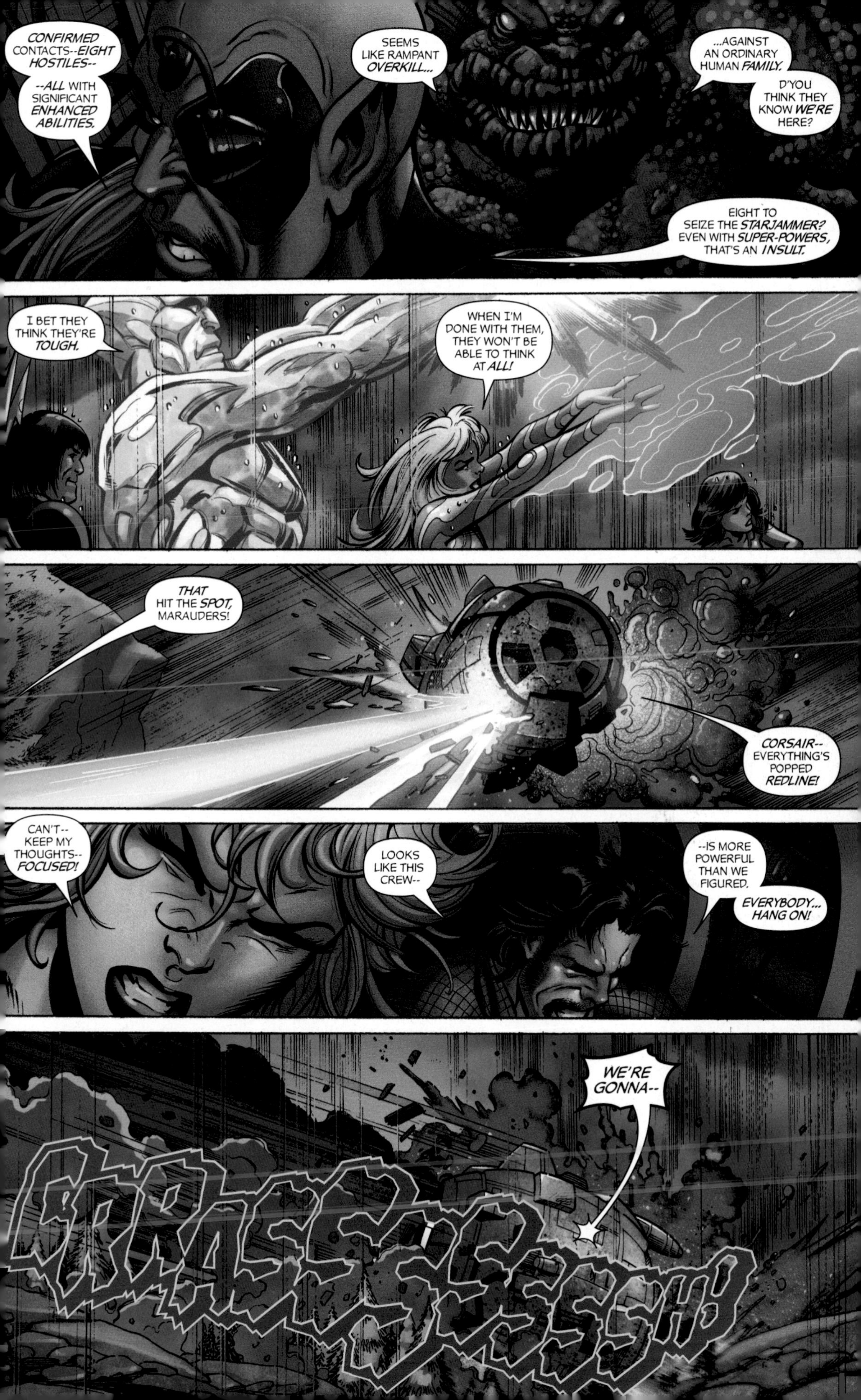
CONFIRMED CONTACTS--EIGHT HOSTILES--
--ALL WITH SIGNIFICANT ENHANCED ABILITIES.
SEEMS LIKE RAMPANT OVERKILL...
...AGAINST AN ORDINARY HUMAN FAMILY.
D'YOU THINK THEY KNOW WE'RE HERE?
EIGHT TO SEIZE THE STARJAMMER? EVEN WITH SUPER-POWERS, THAT'S AN INSULT.
I BET THEY THINK THEY'RE TOUGH.
WHEN I'M DONE WITH THEM, THEY WON'T BE ABLE TO THINK AT ALL!
THAT HIT THE SPOT, MARAUDERS!
CORSAIR-- EVERYTHING'S POPPED REDLINE!
CAN'T-- KEEP MY THOUGHTS-- FOCUSED!
LOOKS LIKE THIS CREW--
--IS MORE POWERFUL THAN WE FIGURED.
EVERYBODY... HANG ON!
WE'RE GONNA--
CRASSSHHH

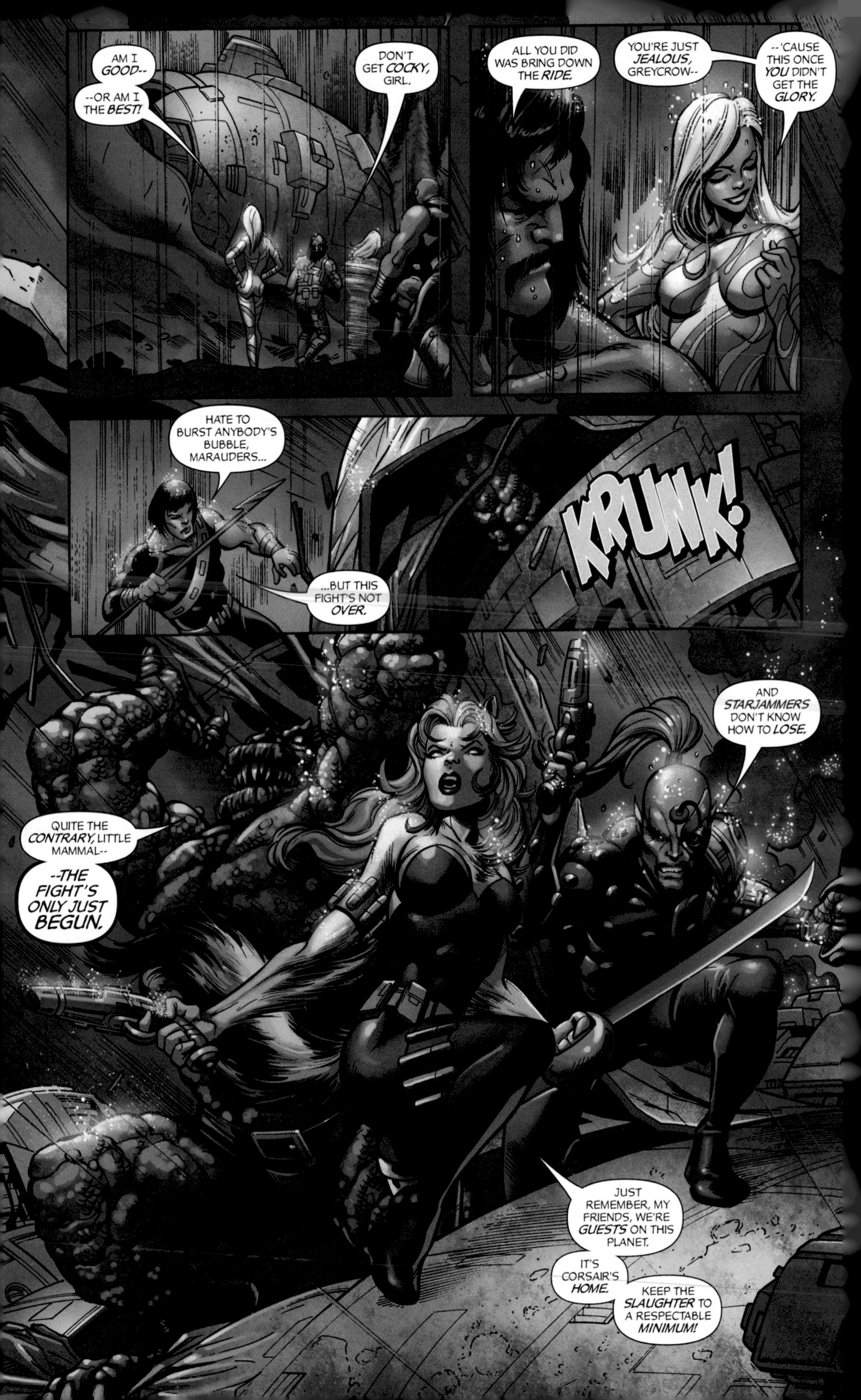
AM I GOOD--
--OR AM I THE BEST!
DON'T GET COCKY, GIRL.
ALL YOU DID WAS BRING DOWN THE RIDE.
YOU'RE JUST JEALOUS, GREYCROW--
--'CAUSE THIS ONCE YOU DIDN'T GET THE GLORY.
HATE TO BURST ANYBODY'S BUBBLE, MARAUDERS...
KRUNK!
...BUT THIS FIGHT'S NOT OVER.
AND STARJAMMERS DON'T KNOW HOW TO LOSE.
QUITE THE CONTRARY, LITTLE MAMMAL--
--THE FIGHT'S ONLY JUST BEGUN.
JUST REMEMBER, MY FRIENDS, WE'RE GUESTS ON THIS PLANET.
IT'S CORSAIR'S HOME.
KEEP THE SLAUGHTER TO A RESPECTABLE MINIMUM!

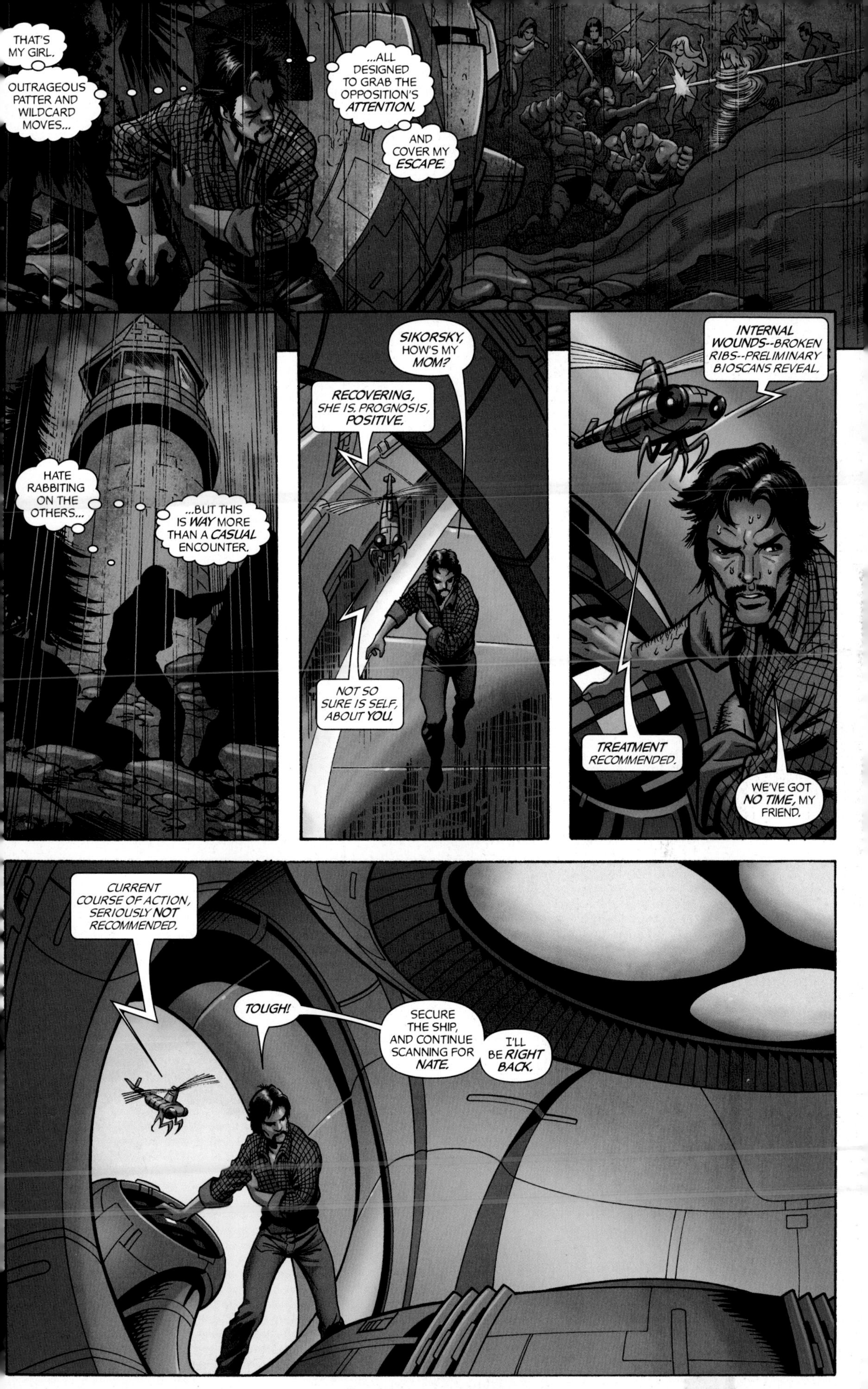
THAT'S MY GIRL.
OUTRAGEOUS PATTER AND WILDCARD MOVES...
...ALL DESIGNED TO GRAB THE OPPOSITION'S ATTENTION.
AND COVER MY ESCAPE.
HATE RABBITING ON THE OTHERS...
...BUT THIS IS WAY MORE THAN A CASUAL ENCOUNTER.
SIKORSKY, HOW'S MY MOM?
RECOVERING, SHE IS. PROGNOSIS, POSITIVE.
NOT SO SURE IS SELF, ABOUT YOU.
INTERNAL WOUNDS--BROKEN RIBS--PRELIMINARY BIOSCANS REVEAL.
TREATMENT RECOMMENDED.
WE'VE GOT NO TIME, MY FRIEND.
CURRENT COURSE OF ACTION, SERIOUSLY NOT RECOMMENDED.
TOUGH!
SECURE THE SHIP, AND CONTINUE SCANNING FOR NATE.
I'LL BE RIGHT BACK.

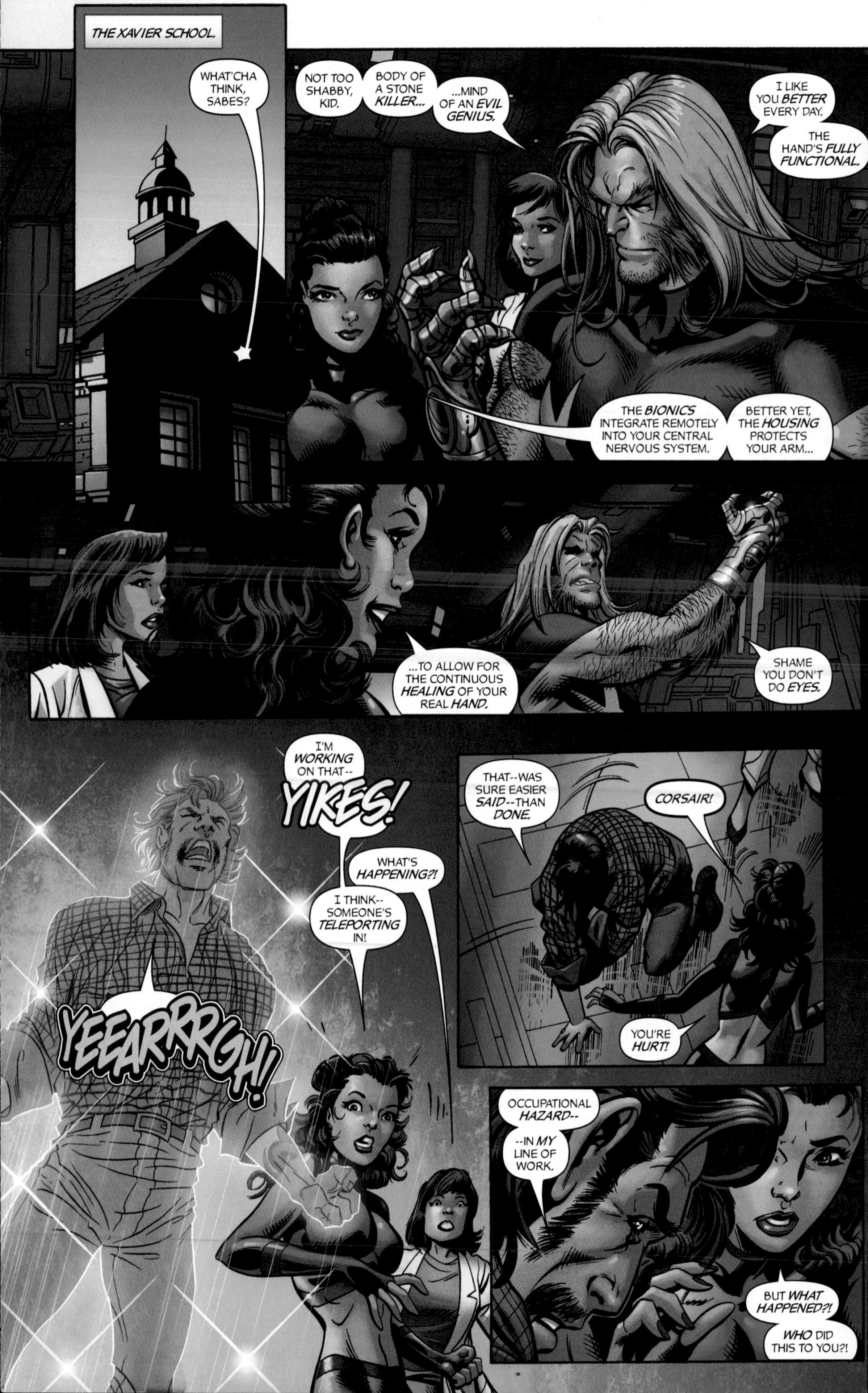

THE XAVIER SCHOOL.
WHAT'CHA THINK, SABES?
NOT TOO SHABBY, KID.
BODY OF A STONE KILLER...
...MIND OF AN EVIL GENIUS.
I LIKE YOU BETTER EVERY DAY.
THE HAND'S FULLY FUNCTIONAL.
THE BIONICS INTEGRATE REMOTELY INTO YOUR CENTRAL NERVOUS SYSTEM.
BETTER YET, THE HOUSING PROTECTS YOUR ARM...
...TO ALLOW FOR THE CONTINUOUS HEALING OF YOUR REAL HAND.
SHAME YOU DON'T DO EYES.
I'M WORKING ON THAT--
YIKES!
WHAT'S HAPPENING?!
I THINK--SOMEONE'S TELEPORTING IN!
YEEARRRGH!
THAT--WAS SURE EASIER SAID--THAN DONE.
CORSAIR!
YOU'RE HURT!
OCCUPATIONAL HAZARD--
--IN MY LINE OF WORK.
BUT WHAT HAPPENED?!
WHO DID THIS TO YOU?!

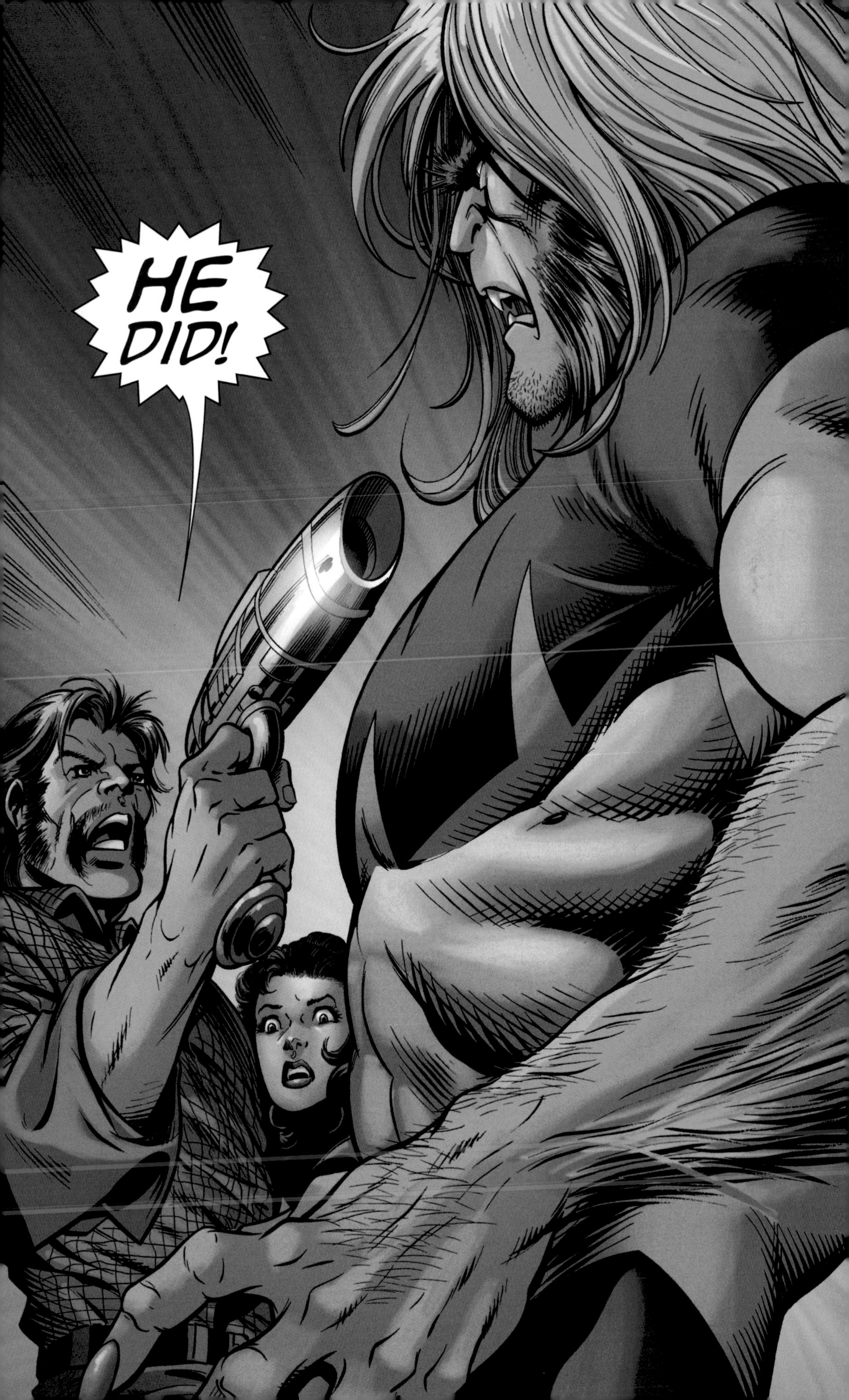
HE DID!

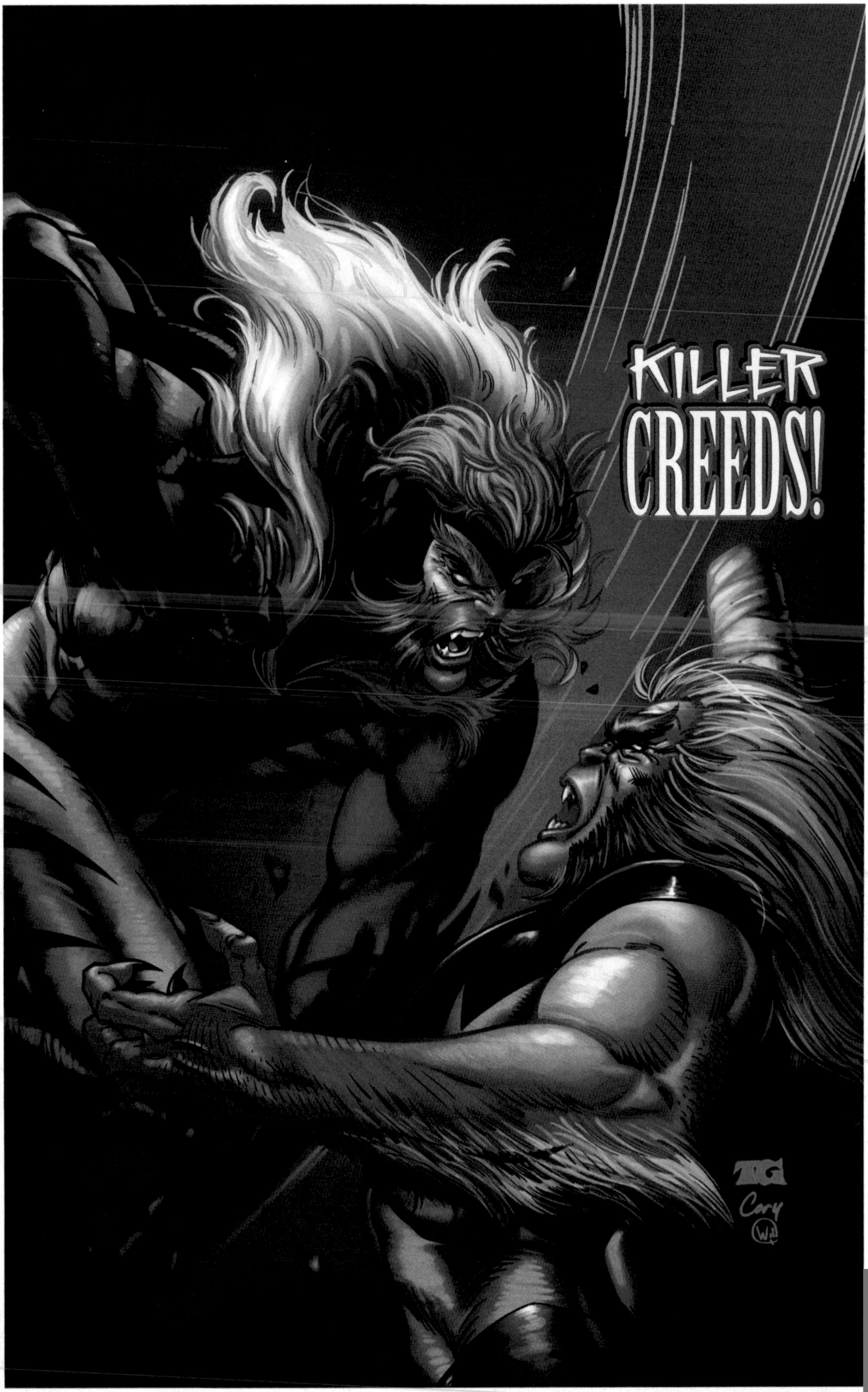
KILLER
CREEDS!

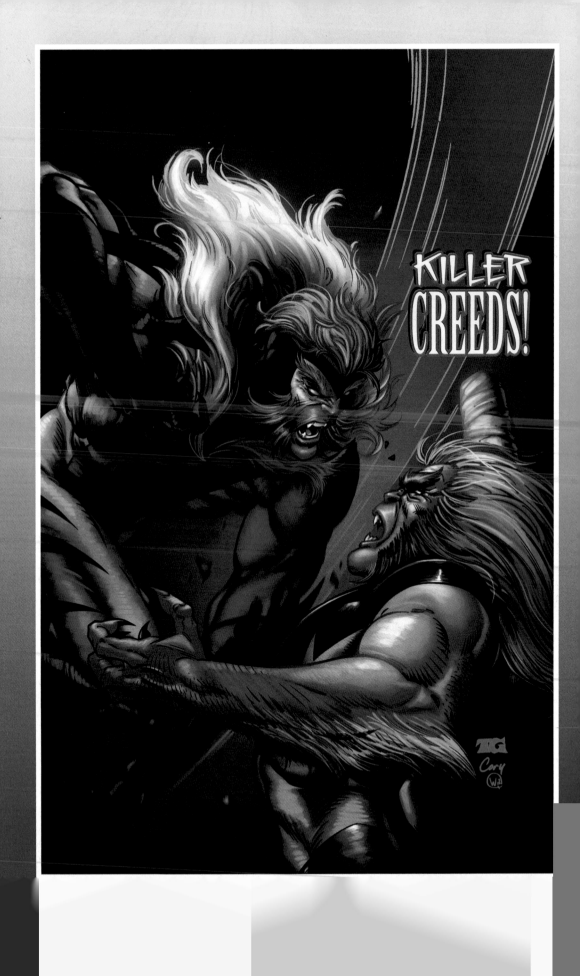

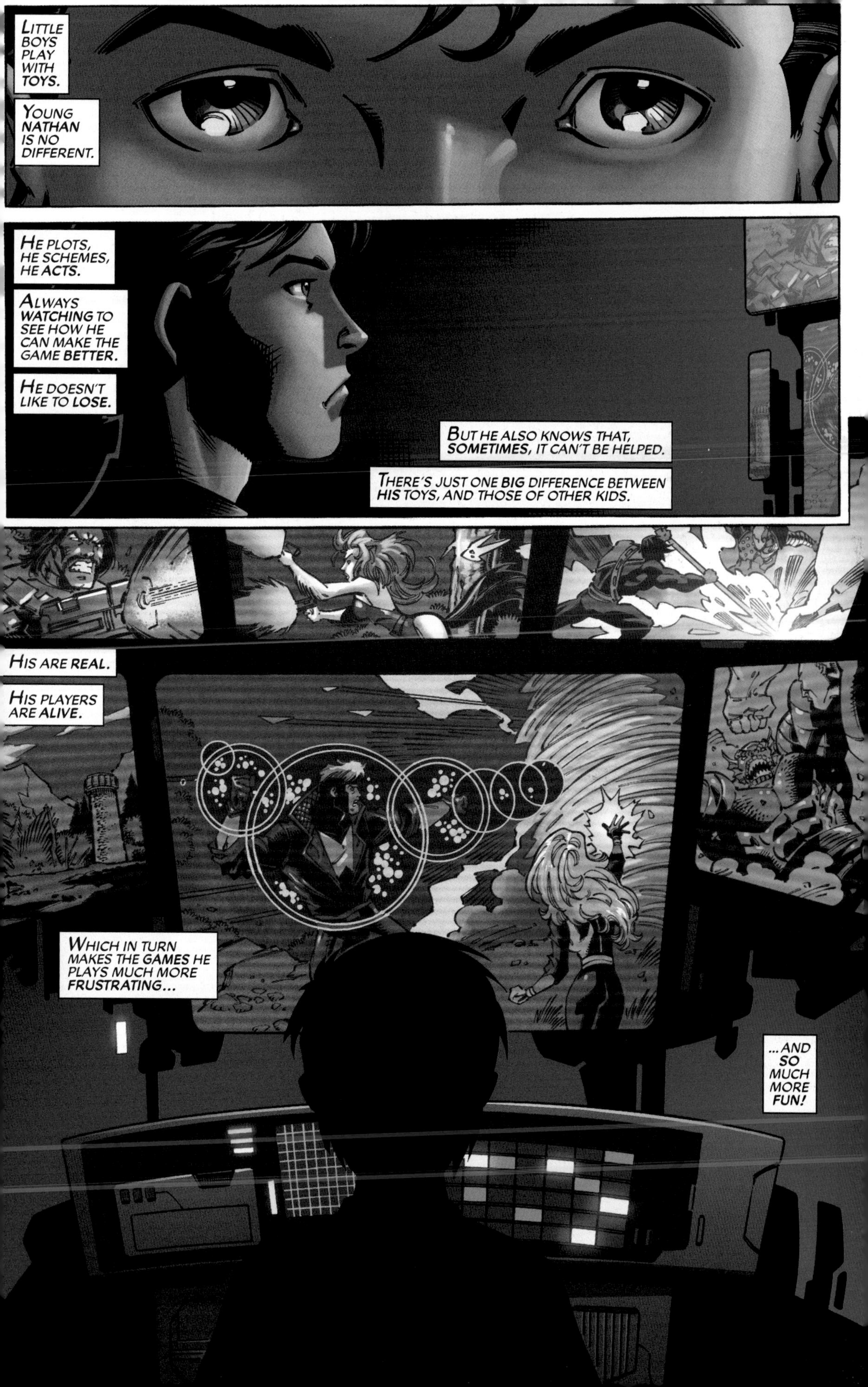
LITTLE BOYS PLAY WITH TOYS.
YOUNG NATHAN IS NO DIFFERENT.
HE PLOTS, HE SCHEMES, HE ACTS.
ALWAYS WATCHING TO SEE HOW HE CAN MAKE THE GAME BETTER.
HE DOESN'T LIKE TO LOSE.
BUT HE ALSO KNOWS THAT, SOMETIMES, IT CAN'T BE HELPED.
THERE'S JUST ONE BIG DIFFERENCE BETWEEN HIS TOYS, AND THOSE OF OTHER KIDS.
HIS ARE REAL.
HIS PLAYERS ARE ALIVE.
WHICH IN TURN MAKES THE GAMES HE PLAYS MUCH MORE FRUSTRATING...
...AND SO MUCH MORE FUN!

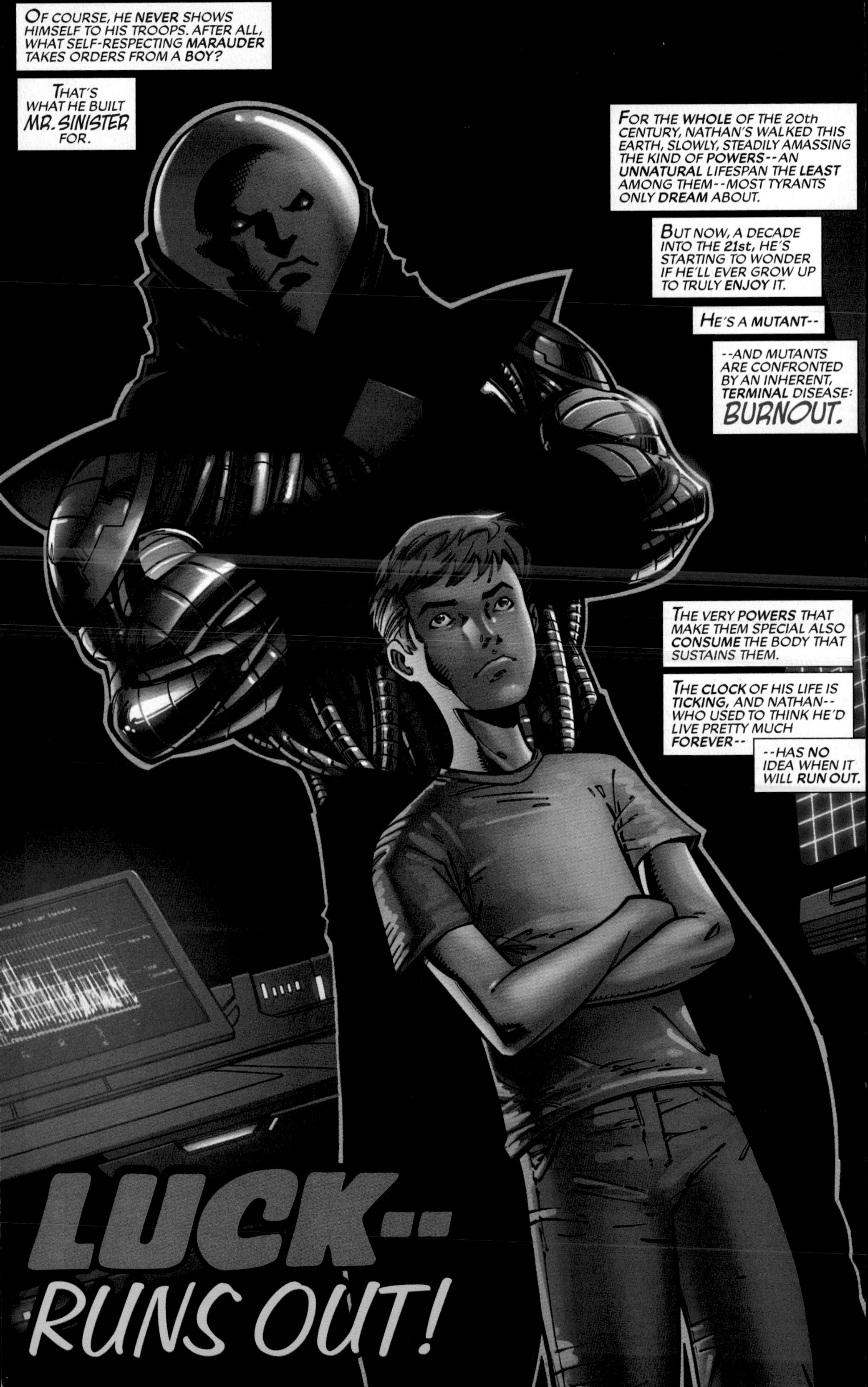
OF COURSE, HE NEVER SHOWS HIMSELF TO HIS TROOPS. AFTER ALL, WHAT SELF-RESPECTING MARAUDER TAKES ORDERS FROM A BOY?
THAT'S WHAT HE BUILT MR. SINISTER FOR.
FOR THE WHOLE OF THE 20th CENTURY, NATHAN'S WALKED THIS EARTH, SLOWLY, STEADILY AMASSING THE KIND OF POWERS--AN UNNATURAL LIFESPAN THE LEAST AMONG THEM--MOST TYRANTS ONLY DREAM ABOUT.
BUT NOW, A DECADE INTO THE 21st, HE'S STARTING TO WONDER IF HE'LL EVER GROW UP TO TRULY ENJOY IT.
HE'S A MUTANT--
--AND MUTANTS ARE CONFRONTED BY AN INHERENT, TERMINAL DISEASE: BURNOUT.
THE VERY POWERS THAT MAKE THEM SPECIAL ALSO CONSUME THE BODY THAT SUSTAINS THEM.
THE CLOCK OF HIS LIFE IS TICKING, AND NATHAN--WHO USED TO THINK HE'D LIVE PRETTY MUCH FOREVER--
--HAS NO IDEA WHEN IT WILL RUN OUT.
LUCK..
RUNS OUT!

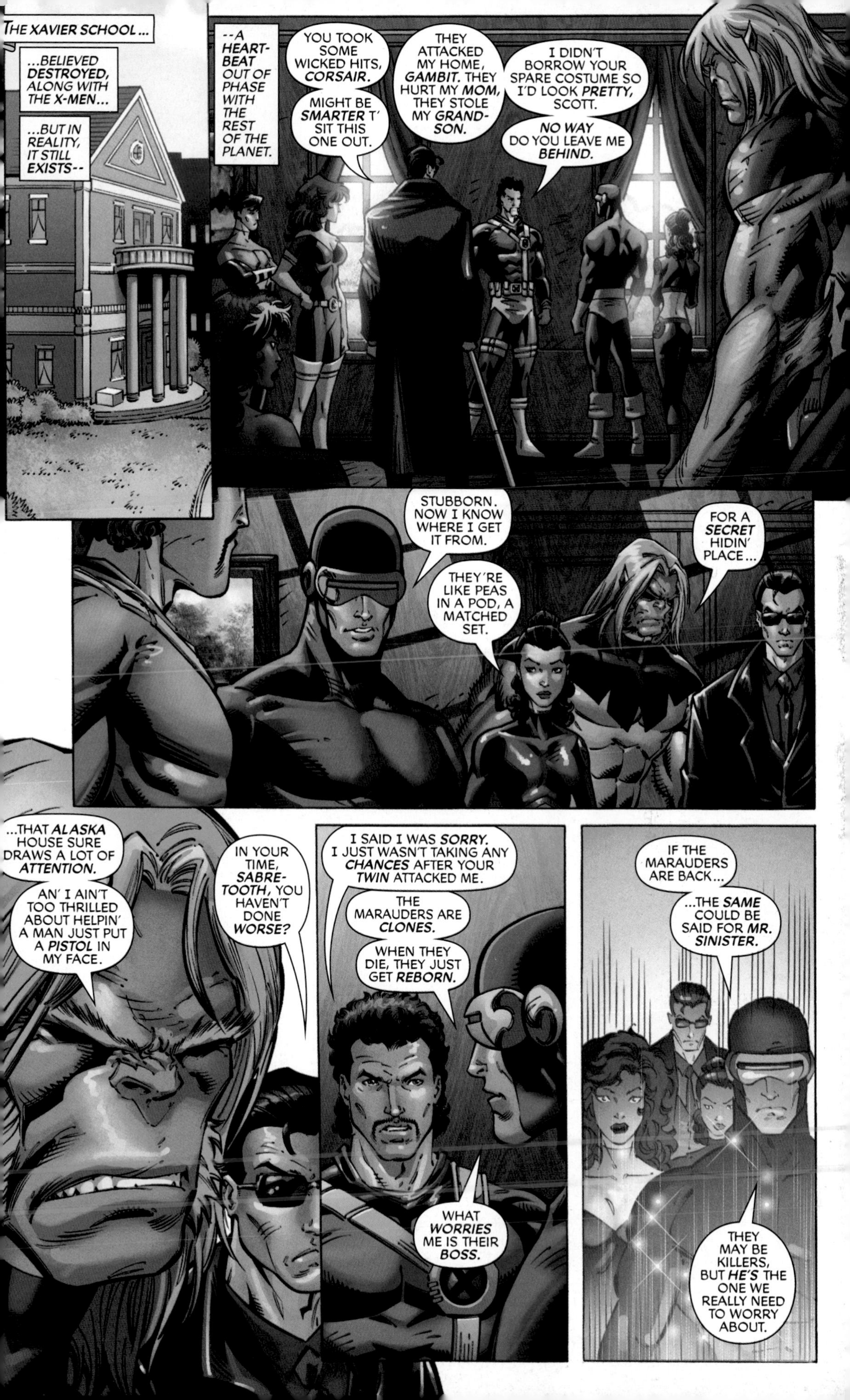
THE XAVIER SCHOOL...
...BELIEVED DESTROYED, ALONG WITH THE X-MEN...
...BUT IN REALITY, IT STILL EXISTS--
--A HEART-BEAT OUT OF PHASE WITH THE REST OF THE PLANET.
YOU TOOK SOME WICKED HITS, CORSAIR.
MIGHT BE SMARTER T' SIT THIS ONE OUT.
THEY ATTACKED MY HOME, GAMBIT. THEY HURT MY MOM, THEY STOLE MY GRAND-SON.
I DIDN'T BORROW YOUR SPARE COSTUME SO I'D LOOK PRETTY, SCOTT.
NO WAY DO YOU LEAVE ME BEHIND.
STUBBORN. NOW I KNOW WHERE I GET IT FROM.
THEY'RE LIKE PEAS IN A POD, A MATCHED SET.
FOR A SECRET HIDIN' PLACE...
...THAT ALASKA HOUSE SURE DRAWS A LOT OF ATTENTION.
AN' I AIN'T TOO THRILLED ABOUT HELPIN' A MAN JUST PUT A PISTOL IN MY FACE.
IN YOUR TIME, SABRE-TOOTH, YOU HAVEN'T DONE WORSE?
I SAID I WAS SORRY. I JUST WASN'T TAKING ANY CHANCES AFTER YOUR TWIN ATTACKED ME.
THE MARAUDERS ARE CLONES.
WHEN THEY DIE, THEY JUST GET REBORN.
WHAT WORRIES ME IS THEIR BOSS.
IF THE MARAUDERS ARE BACK...
...THE SAME COULD BE SAID FOR MR. SINISTER.
THEY MAY BE KILLERS, BUT HE'S THE ONE WE REALLY NEED TO WORRY ABOUT.

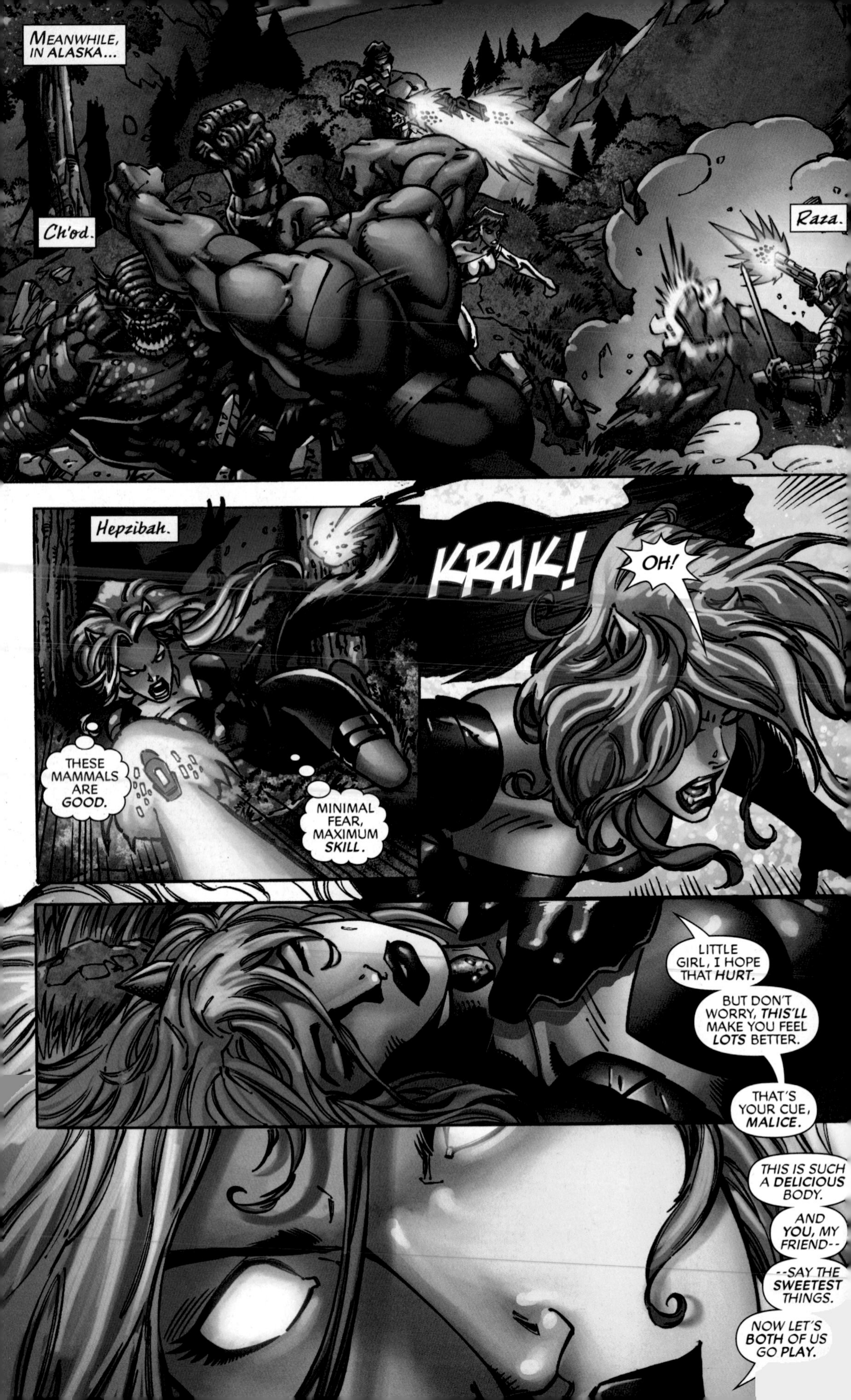
MEANWHILE, IN ALASKA...
Ch'od.
Raza.
Hepzibah.
KRAK!
OH!
THESE MAMMALS ARE GOOD.
MINIMAL FEAR, MAXIMUM SKILL.
LITTLE GIRL, I HOPE THAT HURT.
BUT DON'T WORRY, THIS'LL MAKE YOU FEEL LOTS BETTER.
THAT'S YOUR CUE, MALICE.
THIS IS SUCH A DELICIOUS BODY.
AND YOU, MY FRIEND--
--SAY THE SWEETEST THINGS.
NOW LET'S BOTH OF US GO PLAY.

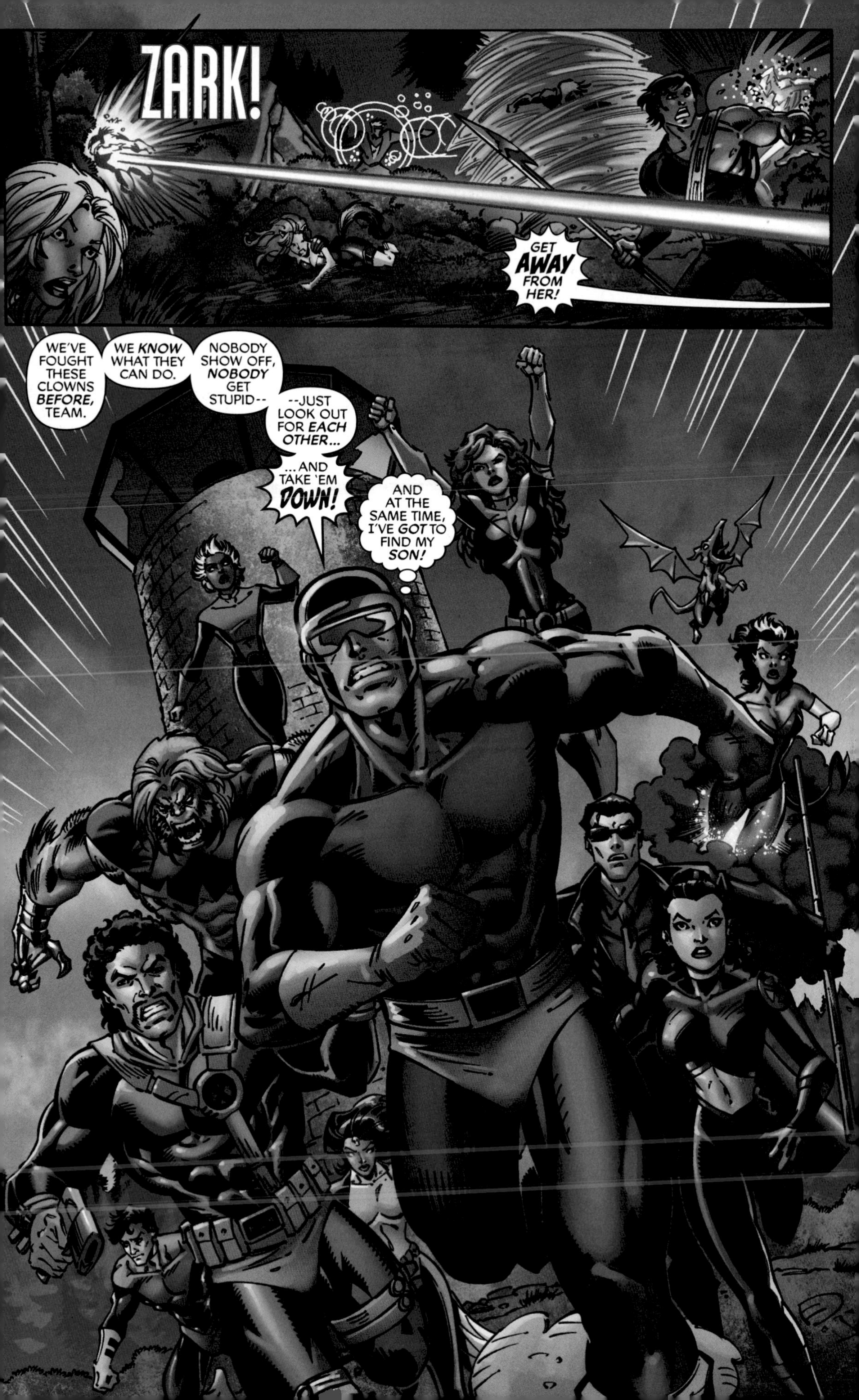
ZARK!
GET AWAY FROM HER!
WE'VE FOUGHT THESE CLOWNS BEFORE, TEAM.
WE KNOW WHAT THEY CAN DO.
NOBODY SHOW OFF, NOBODY GET STUPID--
--JUST LOOK OUT FOR EACH OTHER...
...AND TAKE 'EM DOWN!
AND AT THE SAME TIME, I'VE GOT TO FIND MY SON!

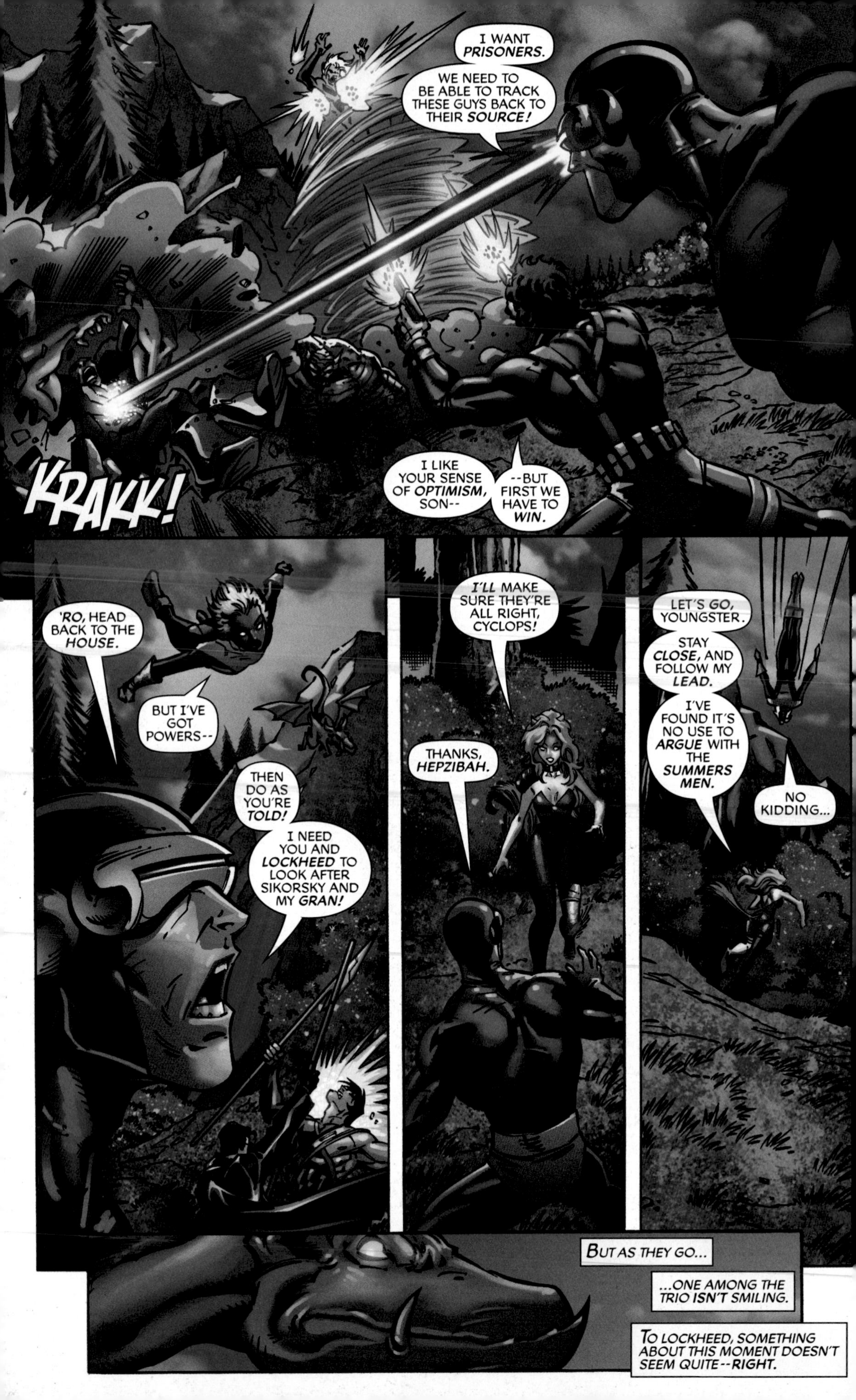
I WANT PRISONERS.
WE NEED TO BE ABLE TO TRACK THESE GUYS BACK TO THEIR SOURCE!
KRAKK!
I LIKE YOUR SENSE OF OPTIMISM, SON--
--BUT FIRST WE HAVE TO WIN.
'RO, HEAD BACK TO THE HOUSE.
BUT I'VE GOT POWERS--
THEN DO AS YOU'RE TOLD!
I NEED YOU AND LOCKHEED TO LOOK AFTER SIKORSKY AND MY GRAN!
I'LL MAKE SURE THEY'RE ALL RIGHT, CYCLOPS!
THANKS, HEPZIBAH.
LET'S GO, YOUNGSTER.
STAY CLOSE, AND FOLLOW MY LEAD.
I'VE FOUND IT'S NO USE TO ARGUE WITH THE SUMMERS MEN.
NO KIDDING...
BUT AS THEY GO...
...ONE AMONG THE TRIO ISN'T SMILING.
TO LOCKHEED, SOMETHING ABOUT THIS MOMENT DOESN'T SEEM QUITE--RIGHT.

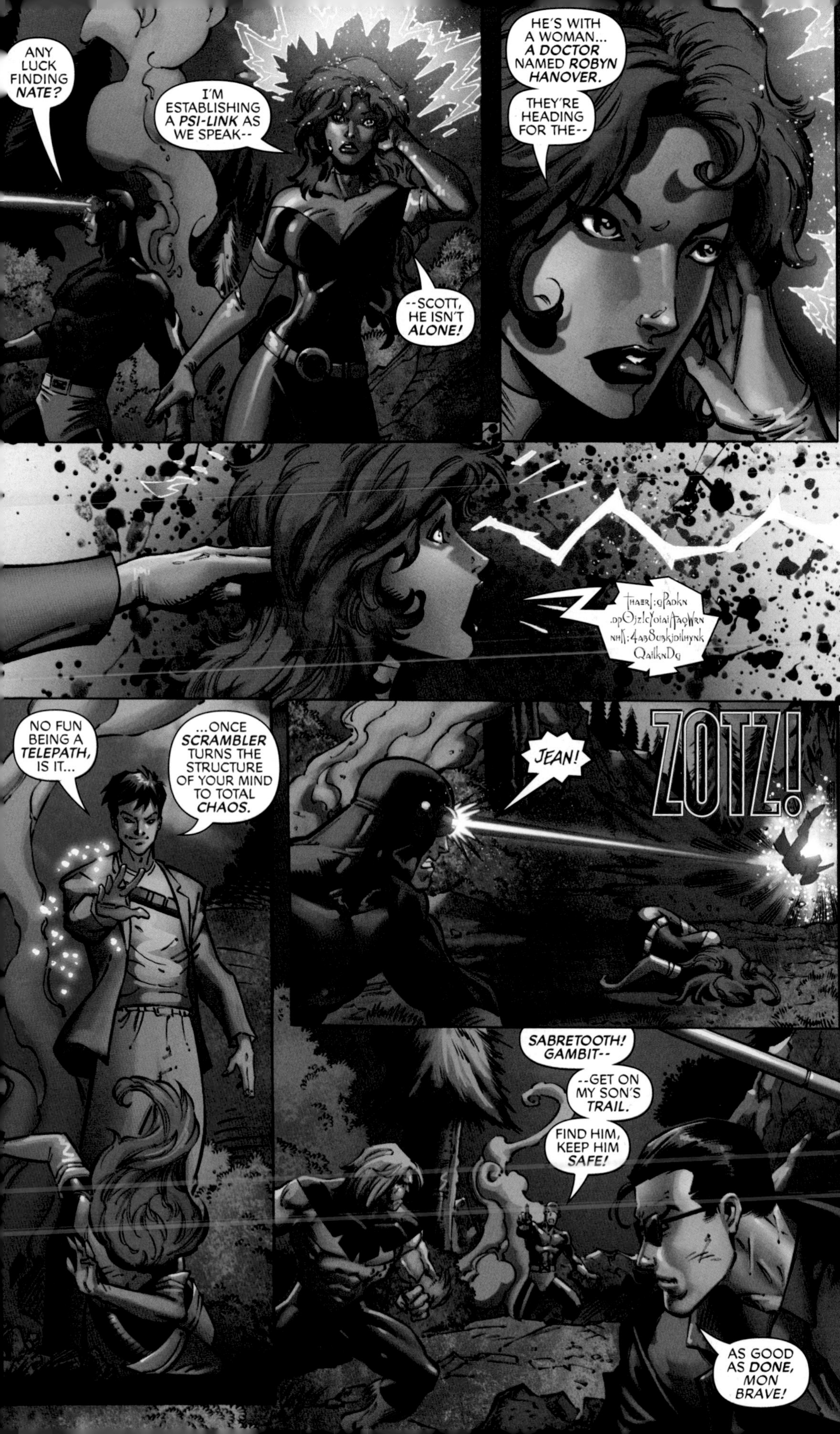
ANY LUCK FINDING NATE?
I'M ESTABLISHING A PSI-LINK AS WE SPEAK--
--SCOTT, HE ISN'T ALONE!
HE'S WITH A WOMAN... A DOCTOR NAMED ROBYN HANOVER.
THEY'RE HEADING FOR THE--
NO FUN BEING A TELEPATH, IS IT...
...ONCE SCRAMBLER TURNS THE STRUCTURE OF YOUR MIND TO TOTAL CHAOS.
JEAN!
ZOTZ!
SABRETOOTH! GAMBIT--
--GET ON MY SON'S TRAIL.
FIND HIM, KEEP HIM SAFE!
AS GOOD AS DONE, MON BRAVE!

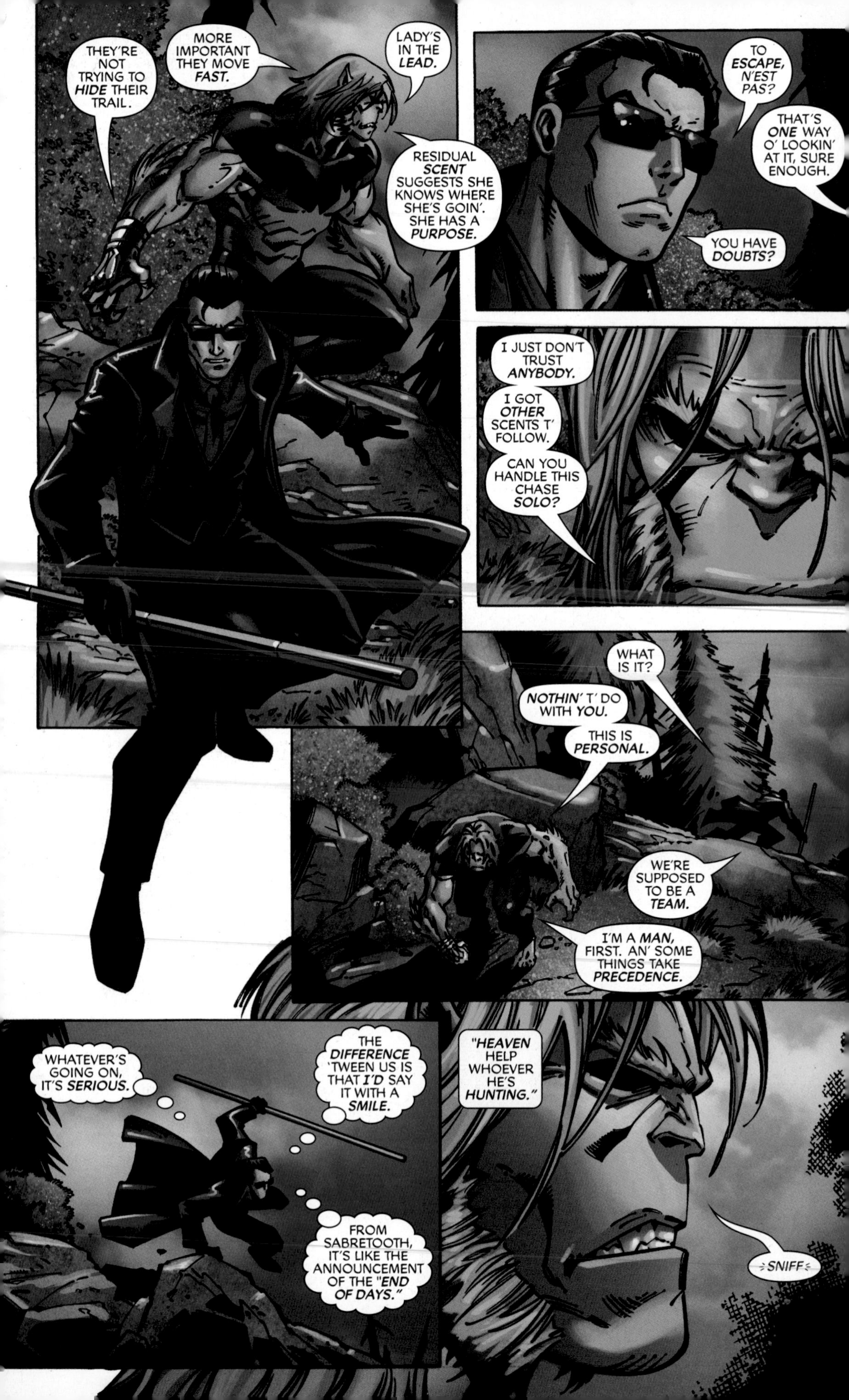
THEY'RE NOT TRYING TO HIDE THEIR TRAIL.
MORE IMPORTANT THEY MOVE FAST.
LADY'S IN THE LEAD.
RESIDUAL SCENT SUGGESTS SHE KNOWS WHERE SHE'S GOIN'. SHE HAS A PURPOSE.
TO ESCAPE, N'EST PAS?
THAT'S ONE WAY O' LOOKIN' AT IT, SURE ENOUGH.
YOU HAVE DOUBTS?
I JUST DON'T TRUST ANYBODY.
I GOT OTHER SCENTS T' FOLLOW.
CAN YOU HANDLE THIS CHASE SOLO?
WHAT IS IT?
NOTHIN' T' DO WITH YOU.
THIS IS PERSONAL.
WE'RE SUPPOSED TO BE A TEAM.
I'M A MAN, FIRST. AN' SOME THINGS TAKE PRECEDENCE.
WHATEVER'S GOING ON, IT'S SERIOUS.
THE DIFFERENCE 'TWEEN US IS THAT I'D SAY IT WITH A SMILE.
FROM SABRETOOTH, IT'S LIKE THE ANNOUNCEMENT OF THE "END OF DAYS."
"HEAVEN HELP WHOEVER HE'S HUNTING."
SNIFF

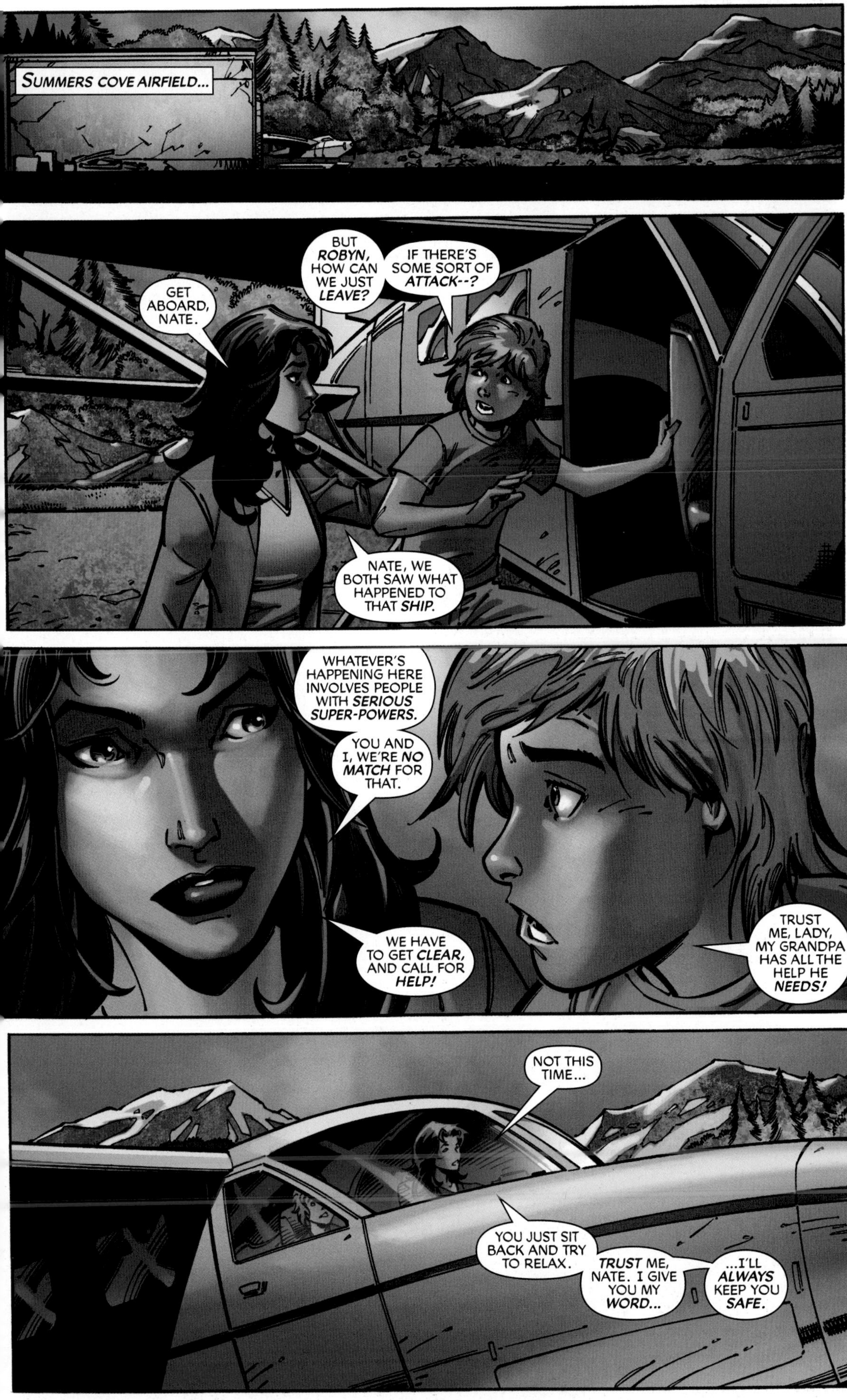
SUMMERS COVE AIRFIELD...
GET ABOARD, NATE.
BUT ROBYN, HOW CAN WE JUST LEAVE?
IF THERE'S SOME SORT OF ATTACK--?
NATE, WE BOTH SAW WHAT HAPPENED TO THAT SHIP.
WHATEVER'S HAPPENING HERE INVOLVES PEOPLE WITH SERIOUS SUPER-POWERS.
YOU AND I, WE'RE NO MATCH FOR THAT.
WE HAVE TO GET CLEAR, AND CALL FOR HELP!
TRUST ME, LADY, MY GRANDPA HAS ALL THE HELP HE NEEDS!
NOT THIS TIME...
YOU JUST SIT BACK AND TRY TO RELAX.
TRUST ME, NATE. I GIVE YOU MY WORD...
...I'LL ALWAYS KEEP YOU SAFE.

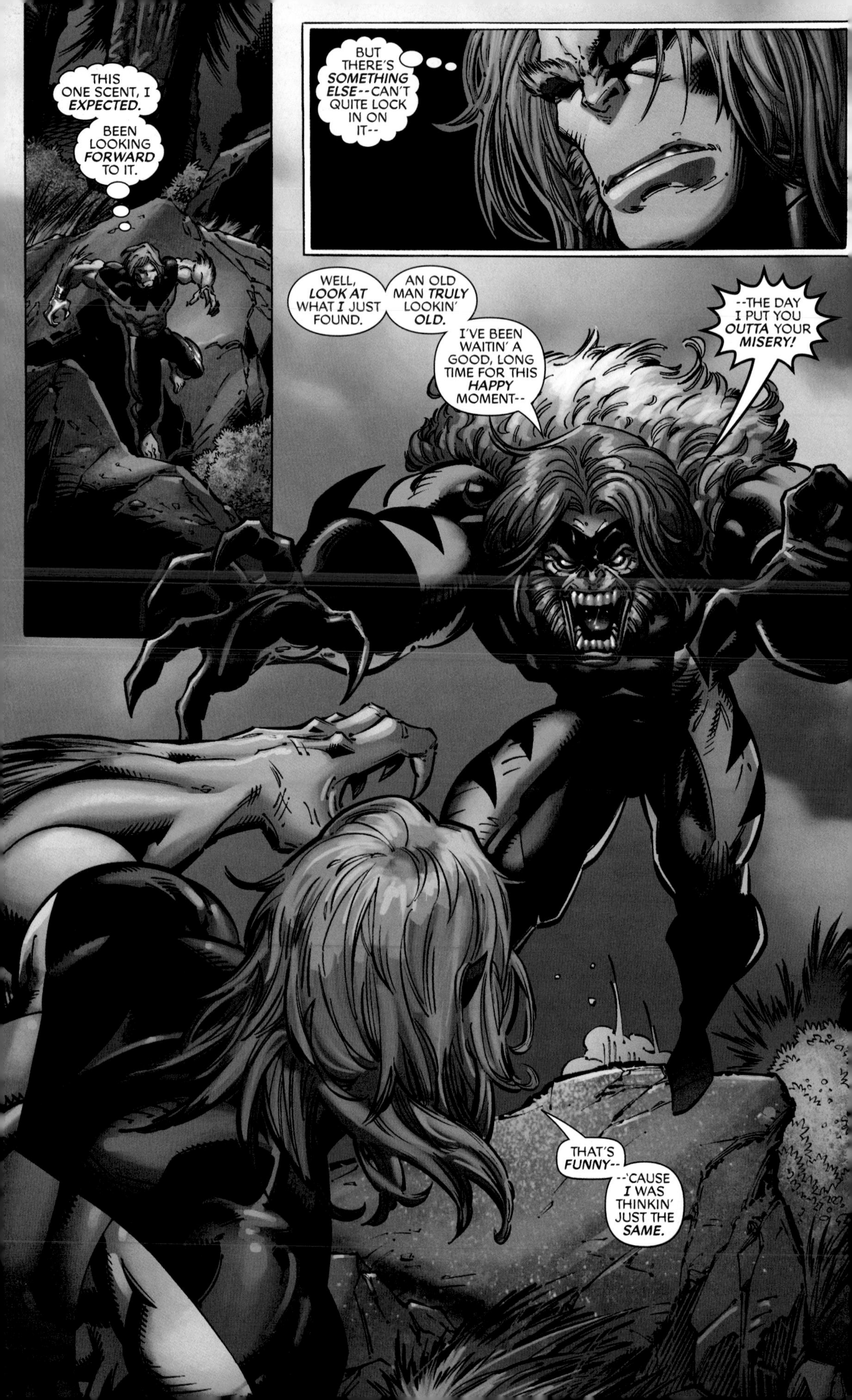

THIS ONE SCENT, I EXPECTED.
BEEN LOOKING FORWARD TO IT.
BUT THERE'S SOMETHING ELSE--CAN'T QUITE LOCK IN ON IT--
WELL, LOOK AT WHAT I JUST FOUND.
AN OLD MAN TRULY LOOKIN' OLD.
I'VE BEEN WAITIN' A GOOD, LONG TIME FOR THIS HAPPY MOMENT--
--THE DAY I PUT YOU OUTTA YOUR MISERY!
THAT'S FUNNY--
--'CAUSE I WAS THINKIN' JUST THE SAME.

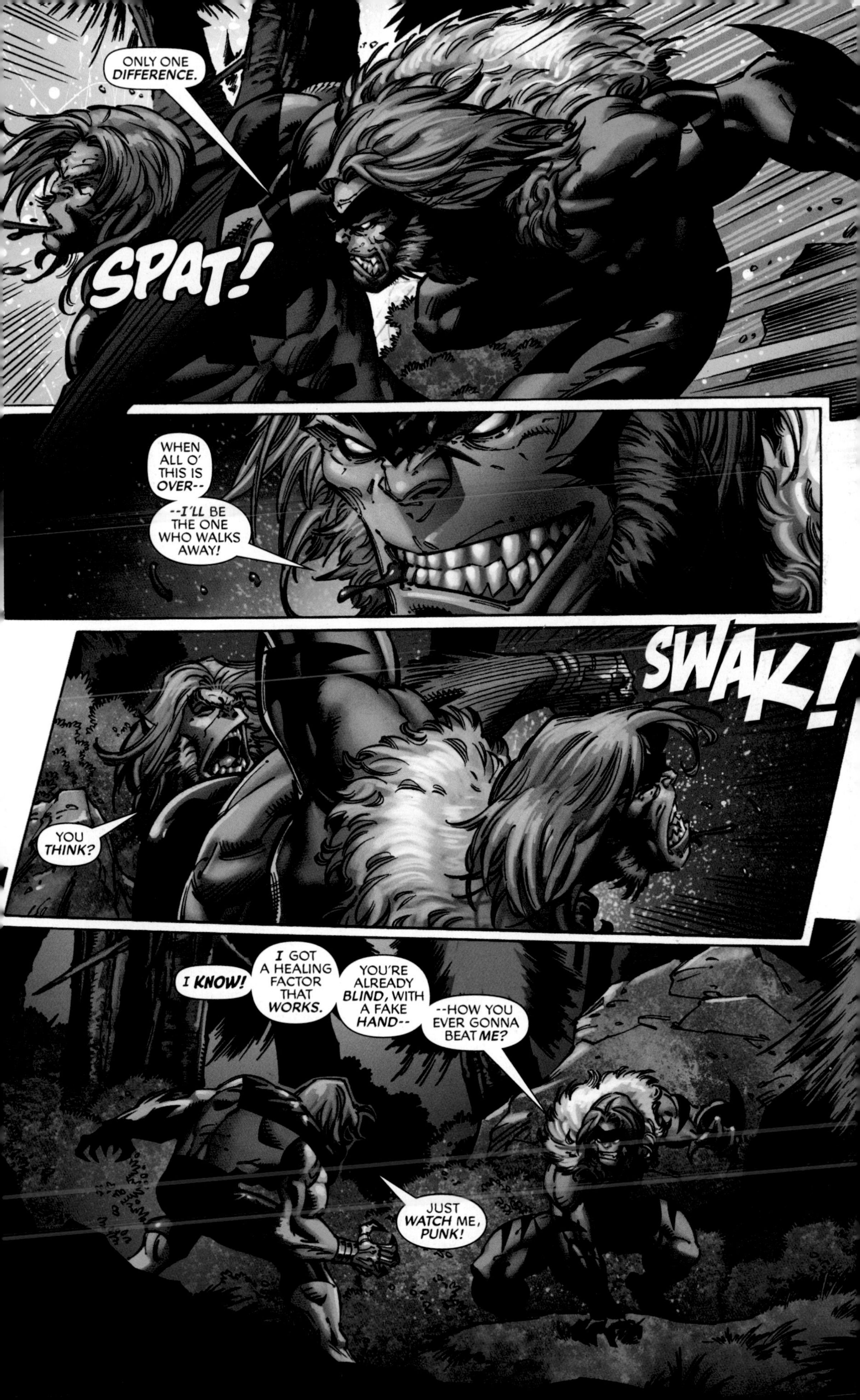
ONLY ONE DIFFERENCE.
SPAT!
WHEN ALL O' THIS IS OVER--
--I'LL BE THE ONE WHO WALKS AWAY!
SWAK!
YOU THINK?
I KNOW!
I GOT A HEALING FACTOR THAT WORKS.
YOU'RE ALREADY BLIND, WITH A FAKE HAND--
--HOW YOU EVER GONNA BEAT ME?
JUST WATCH ME, PUNK!

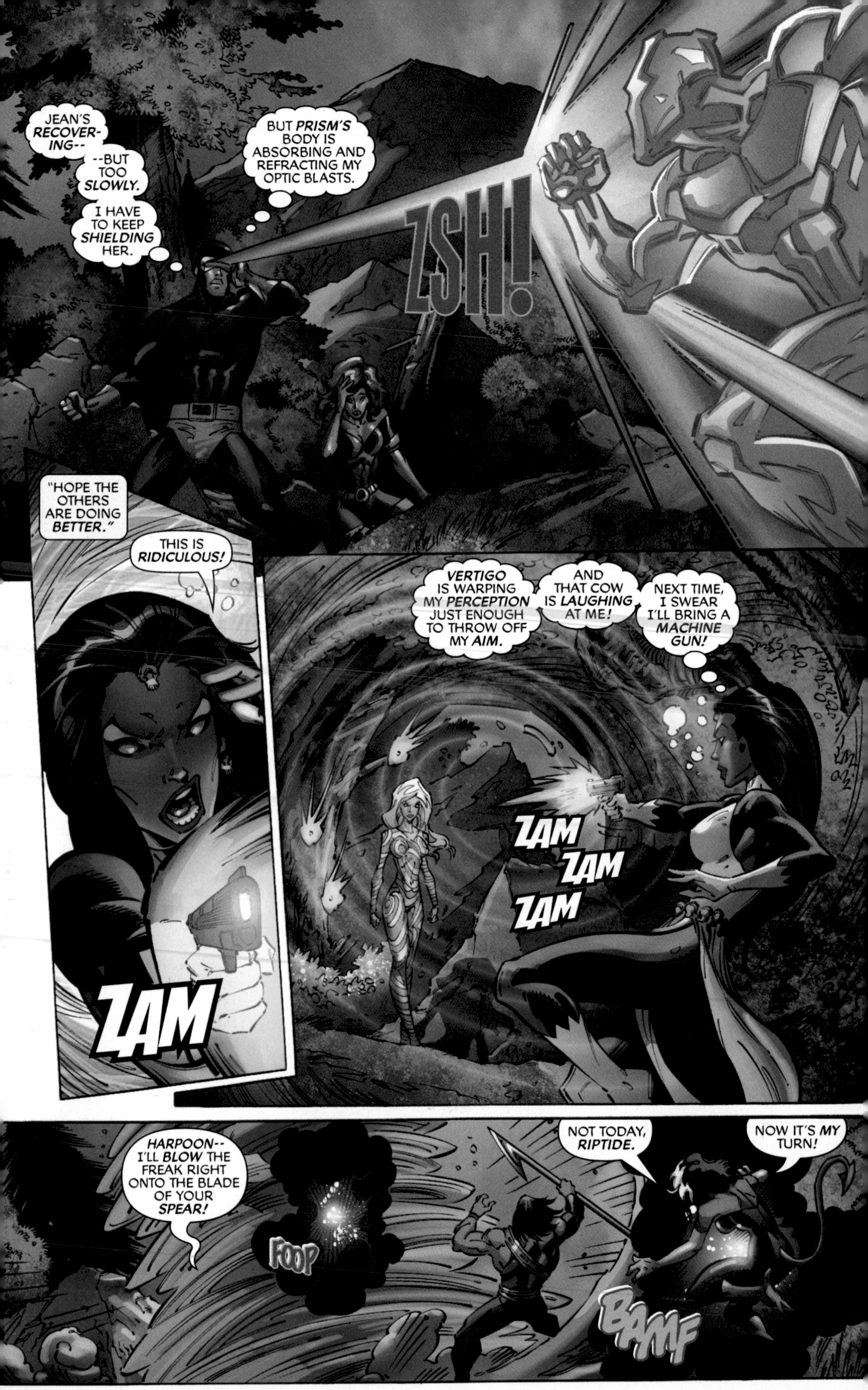

JEAN'S RECOVERING--
--BUT TOO SLOWLY.
I HAVE TO KEEP SHIELDING HER.
BUT PRISM'S BODY IS ABSORBING AND REFRACTING MY OPTIC BLASTS.
ZSH!
"HOPE THE OTHERS ARE DOING BETTER."
THIS IS RIDICULOUS!
ZAM
VERTIGO IS WARPING MY PERCEPTION JUST ENOUGH TO THROW OFF MY AIM.
AND THAT COW IS LAUGHING AT ME!
NEXT TIME, I SWEAR I'LL BRING A MACHINE GUN!
ZAM ZAM ZAM
HARPOON-- I'LL BLOW THE FREAK RIGHT ONTO THE BLADE OF YOUR SPEAR!
FOOP
NOT TODAY, RIPTIDE.
NOW IT'S MY TURN!
BAMF

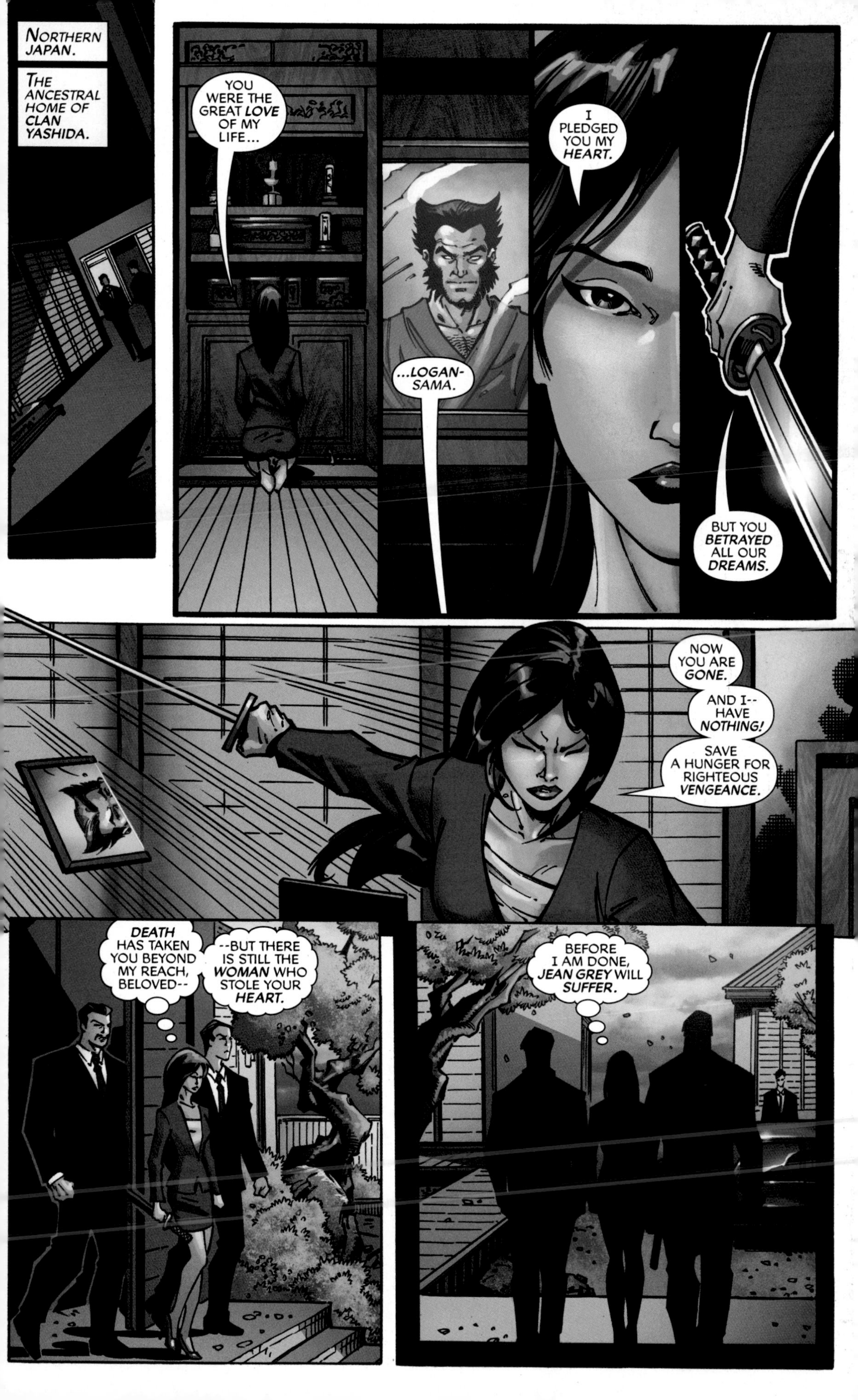
NORTHERN JAPAN.
THE ANCESTRAL HOME OF CLAN YASHIDA.
YOU WERE THE GREAT LOVE OF MY LIFE...
...LOGAN-SAMA.
I PLEDGED YOU MY HEART.
BUT YOU BETRAYED ALL OUR DREAMS.
NOW YOU ARE GONE.
AND I-- HAVE NOTHING!
SAVE A HUNGER FOR RIGHTEOUS VENGEANCE.
DEATH HAS TAKEN YOU BEYOND MY REACH, BELOVED--
--BUT THERE IS STILL THE WOMAN WHO STOLE YOUR HEART.
BEFORE I AM DONE, JEAN GREY WILL SUFFER.

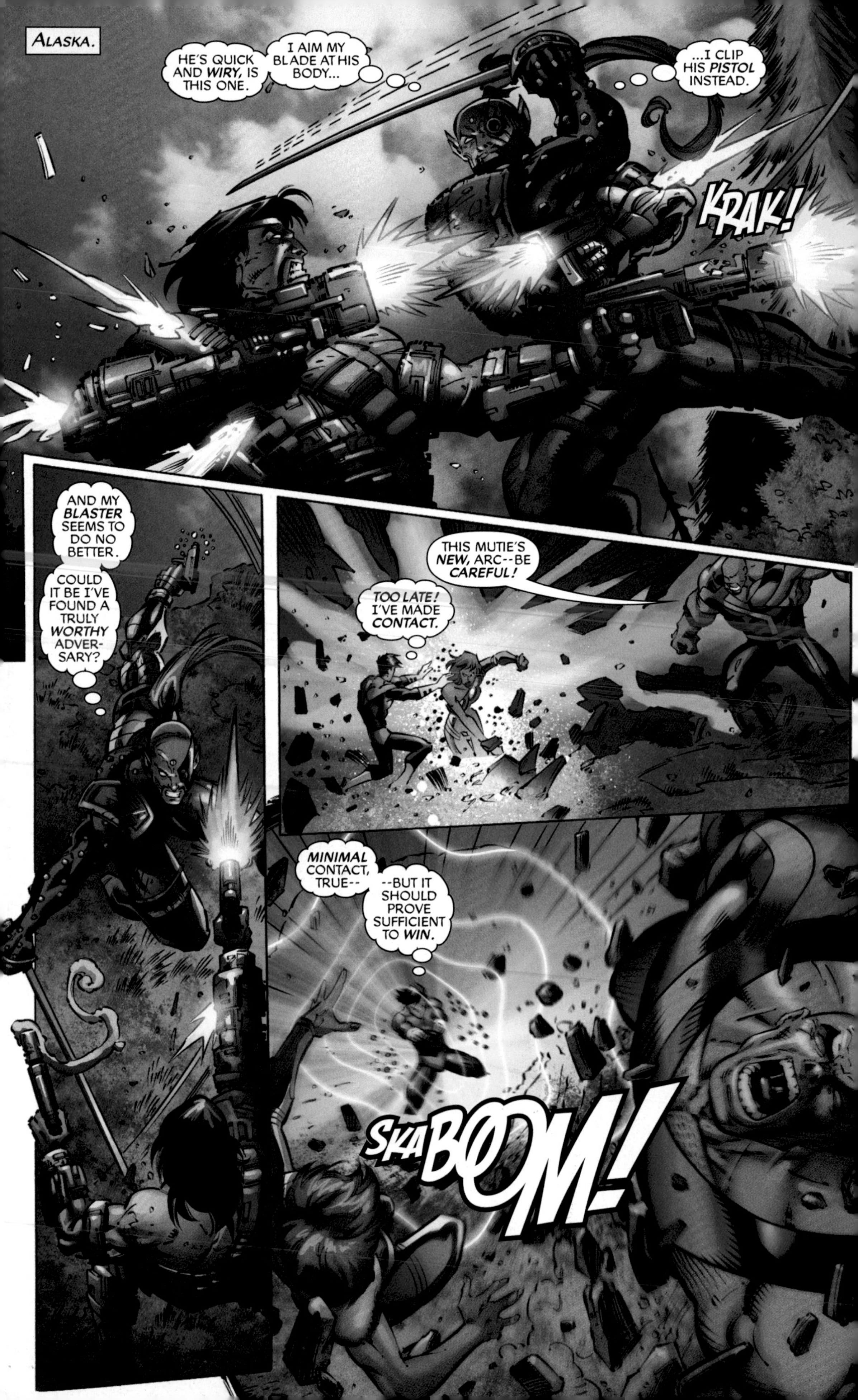

ALASKA.
HE'S QUICK AND WIRY, IS THIS ONE.
I AIM MY BLADE AT HIS BODY...
...I CLIP HIS PISTOL INSTEAD.
KRAK!
AND MY BLASTER SEEMS TO DO NO BETTER.
COULD IT BE I'VE FOUND A TRULY WORTHY ADVER-SARY?
THIS MUTIE'S NEW, ARC--BE CAREFUL!
TOO LATE! I'VE MADE CONTACT.
MINIMAL CONTACT, TRUE--
--BUT IT SHOULD PROVE SUFFICIENT TO WIN.
SKABOOM!

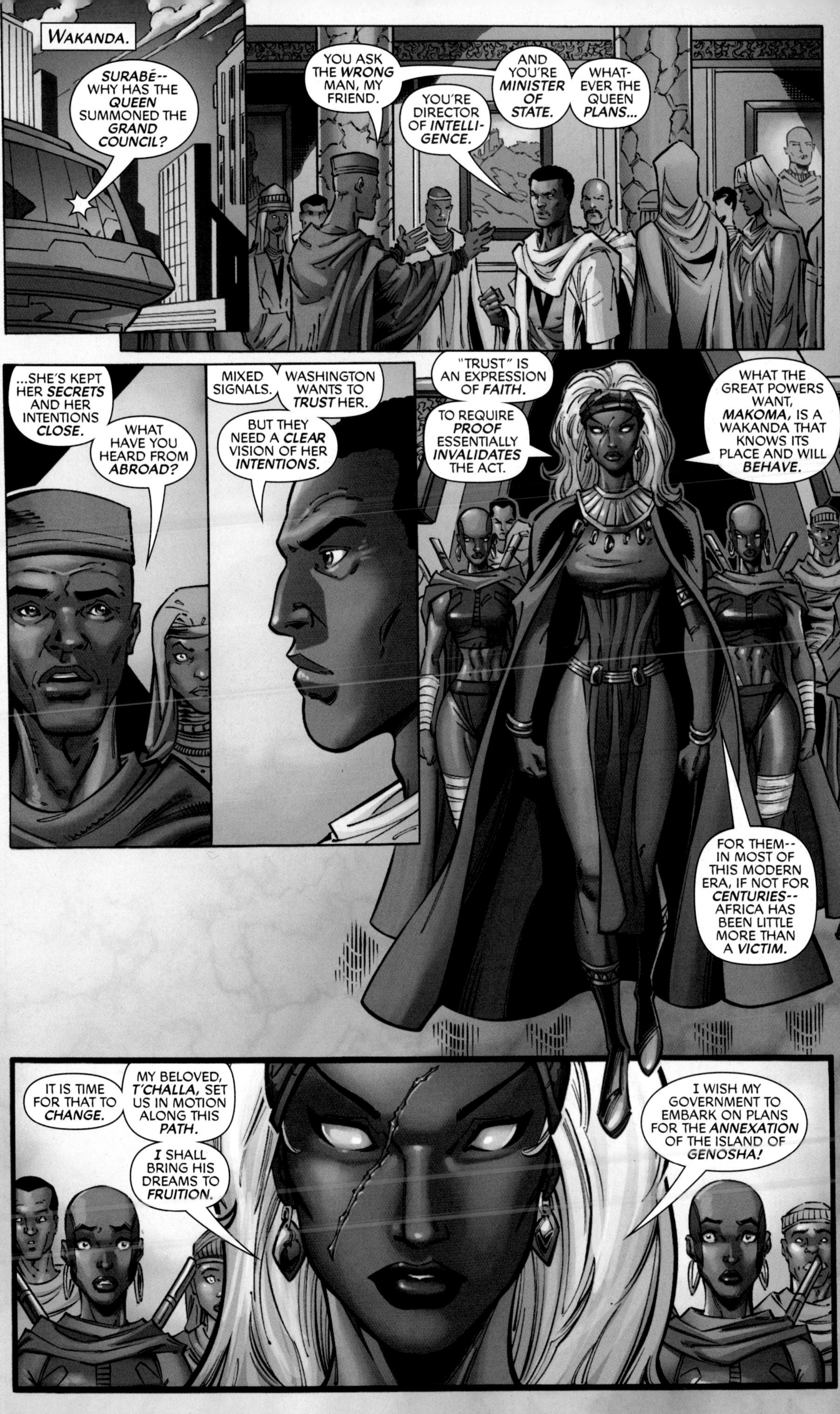
WAKANDA.
SURABÉ-- WHY HAS THE QUEEN SUMMONED THE GRAND COUNCIL?
YOU ASK THE WRONG MAN, MY FRIEND.
YOU'RE DIRECTOR OF INTELLIGENCE.
AND YOU'RE MINISTER OF STATE.
WHATEVER THE QUEEN PLANS...
...SHE'S KEPT HER SECRETS AND HER INTENTIONS CLOSE.
WHAT HAVE YOU HEARD FROM ABROAD?
MIXED SIGNALS.
WASHINGTON WANTS TO TRUST HER.
BUT THEY NEED A CLEAR VISION OF HER INTENTIONS.
"TRUST" IS AN EXPRESSION OF FAITH.
TO REQUIRE PROOF ESSENTIALLY INVALIDATES THE ACT.
WHAT THE GREAT POWERS WANT, MAKOMA, IS A WAKANDA THAT KNOWS ITS PLACE AND WILL BEHAVE.
FOR THEM-- IN MOST OF THIS MODERN ERA, IF NOT FOR CENTURIES-- AFRICA HAS BEEN LITTLE MORE THAN A VICTIM.
IT IS TIME FOR THAT TO CHANGE.
MY BELOVED, T'CHALLA, SET US IN MOTION ALONG THIS PATH.
I SHALL BRING HIS DREAMS TO FRUITION.
I WISH MY GOVERNMENT TO EMBARK ON PLANS FOR THE ANNEXATION OF THE ISLAND OF GENOSHA!

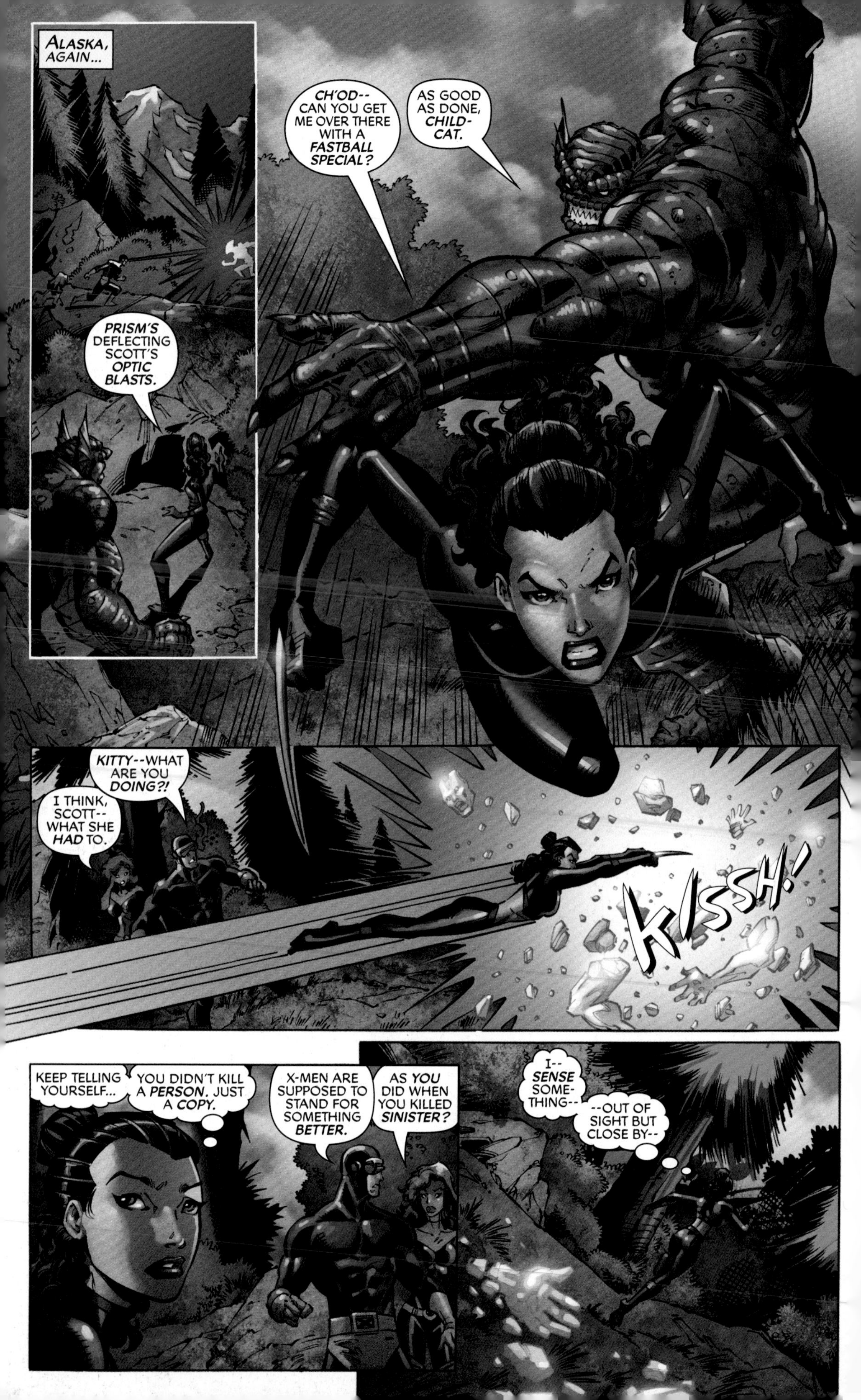

ALASKA, AGAIN...
PRISM'S DEFLECTING SCOTT'S OPTIC BLASTS.
CH'OD-- CAN YOU GET ME OVER THERE WITH A FASTBALL SPECIAL?
AS GOOD AS DONE, CHILD-CAT.
KITTY--WHAT ARE YOU DOING?!
I THINK, SCOTT-- WHAT SHE HAD TO.
KISSH!
KEEP TELLING YOURSELF...
YOU DIDN'T KILL A PERSON. JUST A COPY.
X-MEN ARE SUPPOSED TO STAND FOR SOMETHING BETTER.
AS YOU DID WHEN YOU KILLED SINISTER?
I-- SENSE SOME-THING--
--OUT OF SIGHT BUT CLOSE BY--

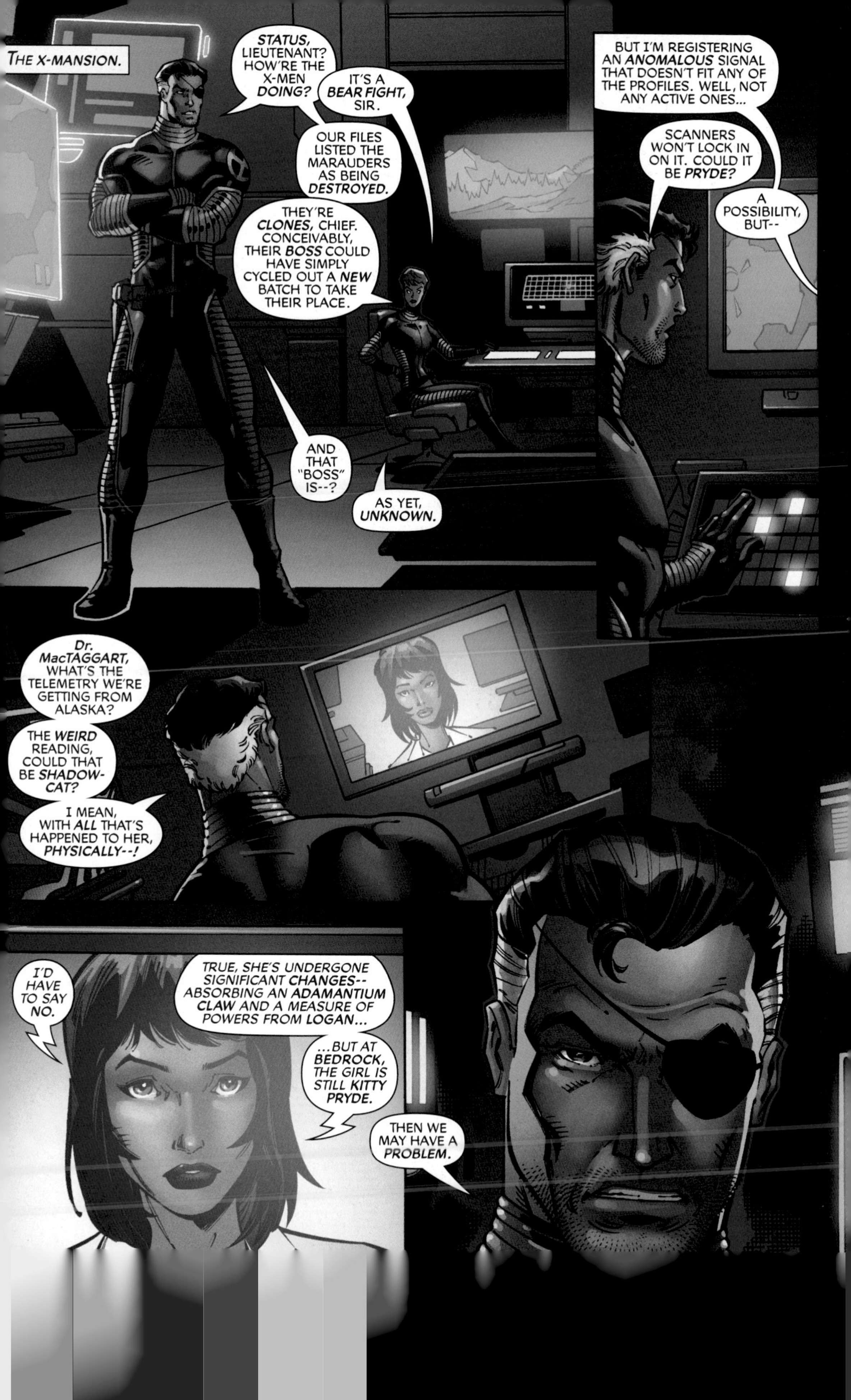
THE X-MANSION.
STATUS, LIEUTENANT? HOW'RE THE X-MEN DOING?
IT'S A BEAR FIGHT, SIR.
OUR FILES LISTED THE MARAUDERS AS BEING DESTROYED.
THEY'RE CLONES, CHIEF. CONCEIVABLY, THEIR BOSS COULD HAVE SIMPLY CYCLED OUT A NEW BATCH TO TAKE THEIR PLACE.
AND THAT "BOSS" IS--?
AS YET, UNKNOWN.
BUT I'M REGISTERING AN ANOMALOUS SIGNAL THAT DOESN'T FIT ANY OF THE PROFILES. WELL, NOT ANY ACTIVE ONES...
SCANNERS WON'T LOCK IN ON IT. COULD IT BE PRYDE?
A POSSIBILITY, BUT--
Dr. MacTAGGART, WHAT'S THE TELEMETRY WE'RE GETTING FROM ALASKA?
THE WEIRD READING, COULD THAT BE SHADOW-CAT?
I MEAN, WITH ALL THAT'S HAPPENED TO HER, PHYSICALLY--!
I'D HAVE TO SAY NO.
TRUE, SHE'S UNDERGONE SIGNIFICANT CHANGES-- ABSORBING AN ADAMANTIUM CLAW AND A MEASURE OF POWERS FROM LOGAN...
...BUT AT BEDROCK, THE GIRL IS STILL KITTY PRYDE.
THEN WE MAY HAVE A PROBLEM.

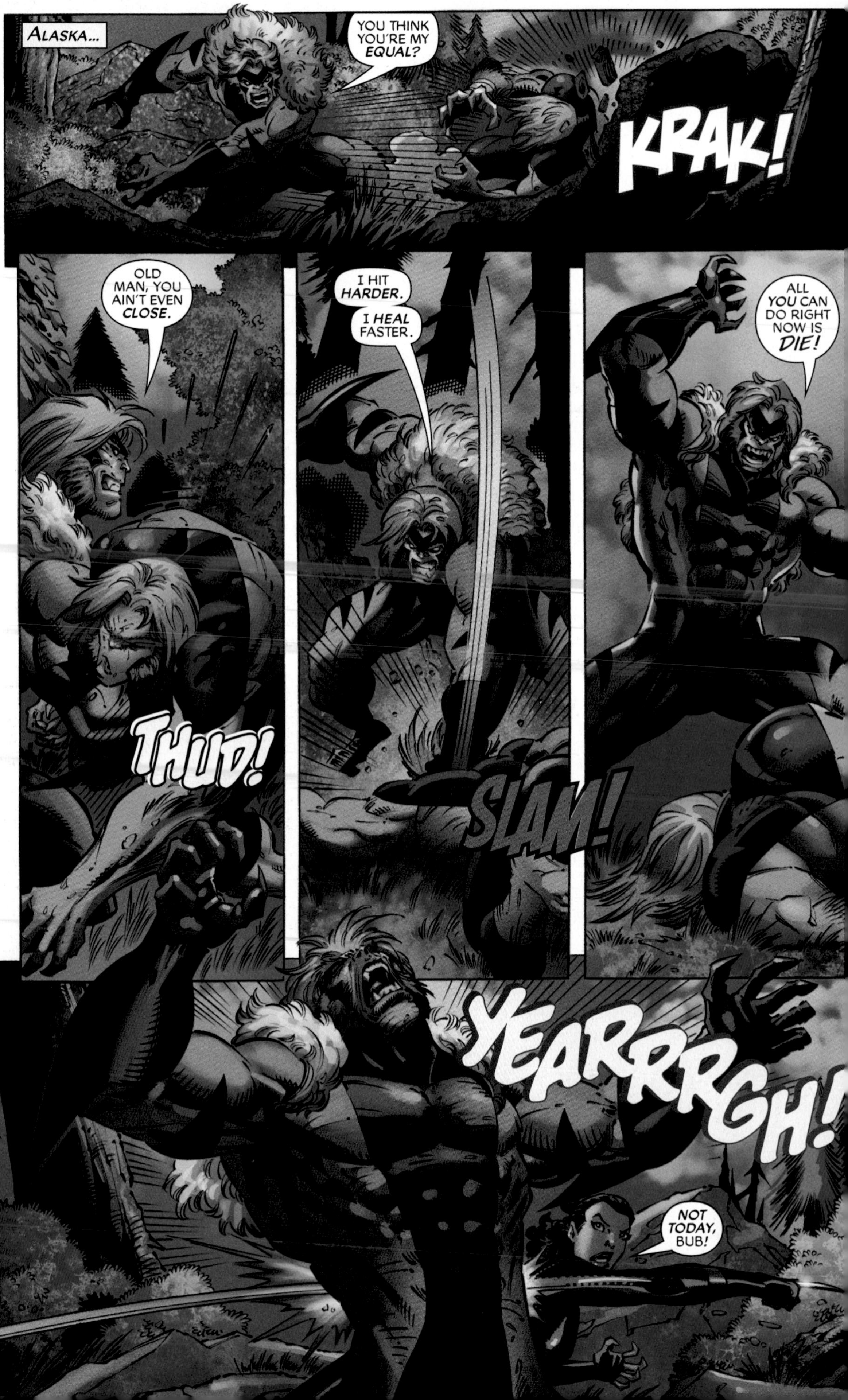

ALASKA...
YOU THINK YOU'RE MY EQUAL?
KRAK!
OLD MAN, YOU AIN'T EVEN CLOSE.
THUD!
I HIT HARDER.
I HEAL FASTER.
SLAM!
ALL YOU CAN DO RIGHT NOW IS DIE!
YEARRRGH!
NOT TODAY, BUB!

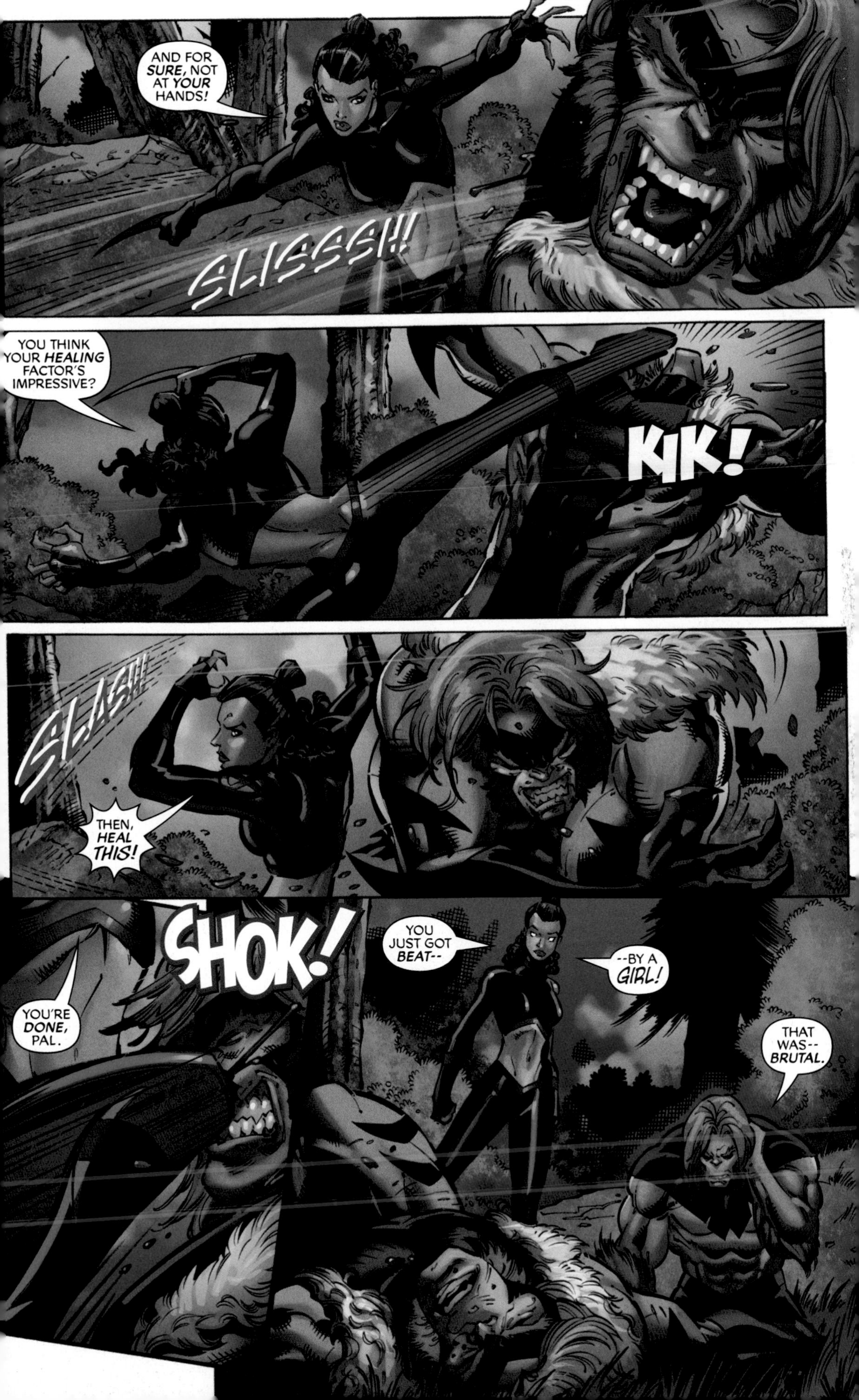
AND FOR SURE, NOT AT YOUR HANDS!
SLISSSH!
YOU THINK YOUR HEALING FACTOR'S IMPRESSIVE?
KIK!
SLASH!!
THEN, HEAL THIS!
SHOK!
YOU'RE DONE, PAL.
YOU JUST GOT BEAT--
--BY A GIRL!
THAT WAS-- BRUTAL.

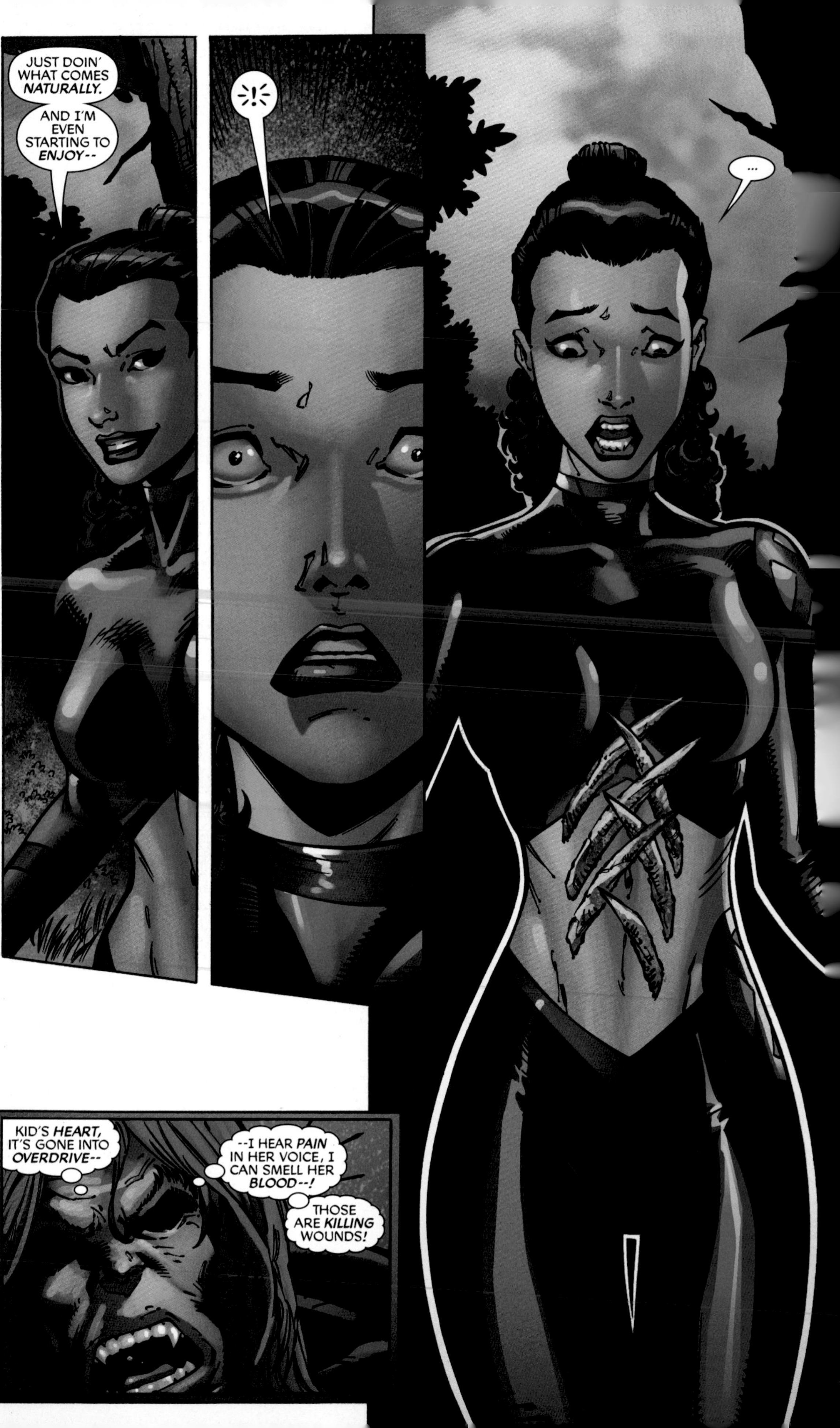
JUST DOIN' WHAT COMES *NATURALLY.*
AND I'M EVEN STARTING TO *ENJOY*--
!
...
KID'S *HEART*, IT'S GONE INTO *OVERDRIVE*--
--I HEAR *PAIN* IN HER VOICE, I CAN SMELL HER *BLOOD*--!
THOSE ARE *KILLING* WOUNDS!

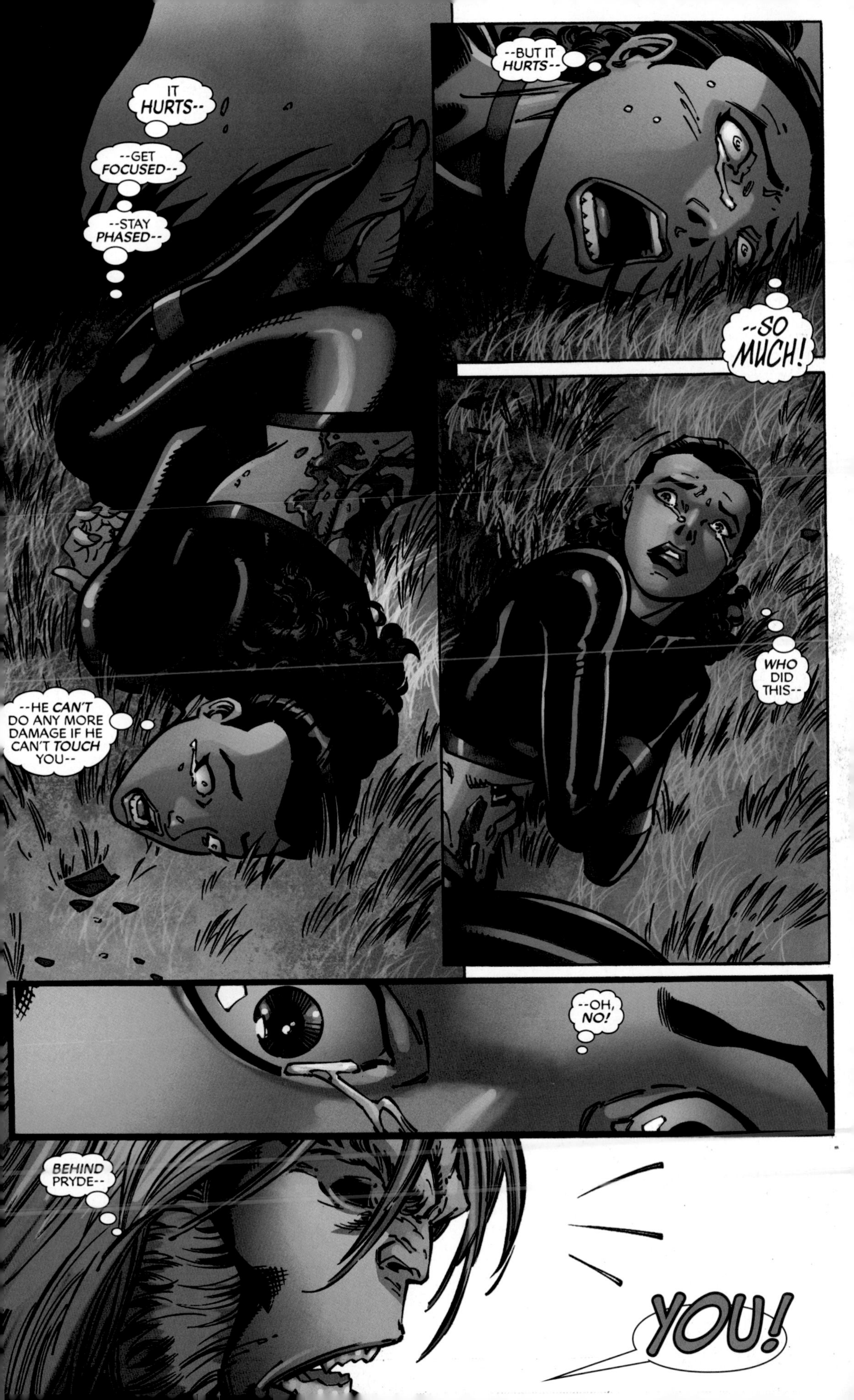
IT HURTS--
--GET FOCUSED--
--STAY PHASED--
--BUT IT HURTS--
--SO MUCH!
--HE CAN'T DO ANY MORE DAMAGE IF HE CAN'T TOUCH YOU--
WHO DID THIS--
--OH, NO!
BEHIND PRYDE--
YOU!

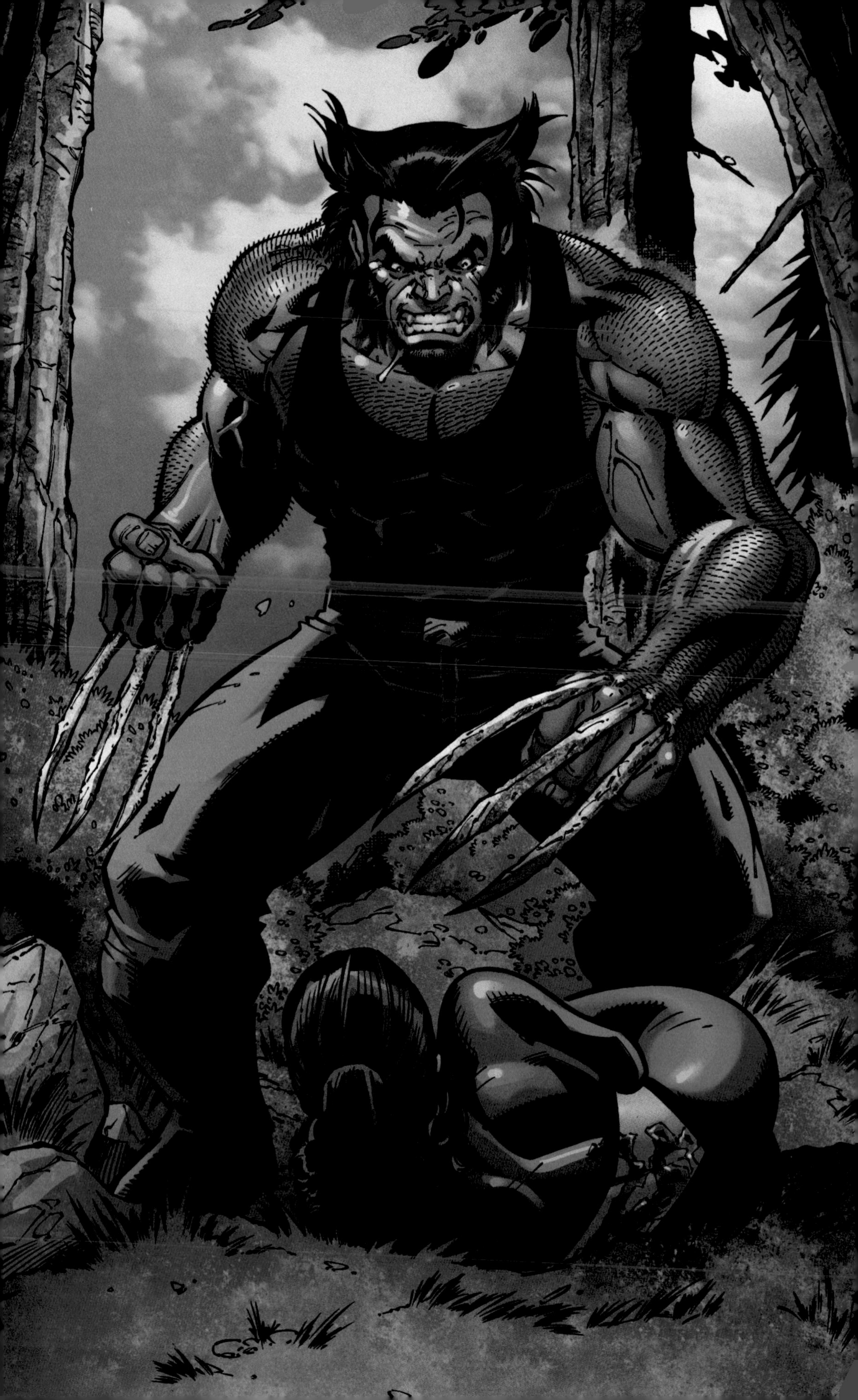

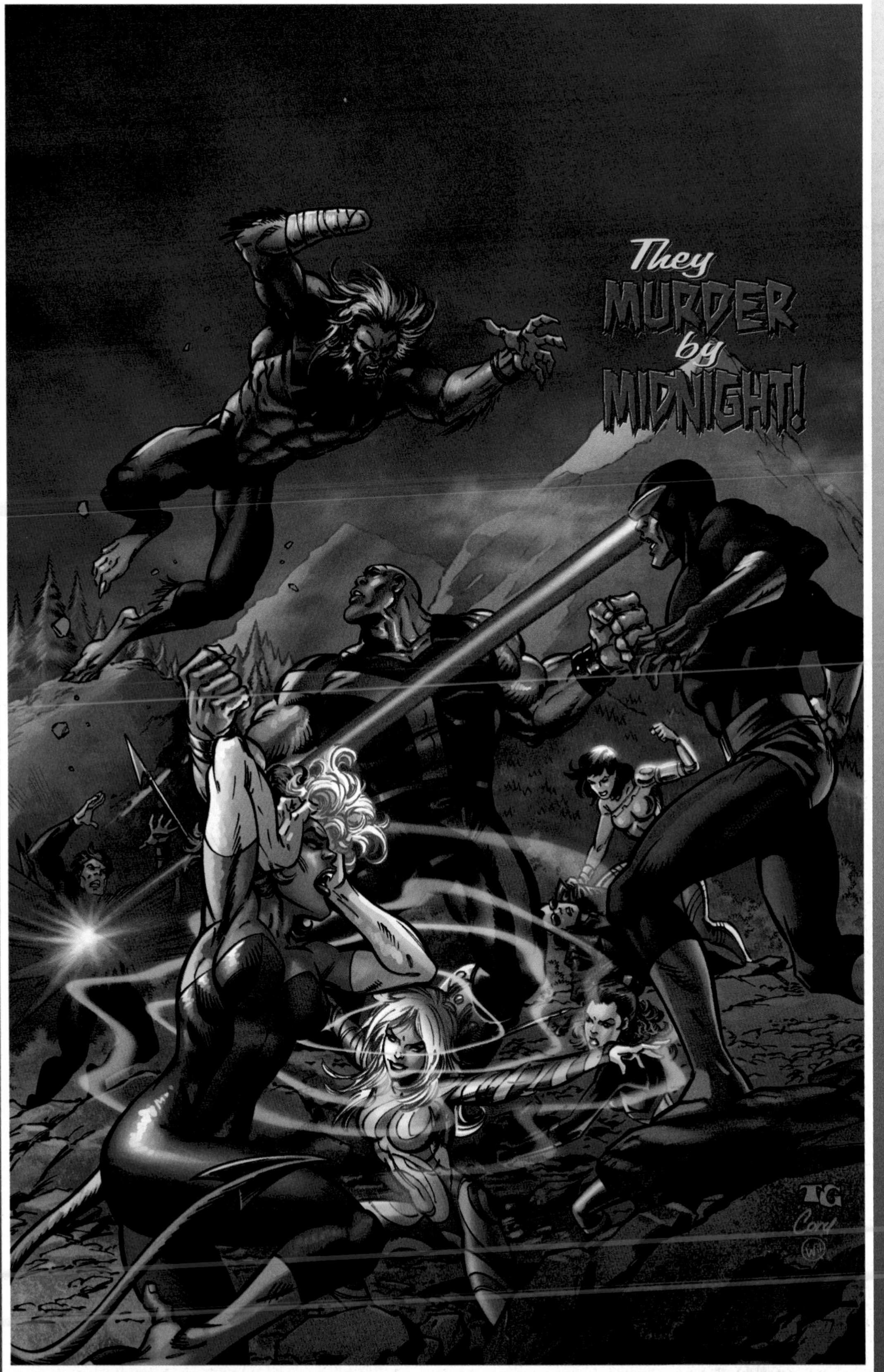
They
MURDER
by
MIDNIGHT!
TG
Cory

EIGHT

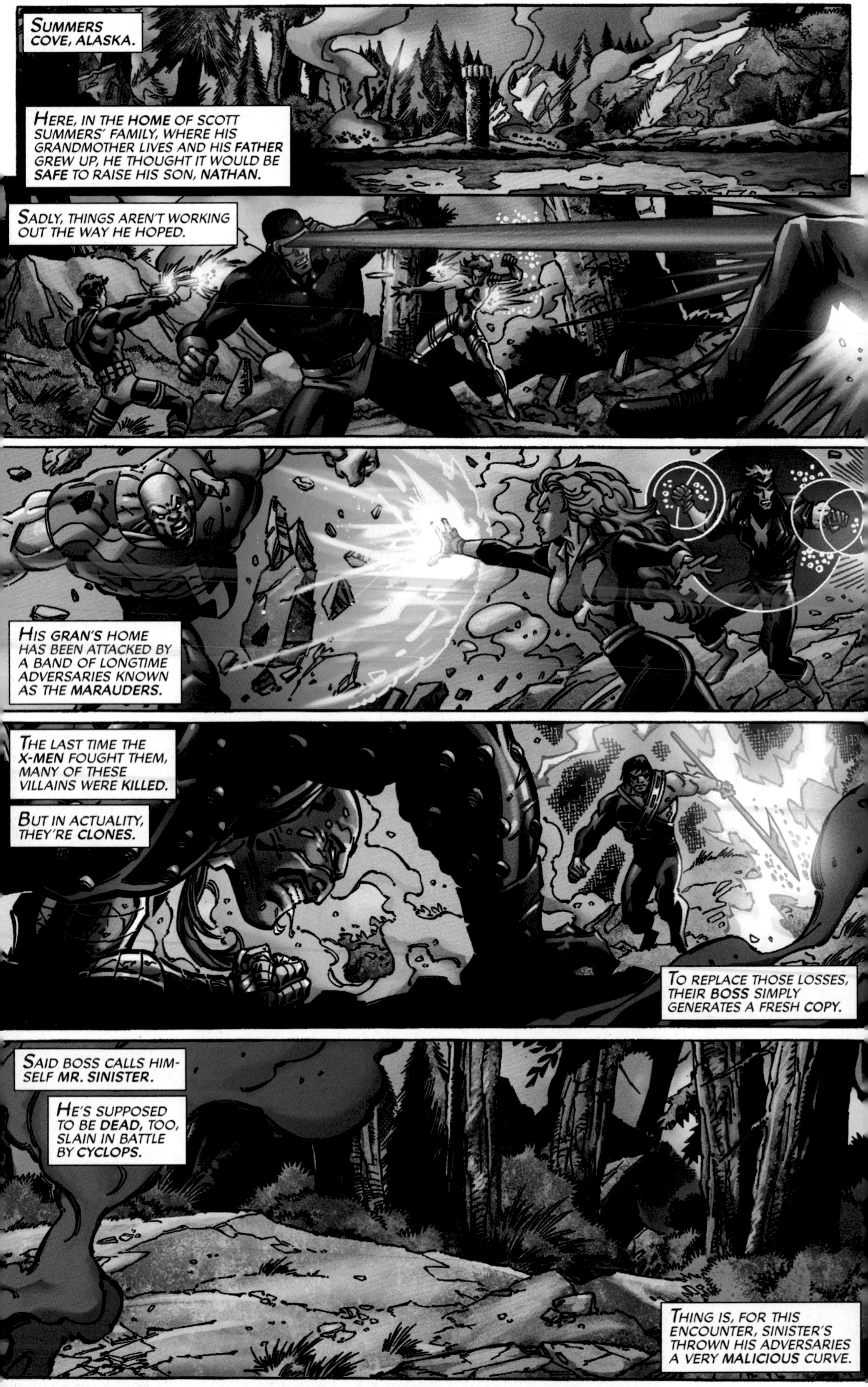
SUMMERS COVE, ALASKA.
HERE, IN THE HOME OF SCOTT SUMMERS' FAMILY, WHERE HIS GRANDMOTHER LIVES AND HIS FATHER GREW UP, HE THOUGHT IT WOULD BE SAFE TO RAISE HIS SON, NATHAN.
SADLY, THINGS AREN'T WORKING OUT THE WAY HE HOPED.
HIS GRAN'S HOME HAS BEEN ATTACKED BY A BAND OF LONGTIME ADVERSARIES KNOWN AS THE MARAUDERS.
THE LAST TIME THE X-MEN FOUGHT THEM, MANY OF THESE VILLAINS WERE KILLED.
BUT IN ACTUALITY, THEY'RE CLONES.
TO REPLACE THOSE LOSSES, THEIR BOSS SIMPLY GENERATES A FRESH COPY.
SAID BOSS CALLS HIMSELF MR. SINISTER.
HE'S SUPPOSED TO BE DEAD, TOO, SLAIN IN BATTLE BY CYCLOPS.
THING IS, FOR THIS ENCOUNTER, SINISTER'S THROWN HIS ADVERSARIES A VERY MALICIOUS CURVE.

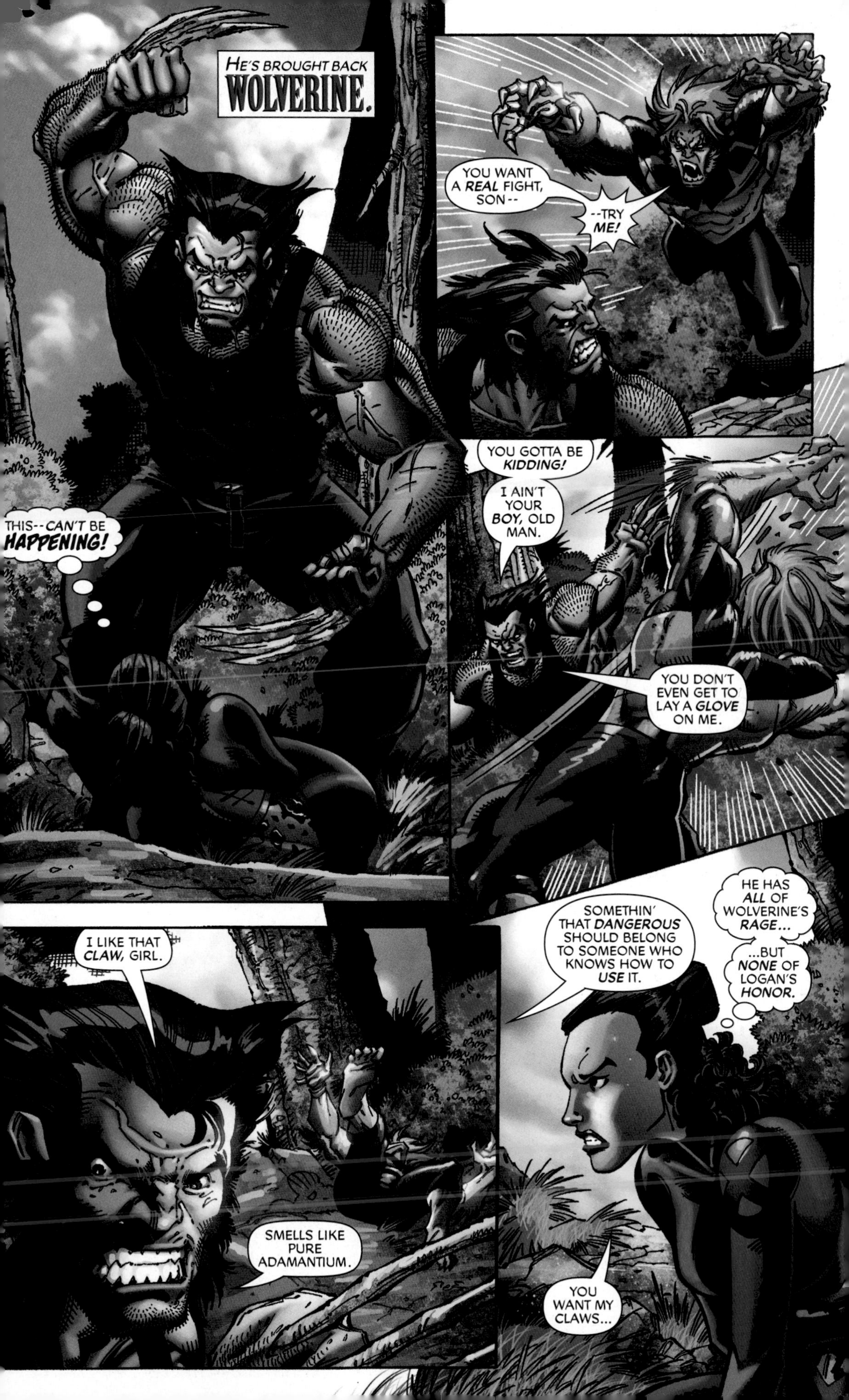

HE'S BROUGHT BACK WOLVERINE.
THIS--CAN'T BE HAPPENING!
YOU WANT A REAL FIGHT, SON--
--TRY ME!
YOU GOTTA BE KIDDING!
I AIN'T YOUR BOY, OLD MAN.
YOU DON'T EVEN GET TO LAY A GLOVE ON ME.
I LIKE THAT CLAW, GIRL.
SMELLS LIKE PURE ADAMANTIUM.
SOMETHIN' THAT DANGEROUS SHOULD BELONG TO SOMEONE WHO KNOWS HOW TO USE IT.
HE HAS ALL OF WOLVERINE'S RAGE...
...BUT NONE OF LOGAN'S HONOR.
YOU WANT MY CLAWS...

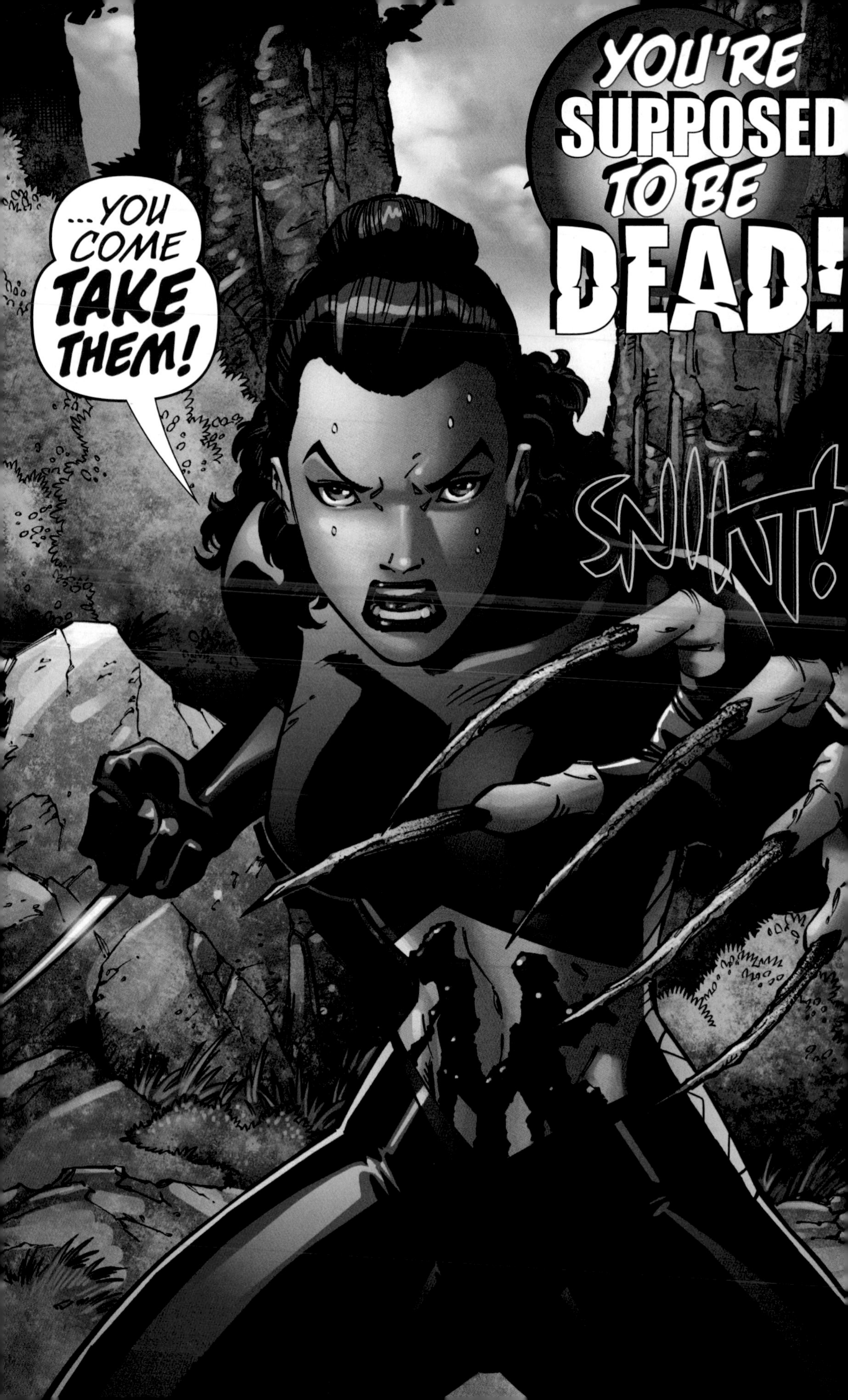

...YOU COME TAKE THEM!
YOU'RE SUPPOSED TO BE DEAD!
SNIKT!

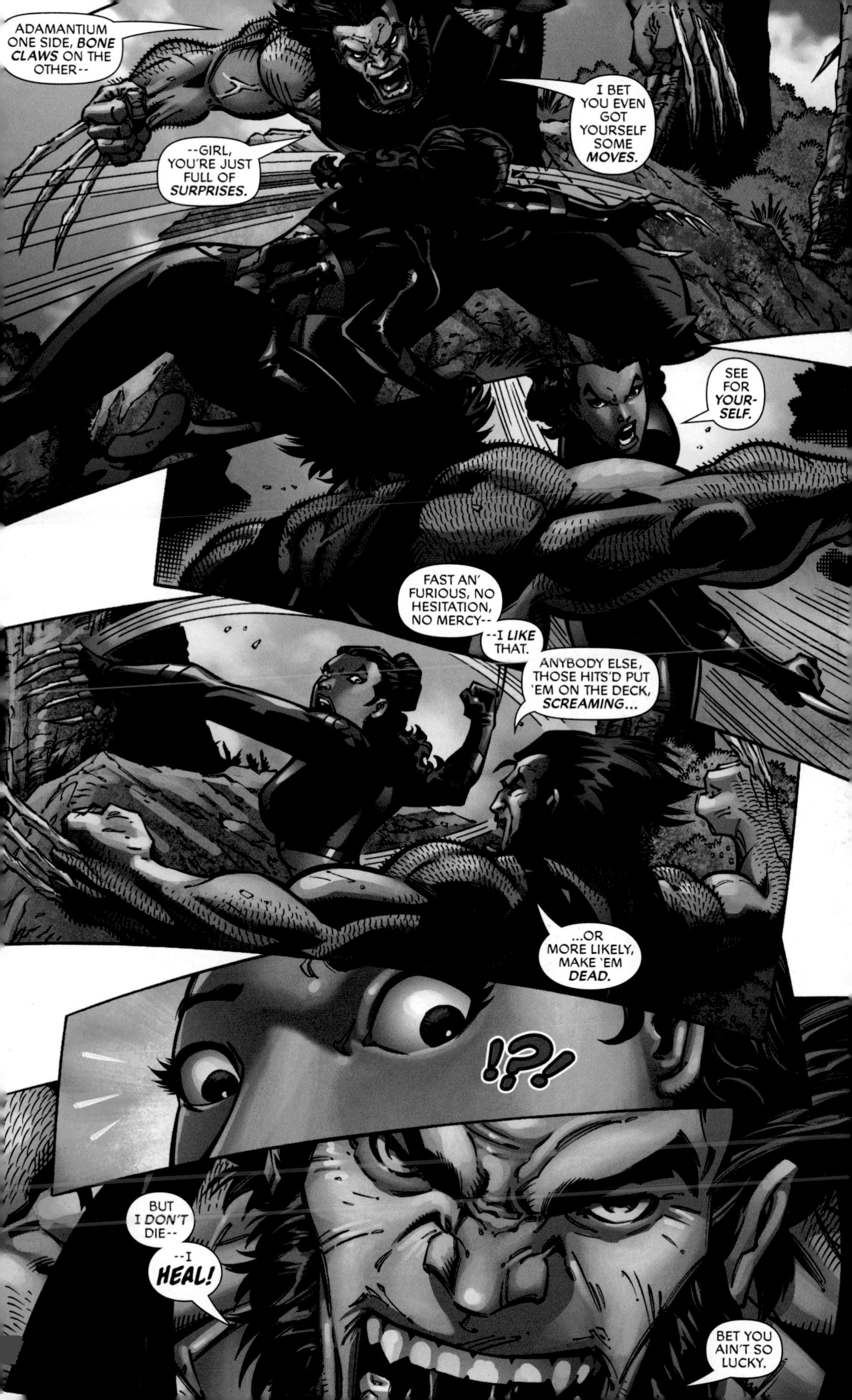
ADAMANTIUM ONE SIDE, BONE CLAWS ON THE OTHER--
--GIRL, YOU'RE JUST FULL OF SURPRISES.
I BET YOU EVEN GOT YOURSELF SOME MOVES.
SEE FOR YOURSELF.
FAST AN' FURIOUS, NO HESITATION, NO MERCY--
--I LIKE THAT.
ANYBODY ELSE, THOSE HITS'D PUT 'EM ON THE DECK, SCREAMING...
...OR MORE LIKELY, MAKE 'EM DEAD.
!?!
BUT I DON'T DIE--
--I HEAL!
BET YOU AIN'T SO LUCKY.

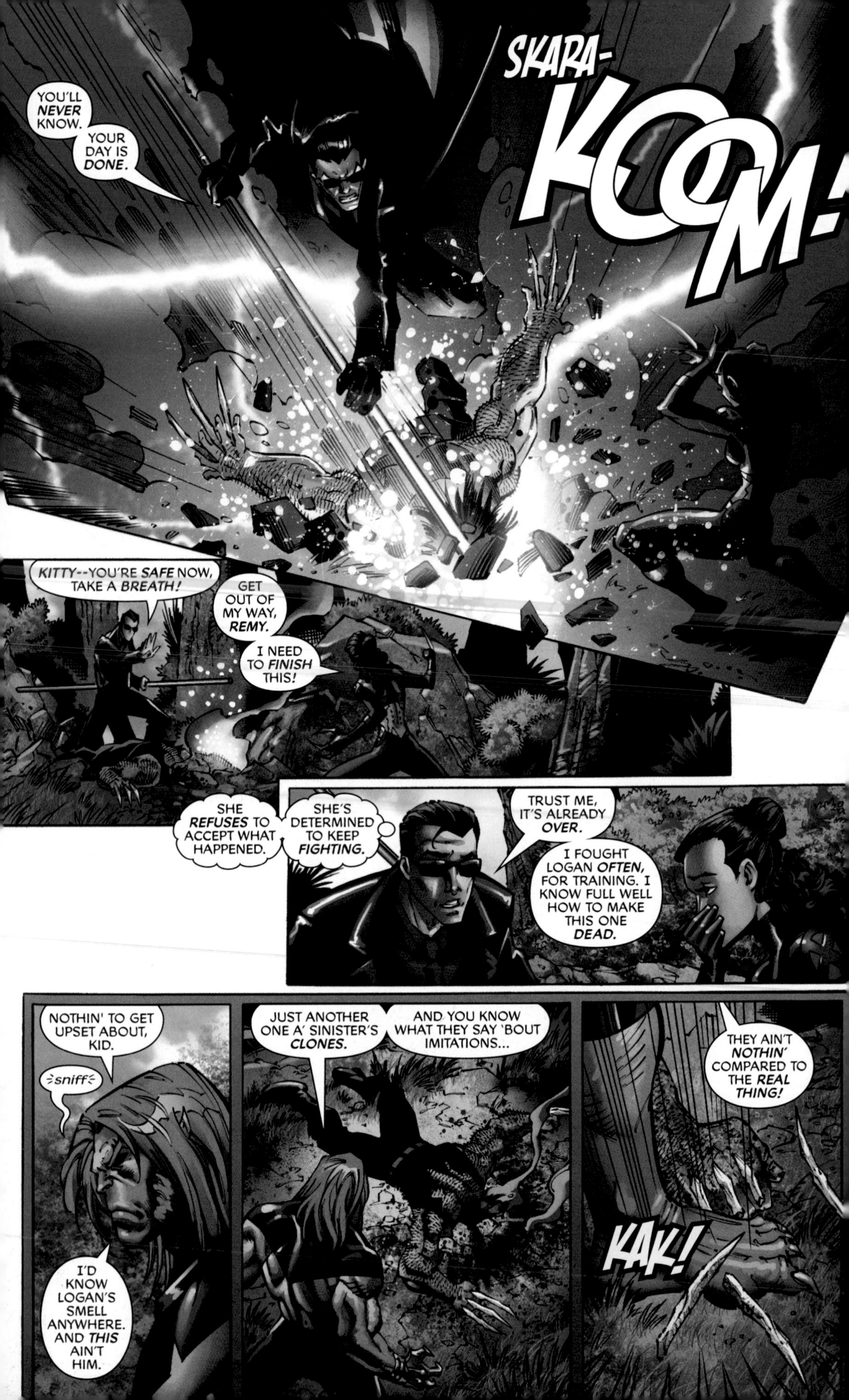
YOU'LL NEVER KNOW.
YOUR DAY IS DONE.
SKARA-KOOM!
KITTY--YOU'RE SAFE NOW, TAKE A BREATH!
GET OUT OF MY WAY, REMY.
I NEED TO FINISH THIS!
SHE REFUSES TO ACCEPT WHAT HAPPENED.
SHE'S DETERMINED TO KEEP FIGHTING.
TRUST ME, IT'S ALREADY OVER.
I FOUGHT LOGAN OFTEN, FOR TRAINING. I KNOW FULL WELL HOW TO MAKE THIS ONE DEAD.
NOTHIN' TO GET UPSET ABOUT, KID.
sniff
I'D KNOW LOGAN'S SMELL ANYWHERE. AND THIS AIN'T HIM.
JUST ANOTHER ONE A' SINISTER'S CLONES.
AND YOU KNOW WHAT THEY SAY 'BOUT IMITATIONS...
THEY AIN'T NOTHIN' COMPARED TO THE REAL THING!
KAK!

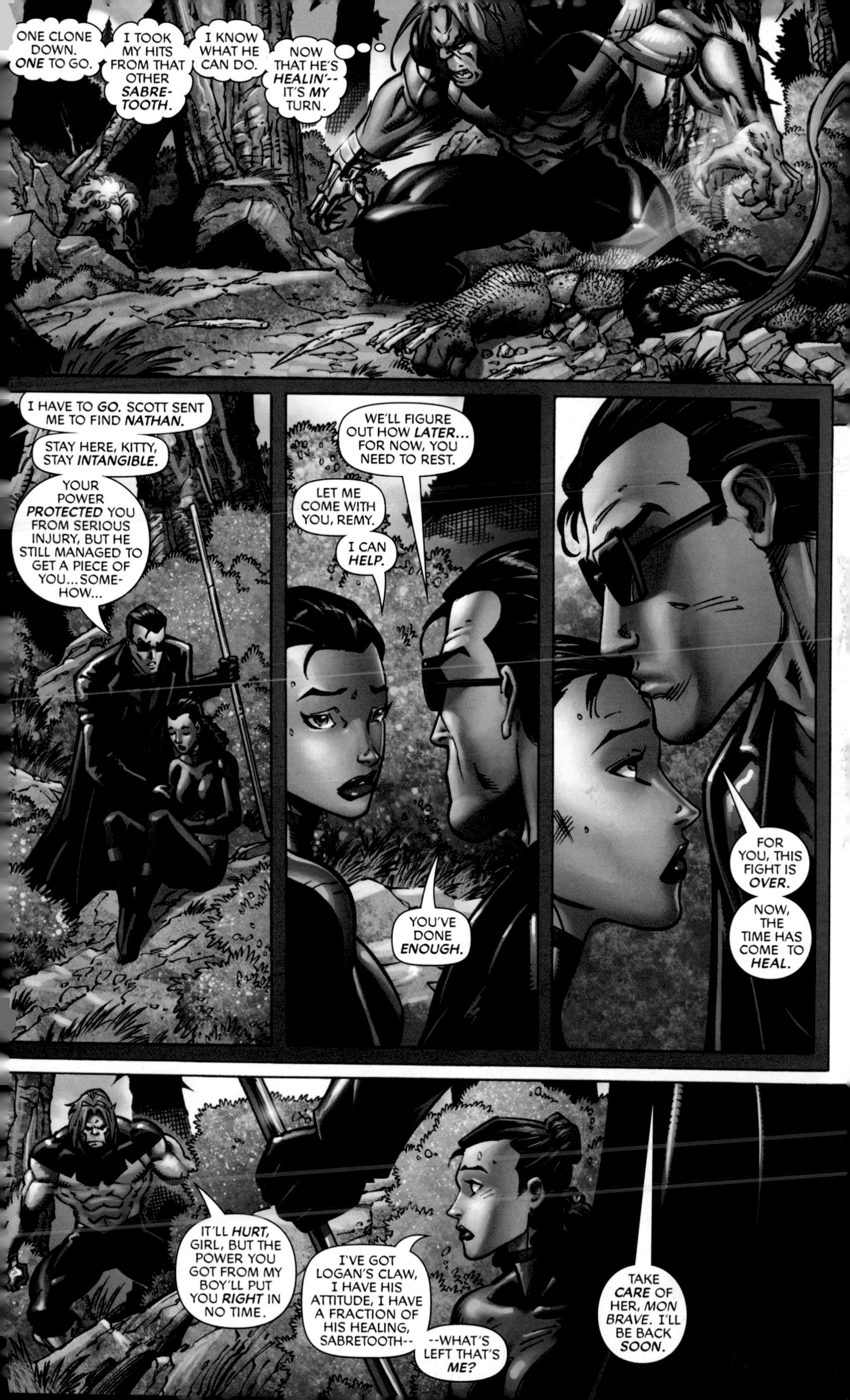
ONE CLONE DOWN. *ONE* TO GO.
I TOOK MY HITS FROM THAT OTHER *SABRETOOTH*.
I KNOW WHAT HE CAN DO.
NOW THAT HE'S *HEALIN'*-- IT'S *MY* TURN.
I HAVE TO *GO.* SCOTT SENT ME TO FIND *NATHAN.*
STAY HERE, KITTY, STAY *INTANGIBLE.*
YOUR POWER *PROTECTED* YOU FROM SERIOUS INJURY, BUT HE STILL MANAGED TO GET A PIECE OF YOU...SOMEHOW...
LET ME COME WITH YOU, REMY.
I CAN *HELP.*
WE'LL FIGURE OUT HOW *LATER...* FOR NOW, YOU NEED TO REST.
YOU'VE DONE *ENOUGH.*
FOR YOU, THIS FIGHT IS *OVER.*
NOW, THE TIME HAS COME TO *HEAL.*
IT'LL *HURT,* GIRL, BUT THE POWER YOU GOT FROM MY BOY'LL PUT YOU *RIGHT* IN NO TIME.
I'VE GOT LOGAN'S CLAW, I HAVE HIS ATTITUDE, I HAVE A FRACTION OF HIS HEALING, SABRETOOTH--
--WHAT'S LEFT THAT'S *ME?*
TAKE *CARE* OF HER, *MON BRAVE.* I'LL BE BACK *SOON.*

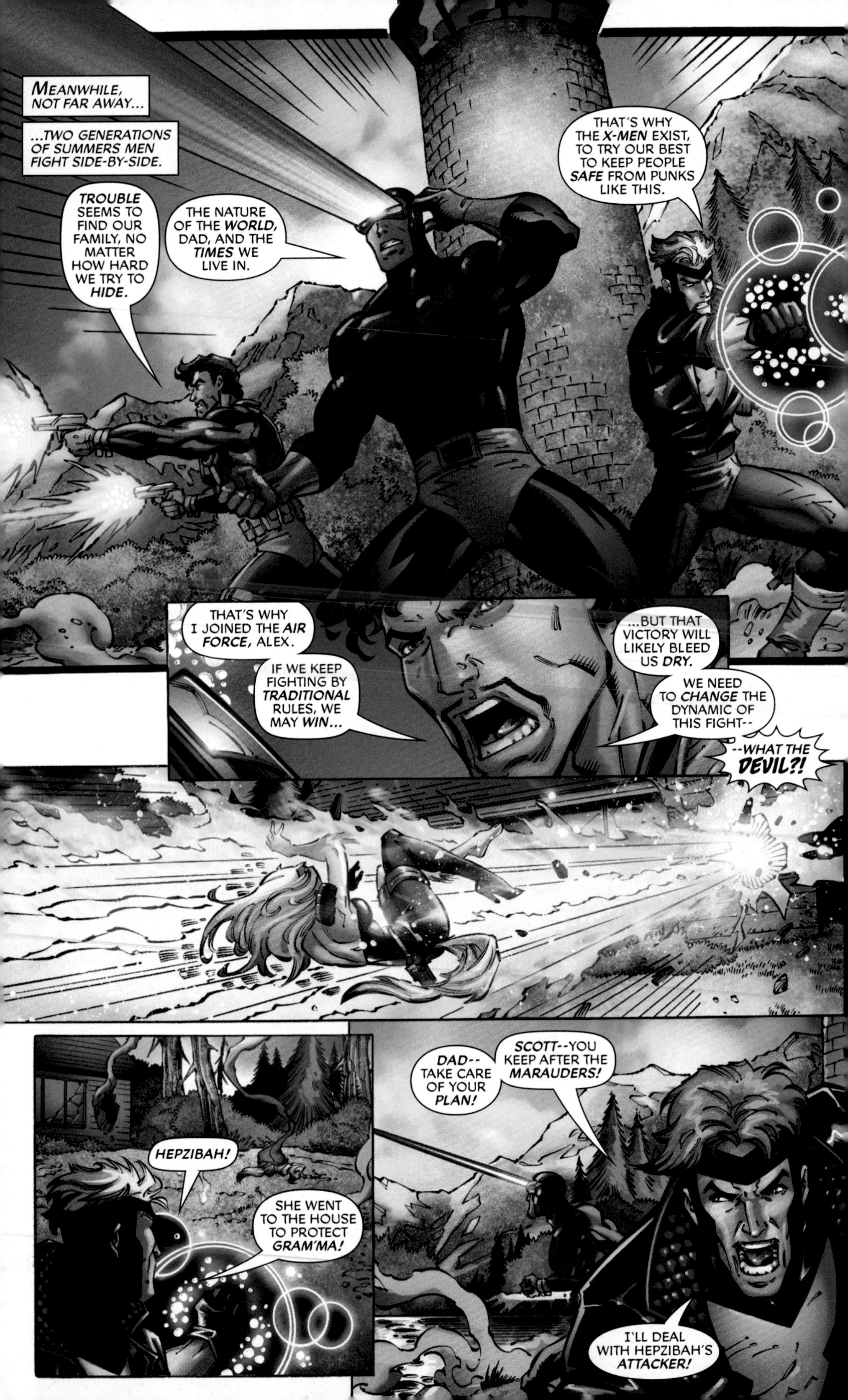
MEANWHILE, NOT FAR AWAY...
...TWO GENERATIONS OF SUMMERS MEN FIGHT SIDE-BY-SIDE.
TROUBLE SEEMS TO FIND OUR FAMILY, NO MATTER HOW HARD WE TRY TO HIDE.
THE NATURE OF THE WORLD, DAD, AND THE TIMES WE LIVE IN.
THAT'S WHY THE X-MEN EXIST, TO TRY OUR BEST TO KEEP PEOPLE SAFE FROM PUNKS LIKE THIS.
THAT'S WHY I JOINED THE AIR FORCE, ALEX.
IF WE KEEP FIGHTING BY TRADITIONAL RULES, WE MAY WIN...
...BUT THAT VICTORY WILL LIKELY BLEED US DRY.
WE NEED TO CHANGE THE DYNAMIC OF THIS FIGHT--
--WHAT THE DEVIL?!
HEPZIBAH!
SHE WENT TO THE HOUSE TO PROTECT GRAM'MA!
DAD-- TAKE CARE OF YOUR PLAN!
SCOTT--YOU KEEP AFTER THE MARAUDERS!
I'LL DEAL WITH HEPZIBAH'S ATTACKER!

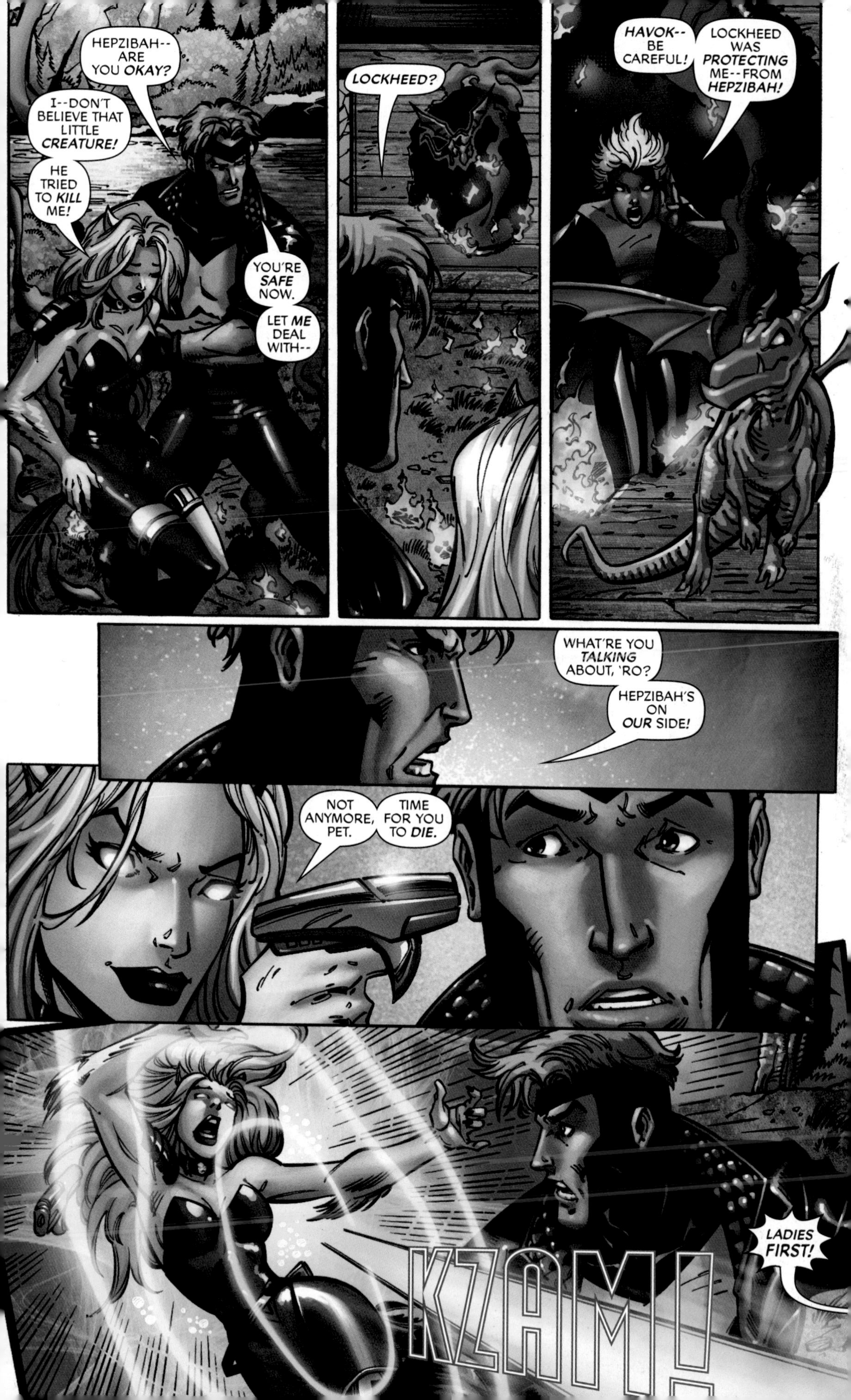
HEPZIBAH-- ARE YOU OKAY?
I--DON'T BELIEVE THAT LITTLE CREATURE!
HE TRIED TO KILL ME!
YOU'RE SAFE NOW.
LET ME DEAL WITH--
LOCKHEED?
HAVOK-- BE CAREFUL!
LOCKHEED WAS PROTECTING ME--FROM HEPZIBAH!
WHAT'RE YOU TALKING ABOUT, 'RO?
HEPZIBAH'S ON OUR SIDE!
NOT ANYMORE, PET.
TIME FOR YOU TO DIE.
LADIES FIRST!
KZAM!

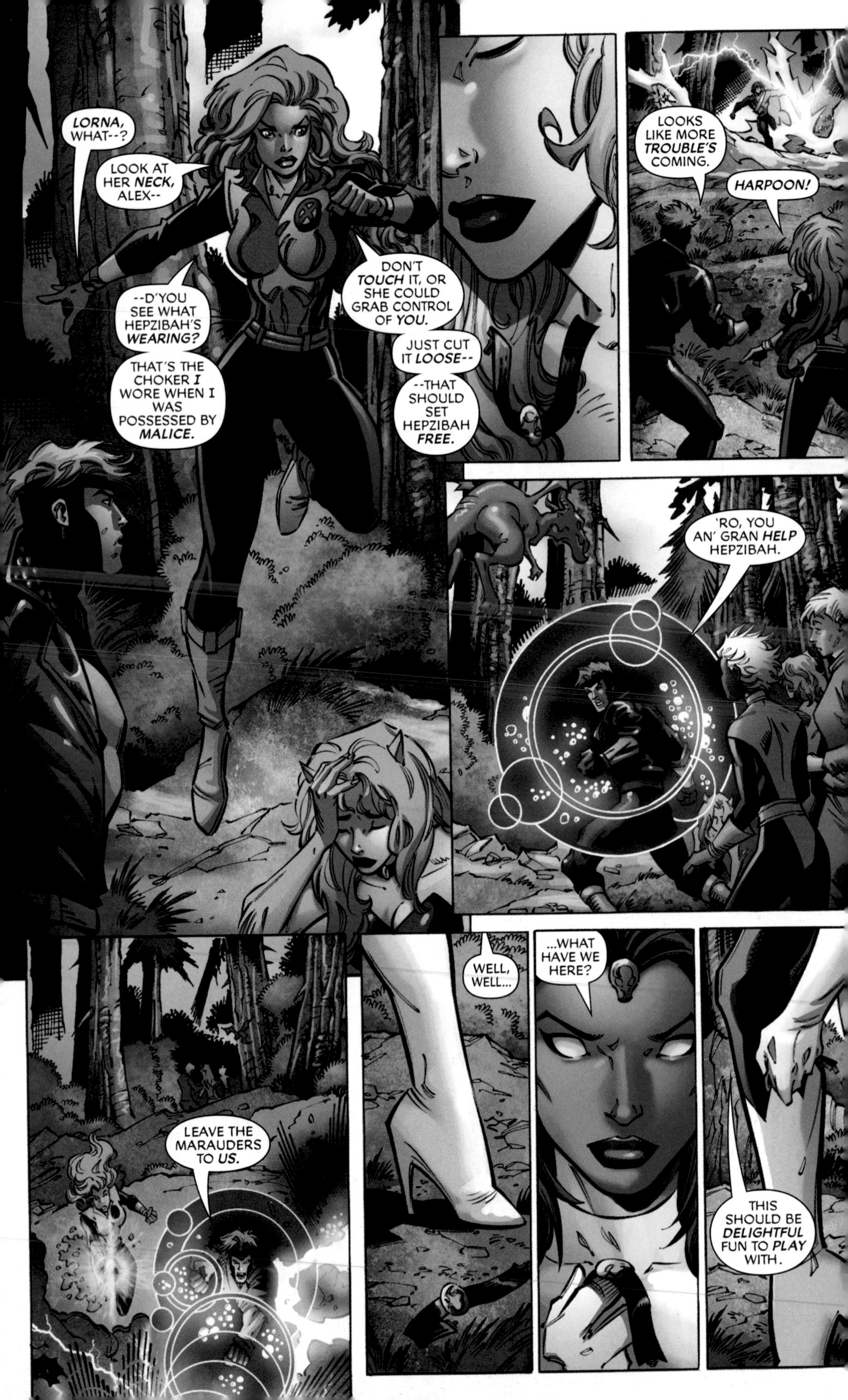
LORNA, WHAT--?
LOOK AT HER NECK, ALEX--
--D'YOU SEE WHAT HEPZIBAH'S WEARING?
THAT'S THE CHOKER I WORE WHEN I WAS POSSESSED BY MALICE.
DON'T TOUCH IT, OR SHE COULD GRAB CONTROL OF YOU.
JUST CUT IT LOOSE--
--THAT SHOULD SET HEPZIBAH FREE.
LOOKS LIKE MORE TROUBLE'S COMING.
HARPOON!
'RO, YOU AN' GRAN HELP HEPZIBAH.
LEAVE THE MARAUDERS TO US.
WELL, WELL...
...WHAT HAVE WE HERE?
THIS SHOULD BE DELIGHTFUL FUN TO PLAY WITH.

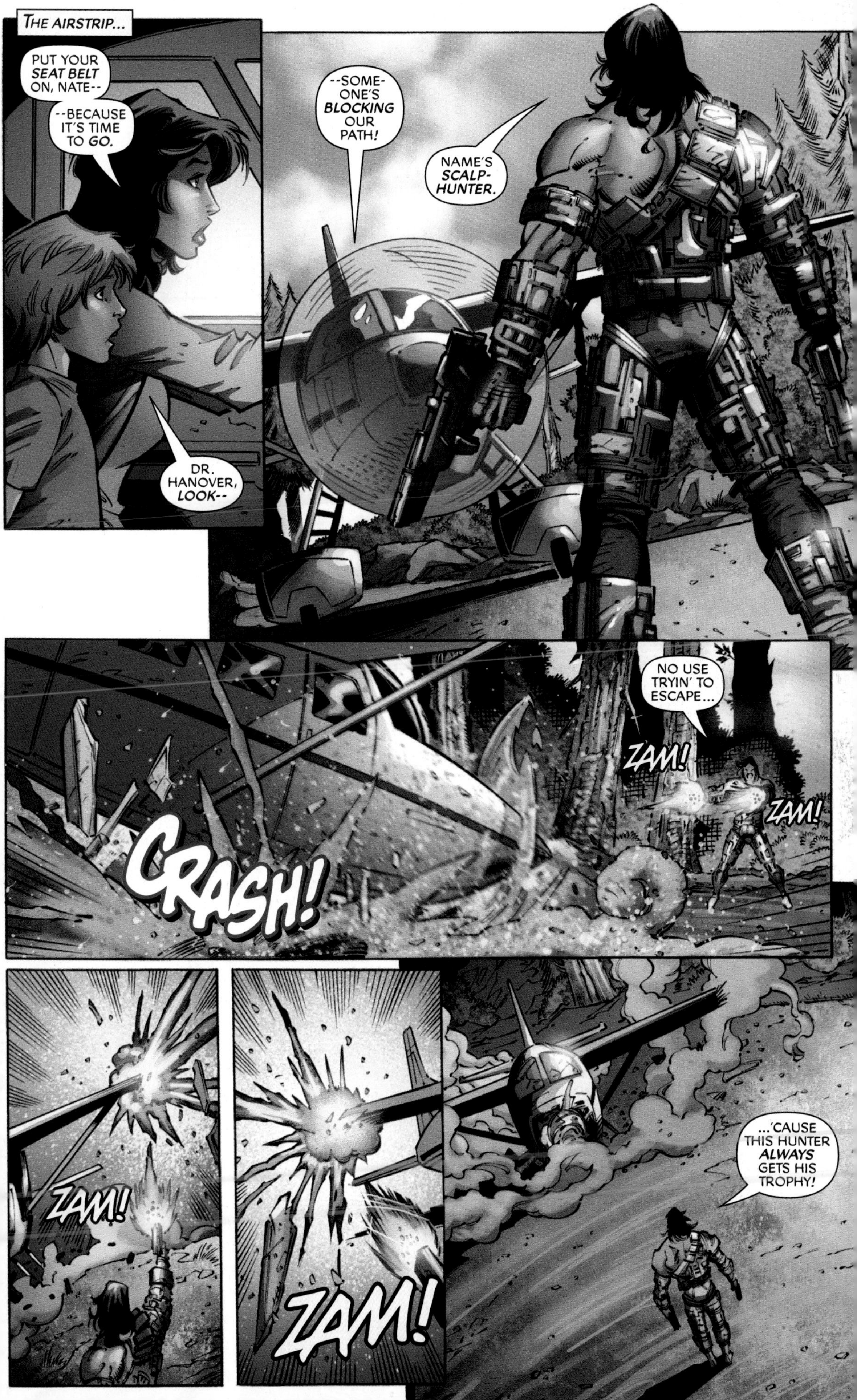
THE AIRSTRIP...
PUT YOUR SEAT BELT ON, NATE--
--BECAUSE IT'S TIME TO GO.
--SOME-ONE'S BLOCKING OUR PATH!
NAME'S SCALP-HUNTER.
DR. HANOVER, LOOK--
NO USE TRYIN' TO ESCAPE...
ZAM!
ZAM!
CRASH!
ZAM!
ZAM!
...'CAUSE THIS HUNTER ALWAYS GETS HIS TROPHY!

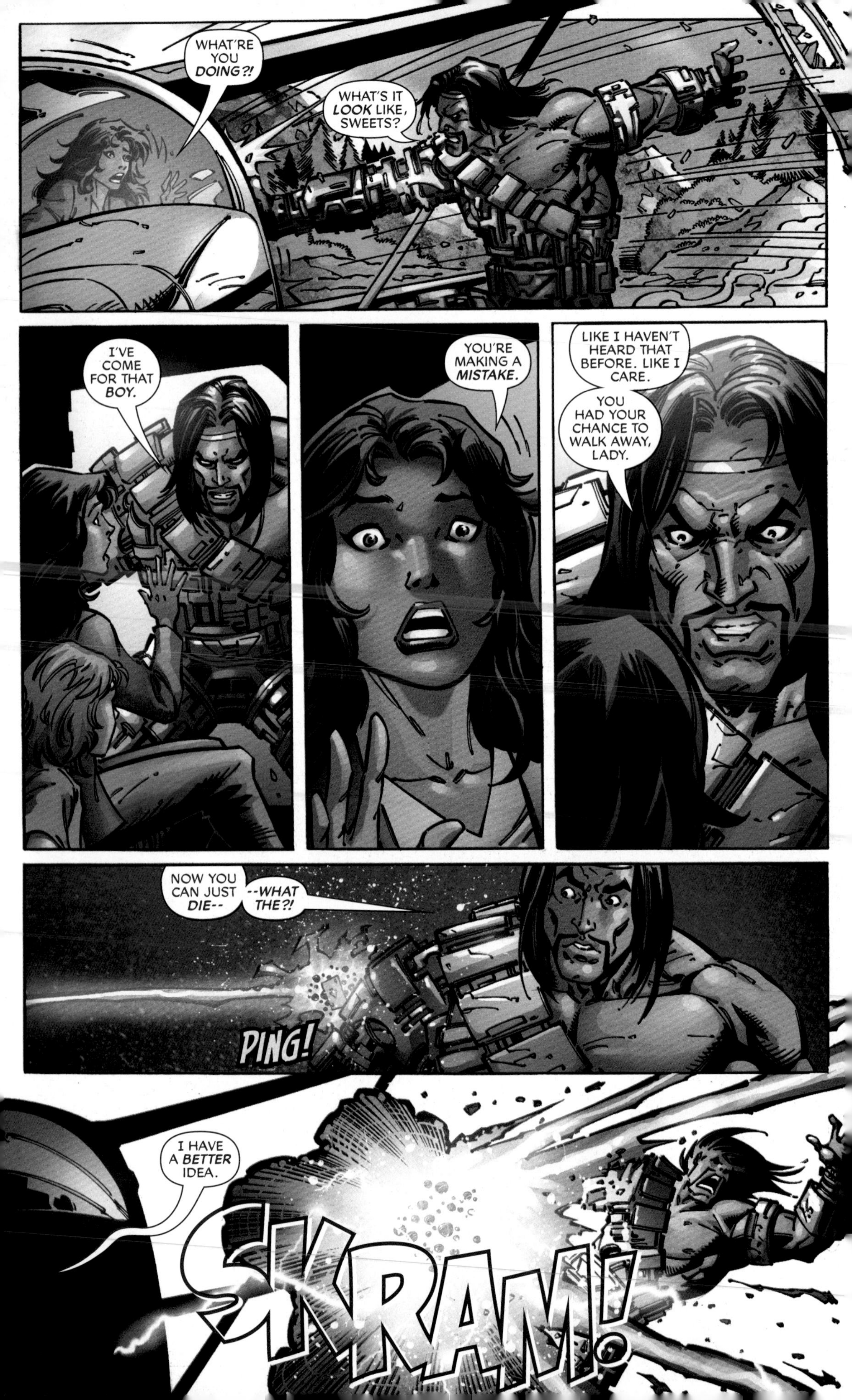
WHAT'RE YOU DOING?!
WHAT'S IT LOOK LIKE, SWEETS?
I'VE COME FOR THAT BOY.
YOU'RE MAKING A MISTAKE.
LIKE I HAVEN'T HEARD THAT BEFORE. LIKE I CARE.
YOU HAD YOUR CHANCE TO WALK AWAY, LADY.
NOW YOU CAN JUST DIE--
--WHAT THE?!
PING!
I HAVE A BETTER IDEA.
SKRAM!

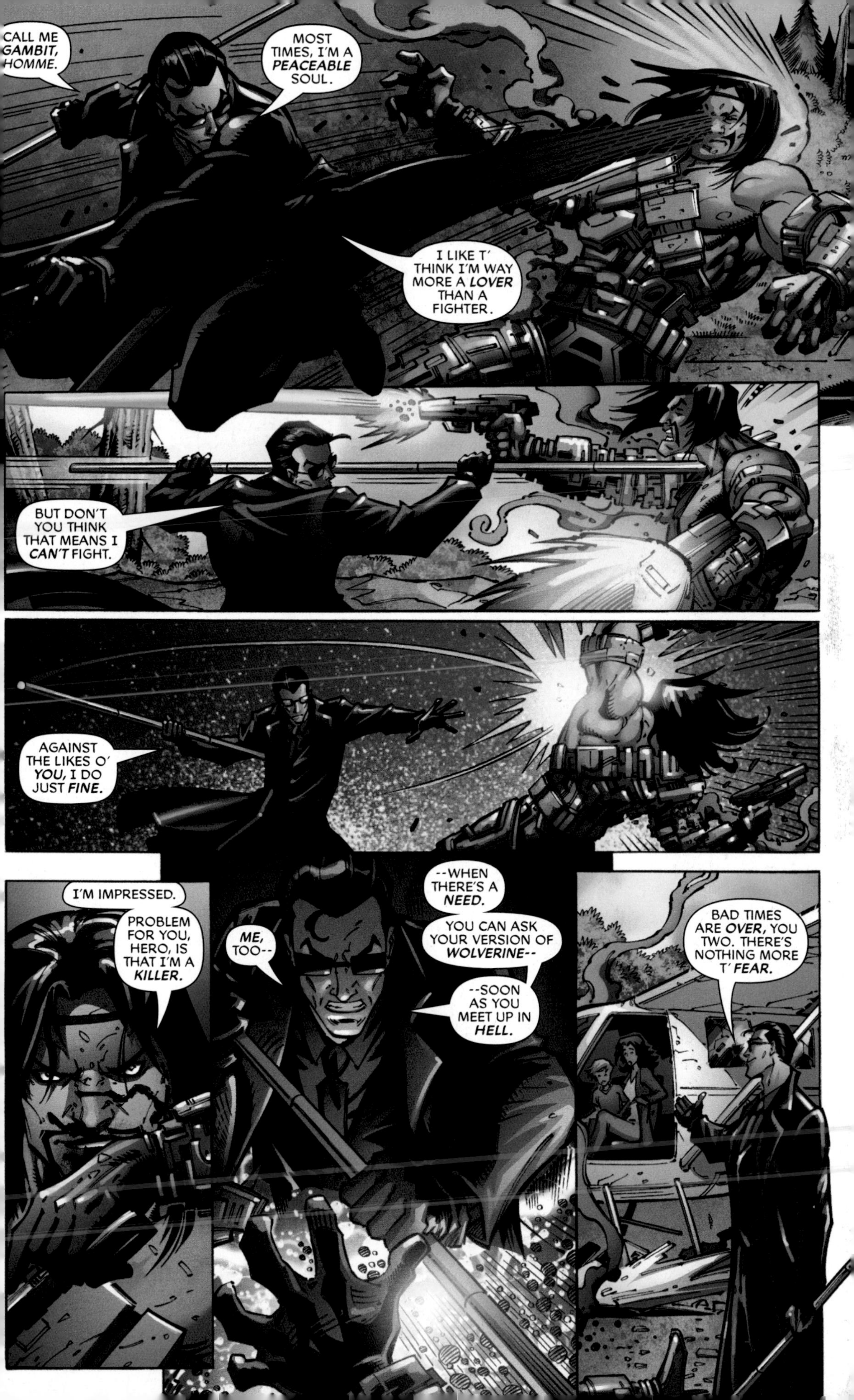
CALL ME GAMBIT, HOMME.
MOST TIMES, I'M A PEACEABLE SOUL.
I LIKE T' THINK I'M WAY MORE A LOVER THAN A FIGHTER.
BUT DON'T YOU THINK THAT MEANS I CAN'T FIGHT.
AGAINST THE LIKES O' YOU, I DO JUST FINE.
I'M IMPRESSED.
PROBLEM FOR YOU, HERO, IS THAT I'M A KILLER.
ME, TOO--
--WHEN THERE'S A NEED.
YOU CAN ASK YOUR VERSION OF WOLVERINE--
--SOON AS YOU MEET UP IN HELL.
BAD TIMES ARE OVER, YOU TWO. THERE'S NOTHING MORE T' FEAR.

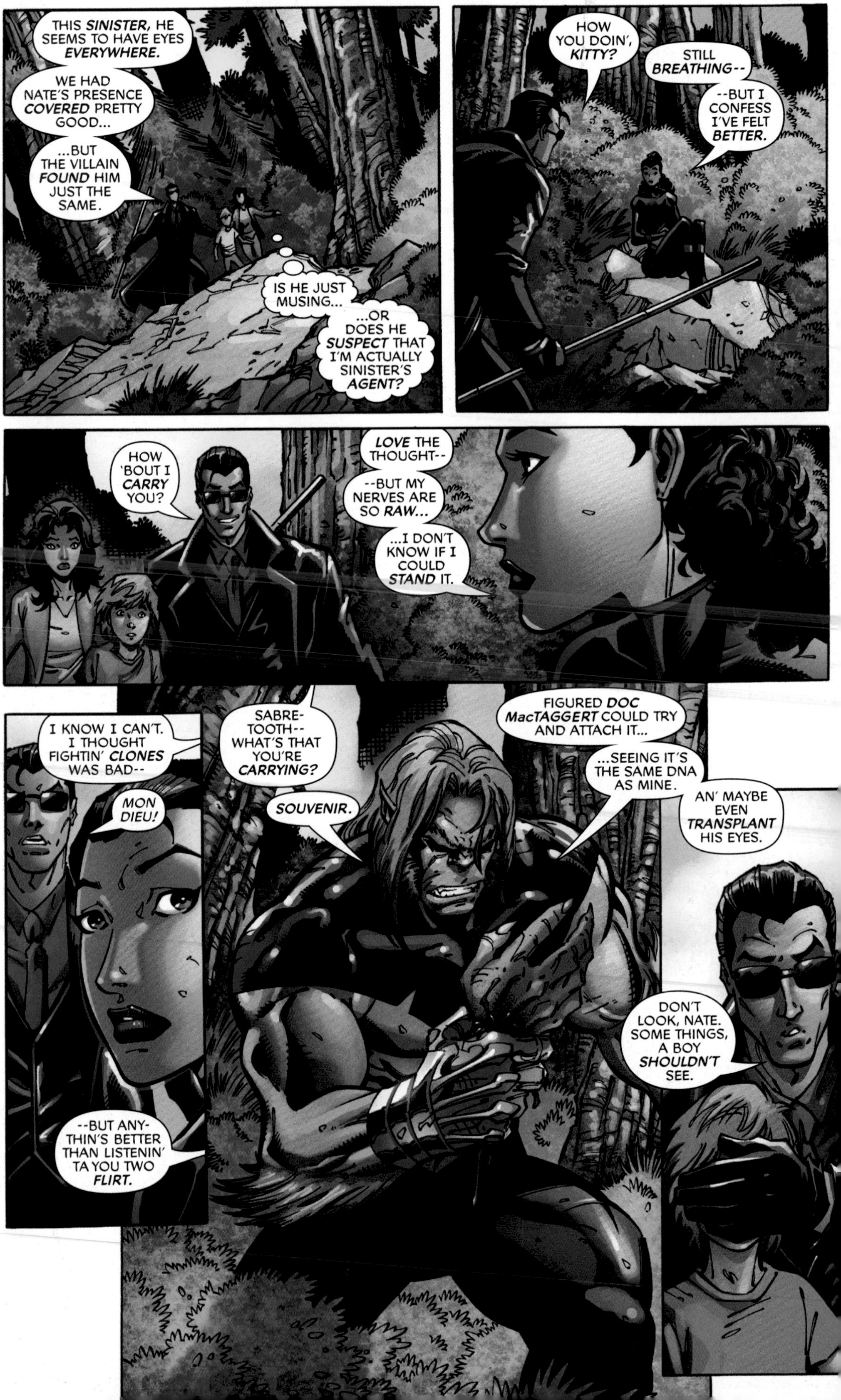

THIS SINISTER, HE SEEMS TO HAVE EYES EVERYWHERE.
WE HAD NATE'S PRESENCE COVERED PRETTY GOOD...
...BUT THE VILLAIN FOUND HIM JUST THE SAME.
IS HE JUST MUSING...
...OR DOES HE SUSPECT THAT I'M ACTUALLY SINISTER'S AGENT?
HOW YOU DOIN', KITTY?
STILL BREATHING--
--BUT I CONFESS I'VE FELT BETTER.
HOW 'BOUT I CARRY YOU?
LOVE THE THOUGHT--
--BUT MY NERVES ARE SO RAW...
...I DON'T KNOW IF I COULD STAND IT.
I KNOW I CAN'T. I THOUGHT FIGHTIN' CLONES WAS BAD--
MON DIEU!
--BUT ANY-THIN'S BETTER THAN LISTENIN' TA YOU TWO FLIRT.
SABRE-TOOTH--WHAT'S THAT YOU'RE CARRYING?
SOUVENIR.
FIGURED DOC MacTAGGERT COULD TRY AND ATTACH IT...
...SEEING IT'S THE SAME DNA AS MINE.
AN' MAYBE EVEN TRANSPLANT HIS EYES.
DON'T LOOK, NATE. SOME THINGS, A BOY SHOULDN'T SEE.

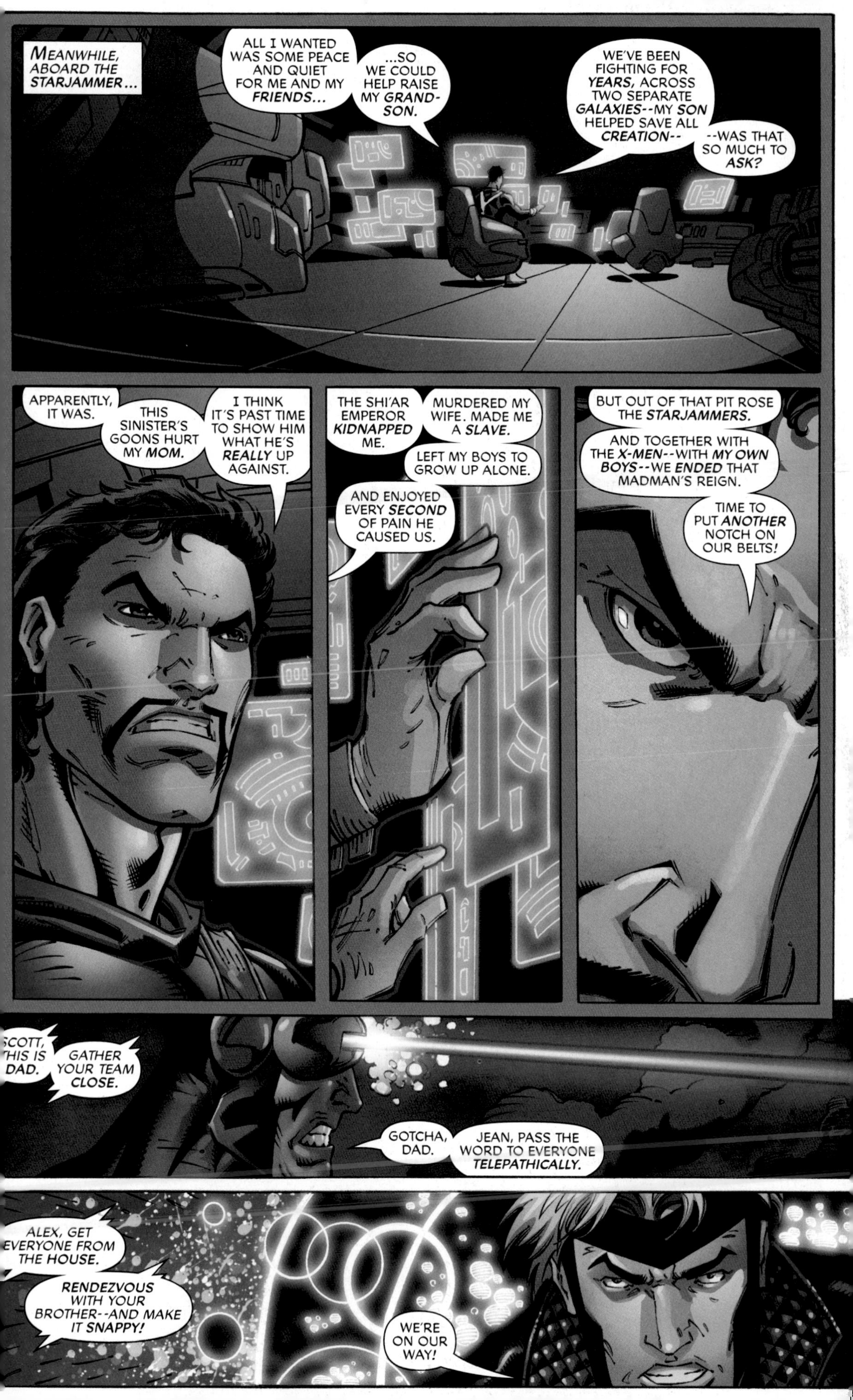
MEANWHILE, ABOARD THE STARJAMMER...
ALL I WANTED WAS SOME PEACE AND QUIET FOR ME AND MY FRIENDS...
...SO WE COULD HELP RAISE MY GRAND-SON.
WE'VE BEEN FIGHTING FOR YEARS, ACROSS TWO SEPARATE GALAXIES--MY SON HELPED SAVE ALL CREATION--
--WAS THAT SO MUCH TO ASK?
APPARENTLY, IT WAS.
THIS SINISTER'S GOONS HURT MY MOM.
I THINK IT'S PAST TIME TO SHOW HIM WHAT HE'S REALLY UP AGAINST.
THE SHI'AR EMPEROR KIDNAPPED ME.
MURDERED MY WIFE. MADE ME A SLAVE.
LEFT MY BOYS TO GROW UP ALONE.
AND ENJOYED EVERY SECOND OF PAIN HE CAUSED US.
BUT OUT OF THAT PIT ROSE THE STARJAMMERS.
AND TOGETHER WITH THE X-MEN--WITH MY OWN BOYS--WE ENDED THAT MADMAN'S REIGN.
TIME TO PUT ANOTHER NOTCH ON OUR BELTS!
SCOTT, THIS IS DAD.
GATHER YOUR TEAM CLOSE.
GOTCHA, DAD.
JEAN, PASS THE WORD TO EVERYONE TELEPATHICALLY.
ALEX, GET EVERYONE FROM THE HOUSE.
RENDEZVOUS WITH YOUR BROTHER--AND MAKE IT SNAPPY!
WE'RE ON OUR WAY!

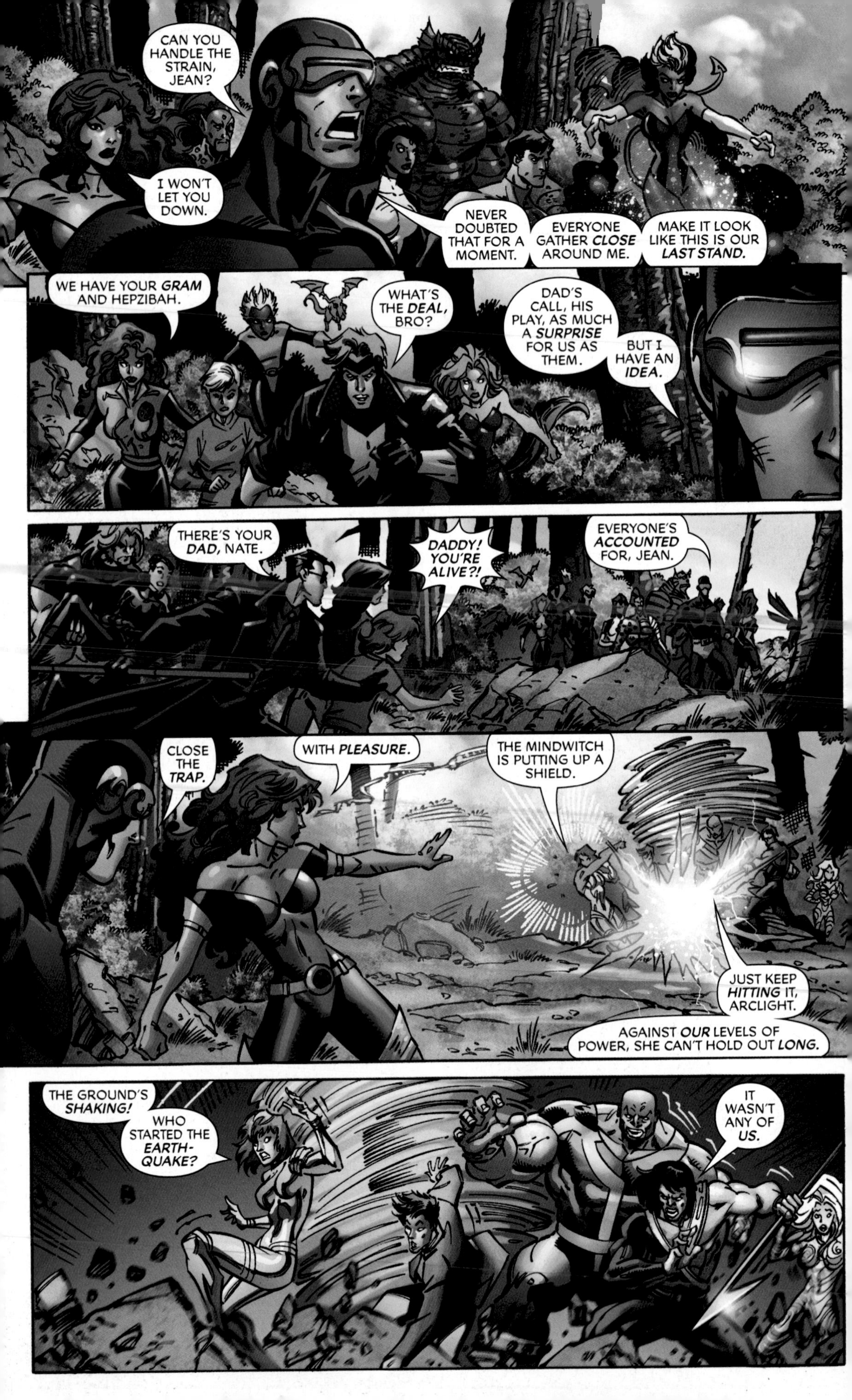
CAN YOU HANDLE THE STRAIN, JEAN?
I WON'T LET YOU DOWN.
NEVER DOUBTED THAT FOR A MOMENT.
EVERYONE GATHER CLOSE AROUND ME.
MAKE IT LOOK LIKE THIS IS OUR LAST STAND.
WE HAVE YOUR GRAM AND HEPZIBAH.
WHAT'S THE DEAL, BRO?
DAD'S CALL, HIS PLAY, AS MUCH A SURPRISE FOR US AS THEM.
BUT I HAVE AN IDEA.
THERE'S YOUR DAD, NATE.
DADDY! YOU'RE ALIVE?!
EVERYONE'S ACCOUNTED FOR, JEAN.
CLOSE THE TRAP.
WITH PLEASURE.
THE MINDWITCH IS PUTTING UP A SHIELD.
JUST KEEP HITTING IT, ARCLIGHT.
AGAINST OUR LEVELS OF POWER, SHE CAN'T HOLD OUT LONG.
THE GROUND'S SHAKING!
WHO STARTED THE EARTH-QUAKE?
IT WASN'T ANY OF US.

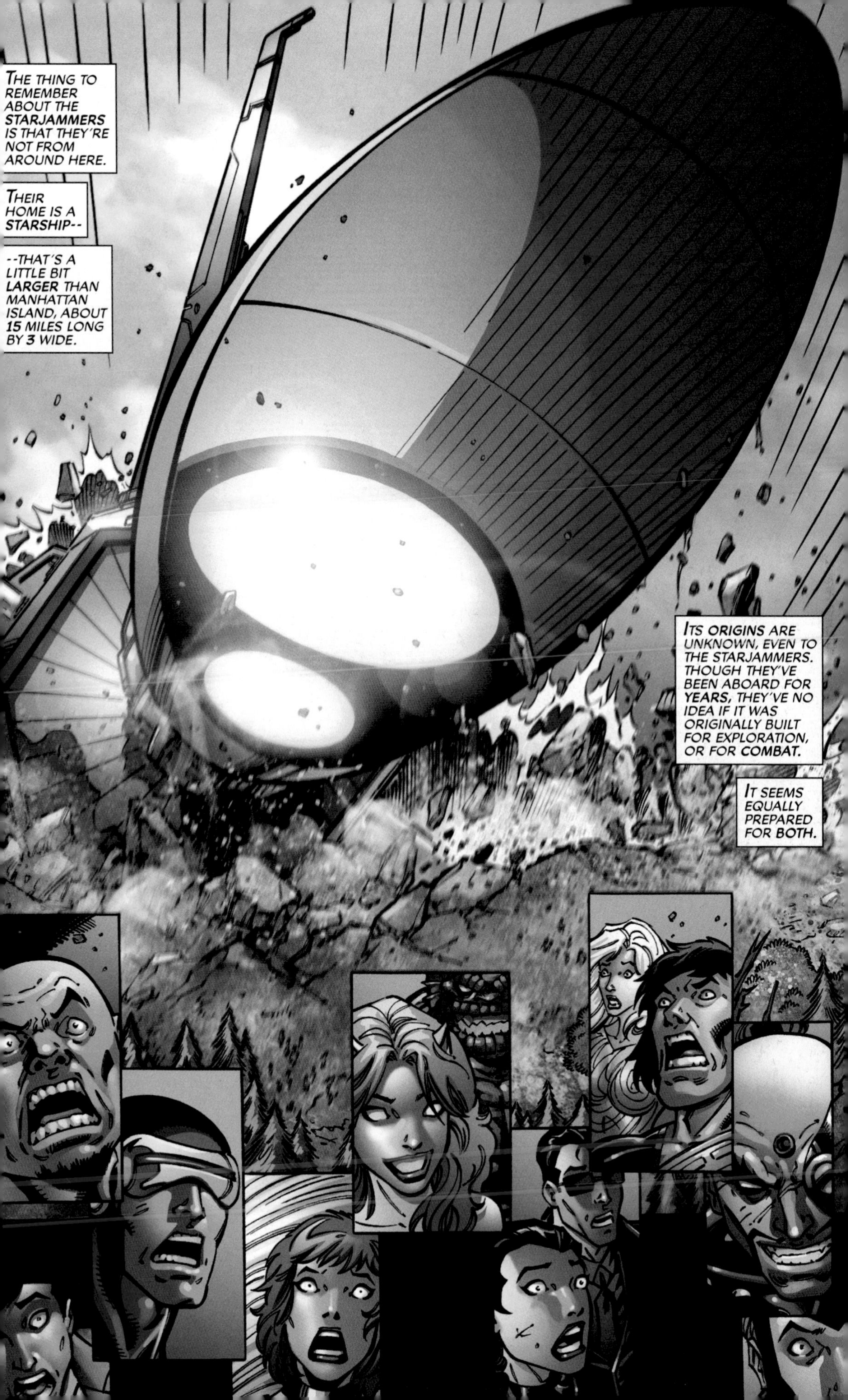
THE THING TO REMEMBER ABOUT THE STARJAMMERS IS THAT THEY'RE NOT FROM AROUND HERE.
THEIR HOME IS A STARSHIP--
--THAT'S A LITTLE BIT LARGER THAN MANHATTAN ISLAND, ABOUT 15 MILES LONG BY 3 WIDE.
ITS ORIGINS ARE UNKNOWN, EVEN TO THE STARJAMMERS. THOUGH THEY'VE BEEN ABOARD FOR YEARS, THEY'VE NO IDEA IF IT WAS ORIGINALLY BUILT FOR EXPLORATION, OR FOR COMBAT.
IT SEEMS EQUALLY PREPARED FOR BOTH.

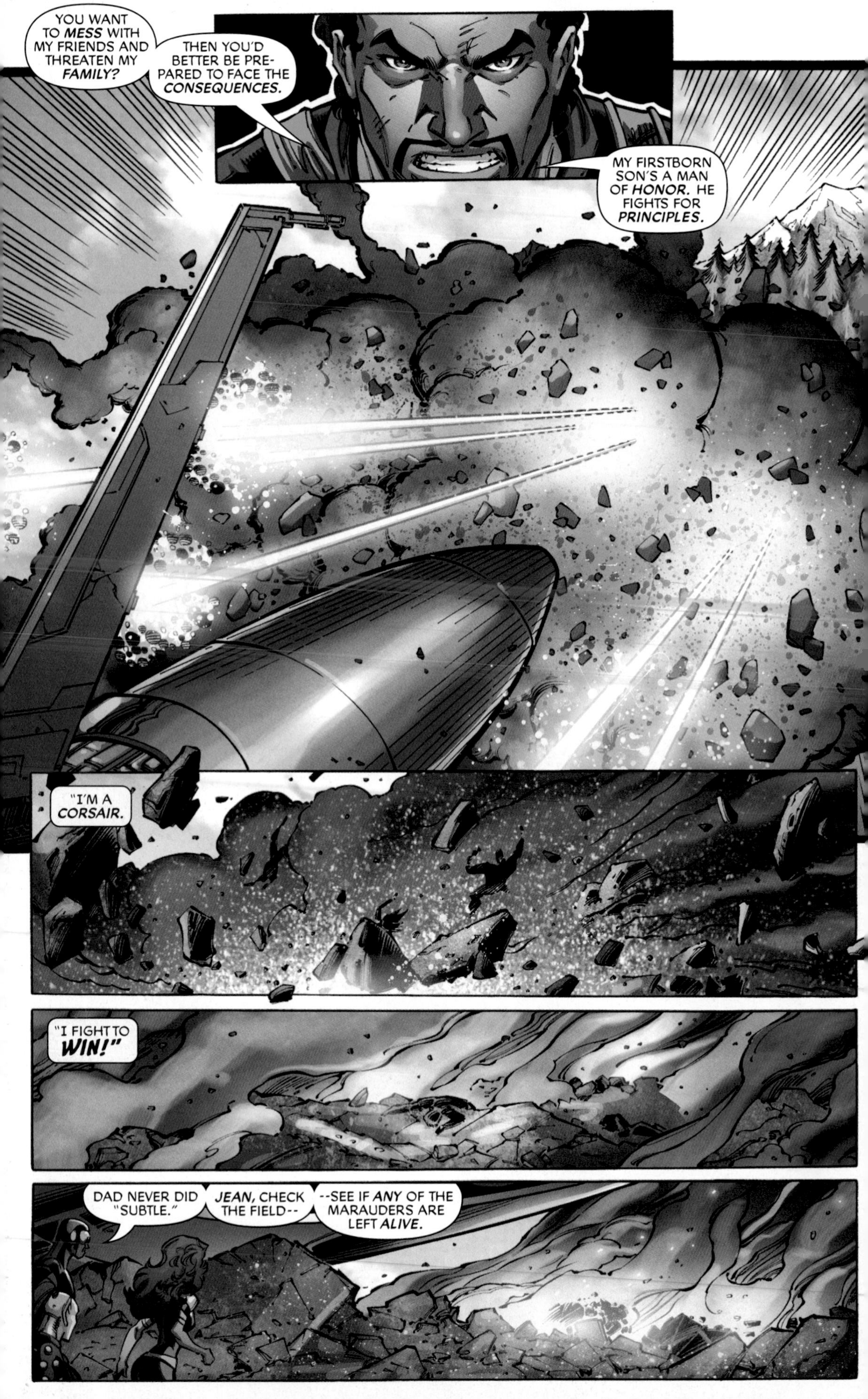
YOU WANT TO MESS WITH MY FRIENDS AND THREATEN MY FAMILY?
THEN YOU'D BETTER BE PRE-PARED TO FACE THE CONSEQUENCES.
MY FIRSTBORN SON'S A MAN OF HONOR. HE FIGHTS FOR PRINCIPLES.
"I'M A CORSAIR.
"I FIGHT TO WIN!"
DAD NEVER DID "SUBTLE."
JEAN, CHECK THE FIELD--
--SEE IF ANY OF THE MARAUDERS ARE LEFT ALIVE.

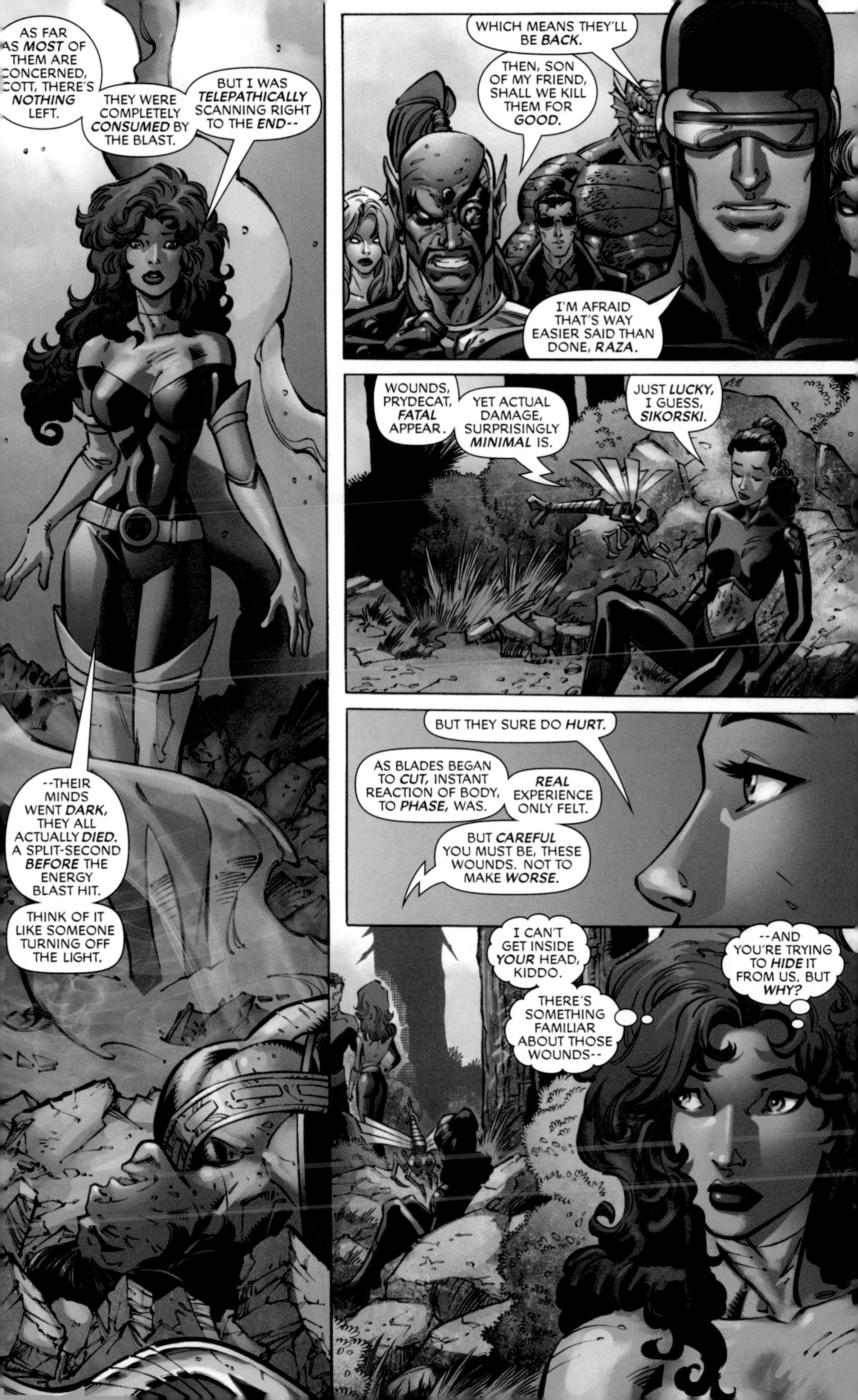
AS FAR AS MOST OF THEM ARE CONCERNED, COTT, THERE'S NOTHING LEFT.
THEY WERE COMPLETELY CONSUMED BY THE BLAST.
BUT I WAS TELEPATHICALLY SCANNING RIGHT TO THE END--
--THEIR MINDS WENT DARK, THEY ALL ACTUALLY DIED. A SPLIT-SECOND BEFORE THE ENERGY BLAST HIT.
THINK OF IT LIKE SOMEONE TURNING OFF THE LIGHT.
WHICH MEANS THEY'LL BE BACK.
THEN, SON OF MY FRIEND, SHALL WE KILL THEM FOR GOOD.
I'M AFRAID THAT'S WAY EASIER SAID THAN DONE, RAZA.
WOUNDS, PRYDECAT, FATAL APPEAR.
YET ACTUAL DAMAGE, SURPRISINGLY MINIMAL IS.
JUST LUCKY, I GUESS, SIKORSKI.
BUT THEY SURE DO HURT.
AS BLADES BEGAN TO CUT, INSTANT REACTION OF BODY, TO PHASE, WAS.
REAL EXPERIENCE ONLY FELT.
BUT CAREFUL YOU MUST BE, THESE WOUNDS. NOT TO MAKE WORSE.
I CAN'T GET INSIDE YOUR HEAD, KIDDO.
THERE'S SOMETHING FAMILIAR ABOUT THOSE WOUNDS--
--AND YOU'RE TRYING TO HIDE IT FROM US. BUT WHY?

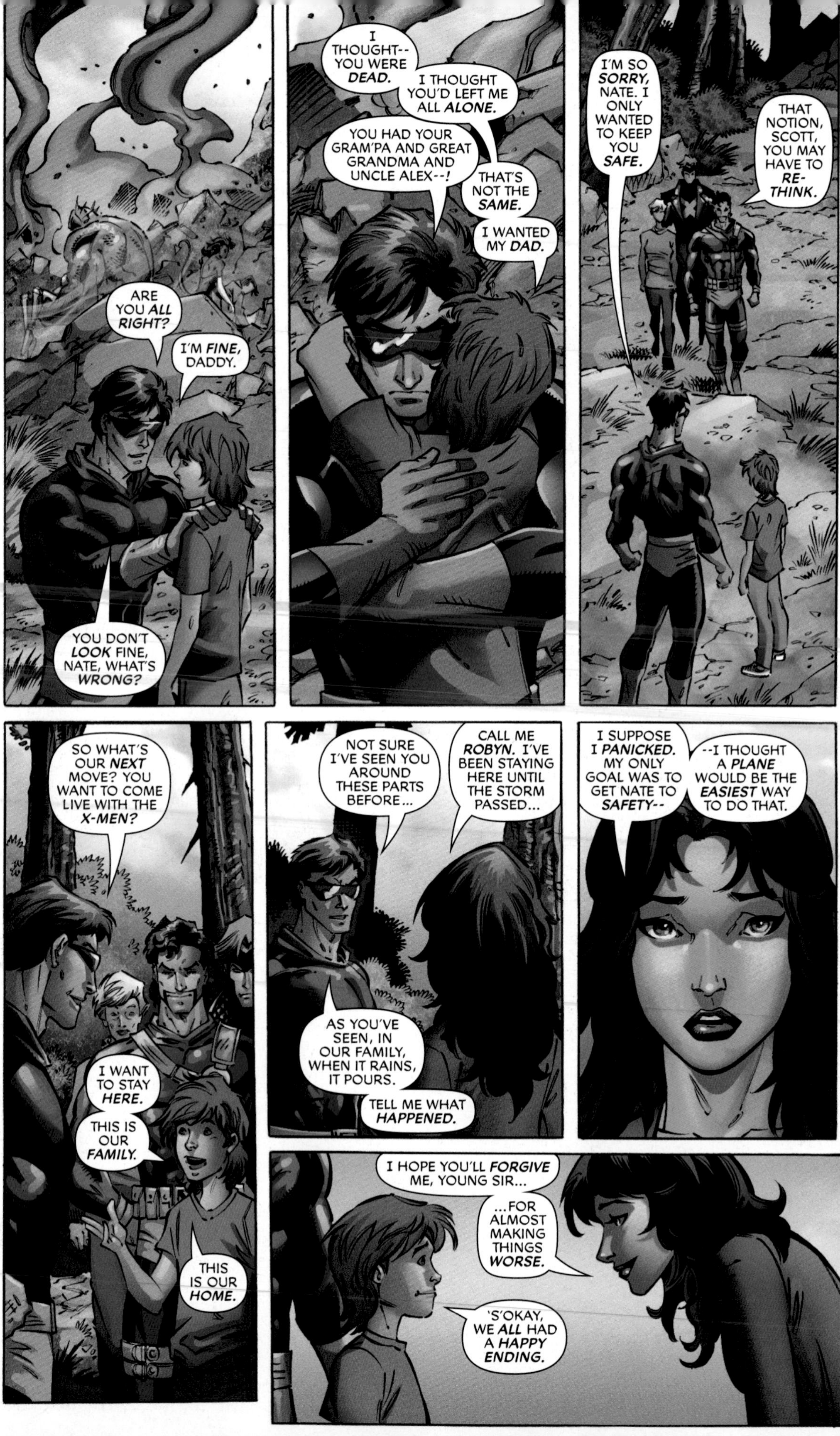
ARE YOU ALL RIGHT?
I'M FINE, DADDY.
YOU DON'T LOOK FINE, NATE, WHAT'S WRONG?
I THOUGHT-- YOU WERE DEAD.
I THOUGHT YOU'D LEFT ME ALL ALONE.
YOU HAD YOUR GRAM'PA AND GREAT GRANDMA AND UNCLE ALEX--!
THAT'S NOT THE SAME.
I WANTED MY DAD.
I'M SO SORRY, NATE. I ONLY WANTED TO KEEP YOU SAFE.
THAT NOTION, SCOTT, YOU MAY HAVE TO RE-THINK.
SO WHAT'S OUR NEXT MOVE? YOU WANT TO COME LIVE WITH THE X-MEN?
I WANT TO STAY HERE.
THIS IS OUR FAMILY.
THIS IS OUR HOME.
NOT SURE I'VE SEEN YOU AROUND THESE PARTS BEFORE...
CALL ME ROBYN. I'VE BEEN STAYING HERE UNTIL THE STORM PASSED...
AS YOU'VE SEEN, IN OUR FAMILY, WHEN IT RAINS, IT POURS.
TELL ME WHAT HAPPENED.
I SUPPOSE I PANICKED. MY ONLY GOAL WAS TO GET NATE TO SAFETY--
--I THOUGHT A PLANE WOULD BE THE EASIEST WAY TO DO THAT.
I HOPE YOU'LL FORGIVE ME, YOUNG SIR...
...FOR ALMOST MAKING THINGS WORSE.
'S'OKAY, WE ALL HAD A HAPPY ENDING.

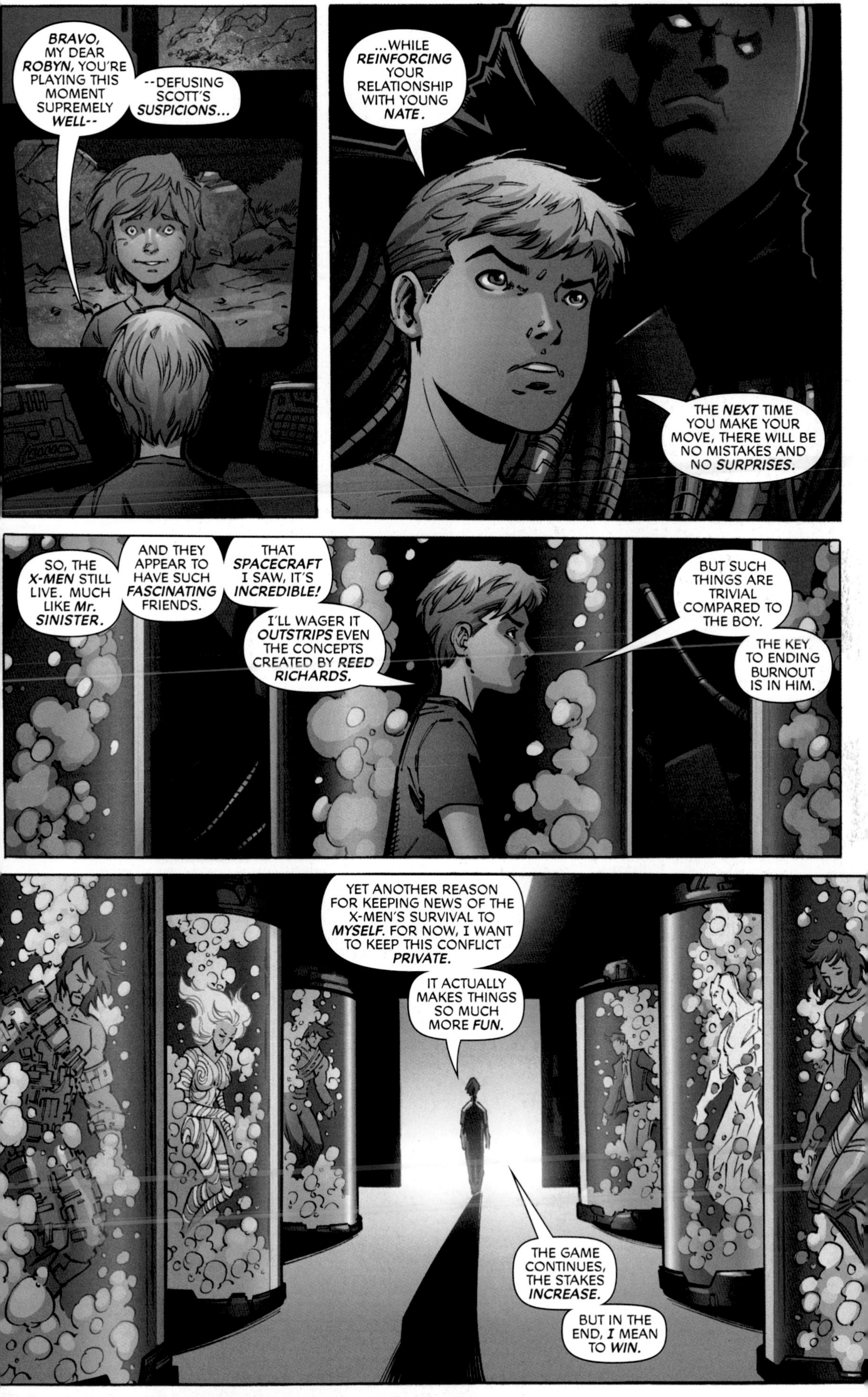
BRAVO, MY DEAR ROBYN, YOU'RE PLAYING THIS MOMENT SUPREMELY WELL--
--DEFUSING SCOTT'S SUSPICIONS...
...WHILE REINFORCING YOUR RELATIONSHIP WITH YOUNG NATE.
THE NEXT TIME YOU MAKE YOUR MOVE, THERE WILL BE NO MISTAKES AND NO SURPRISES.
SO, THE X-MEN STILL LIVE. MUCH LIKE Mr. SINISTER.
AND THEY APPEAR TO HAVE SUCH FASCINATING FRIENDS.
THAT SPACECRAFT I SAW, IT'S INCREDIBLE!
I'LL WAGER IT OUTSTRIPS EVEN THE CONCEPTS CREATED BY REED RICHARDS.
BUT SUCH THINGS ARE TRIVIAL COMPARED TO THE BOY.
THE KEY TO ENDING BURNOUT IS IN HIM.
YET ANOTHER REASON FOR KEEPING NEWS OF THE X-MEN'S SURVIVAL TO MYSELF. FOR NOW, I WANT TO KEEP THIS CONFLICT PRIVATE.
IT ACTUALLY MAKES THINGS SO MUCH MORE FUN.
THE GAME CONTINUES, THE STAKES INCREASE.
BUT IN THE END, I MEAN TO WIN.

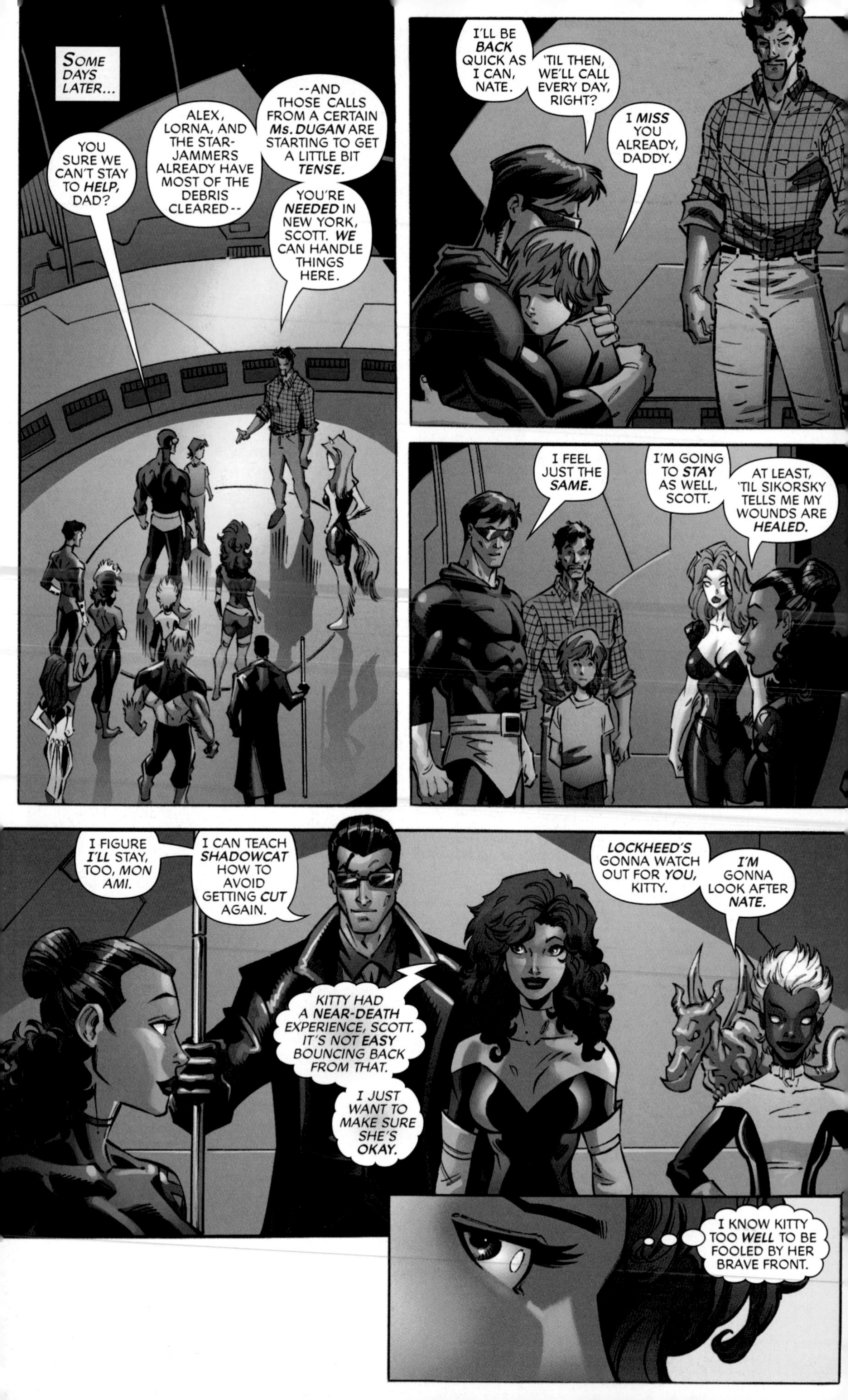
SOME DAYS LATER...
YOU SURE WE CAN'T STAY TO *HELP,* DAD?
ALEX, LORNA, AND THE STAR-JAMMERS ALREADY HAVE MOST OF THE DEBRIS CLEARED--
--AND THOSE CALLS FROM A CERTAIN *Ms. DUGAN* ARE STARTING TO GET A LITTLE BIT *TENSE.*
YOU'RE *NEEDED* IN NEW YORK, SCOTT. *WE* CAN HANDLE THINGS HERE.
I'LL BE *BACK* QUICK AS I CAN, NATE.
'TIL THEN, WE'LL CALL EVERY DAY, RIGHT?
I *MISS* YOU ALREADY, DADDY.
I FEEL JUST THE *SAME.*
I'M GOING TO *STAY* AS WELL, SCOTT.
AT LEAST, 'TIL SIKORSKY TELLS ME MY WOUNDS ARE *HEALED.*
I FIGURE *I'LL* STAY, TOO, *MON AMI.*
I CAN TEACH *SHADOWCAT* HOW TO AVOID GETTING *CUT* AGAIN.
KITTY HAD A *NEAR-DEATH* EXPERIENCE, SCOTT. IT'S NOT *EASY* BOUNCING BACK FROM THAT.
I JUST WANT TO MAKE SURE SHE'S *OKAY.*
LOCKHEED'S GONNA WATCH OUT FOR *YOU,* KITTY.
I'M GONNA LOOK AFTER *NATE.*
I KNOW KITTY TOO *WELL* TO BE FOOLED BY HER BRAVE FRONT.

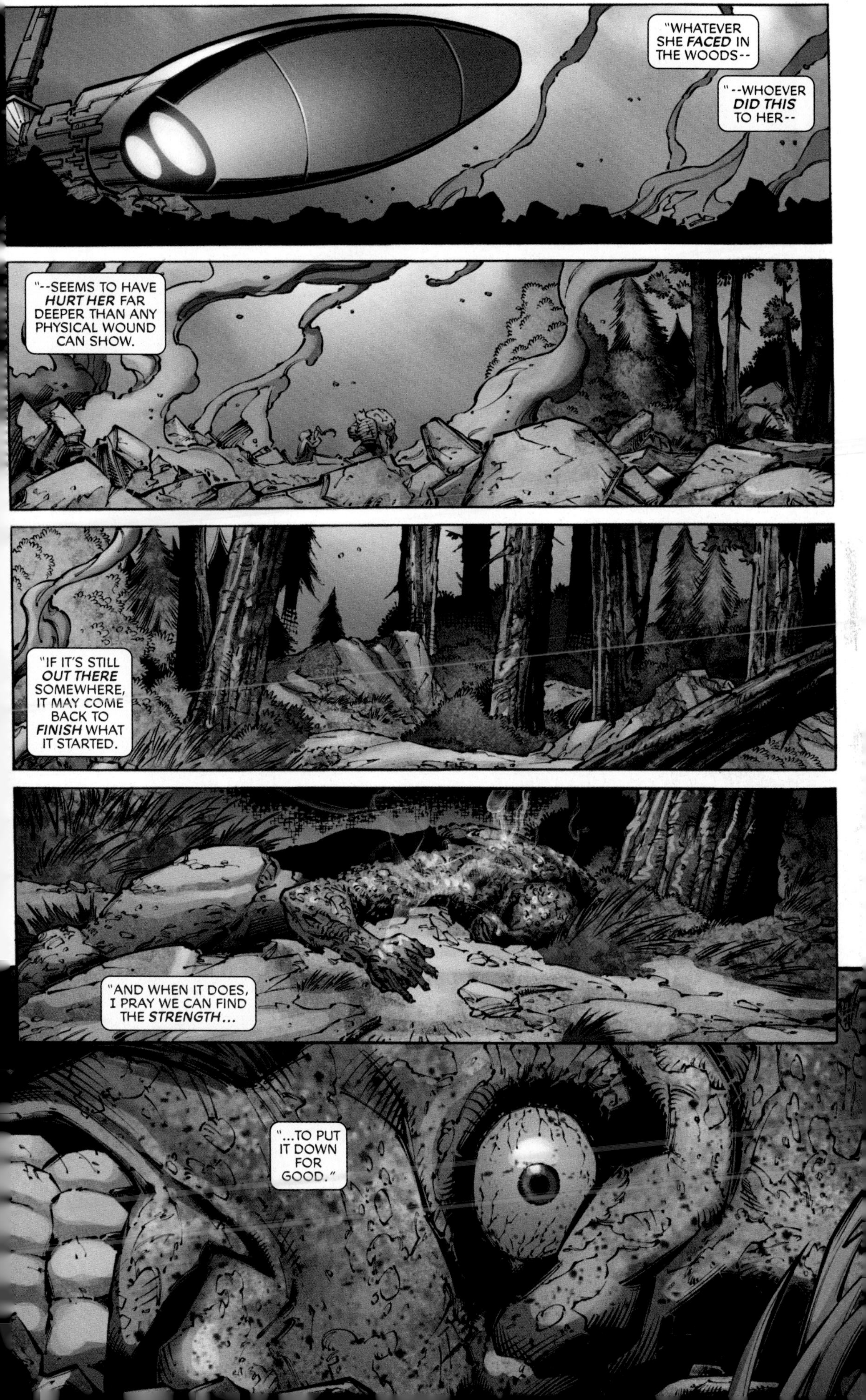
"WHATEVER SHE FACED IN THE WOODS--
"--WHOEVER DID THIS TO HER--
"--SEEMS TO HAVE HURT HER FAR DEEPER THAN ANY PHYSICAL WOUND CAN SHOW.
"IF IT'S STILL OUT THERE SOMEWHERE, IT MAY COME BACK TO FINISH WHAT IT STARTED.
"AND WHEN IT DOES, I PRAY WE CAN FIND THE STRENGTH...
"...TO PUT IT DOWN FOR GOOD."

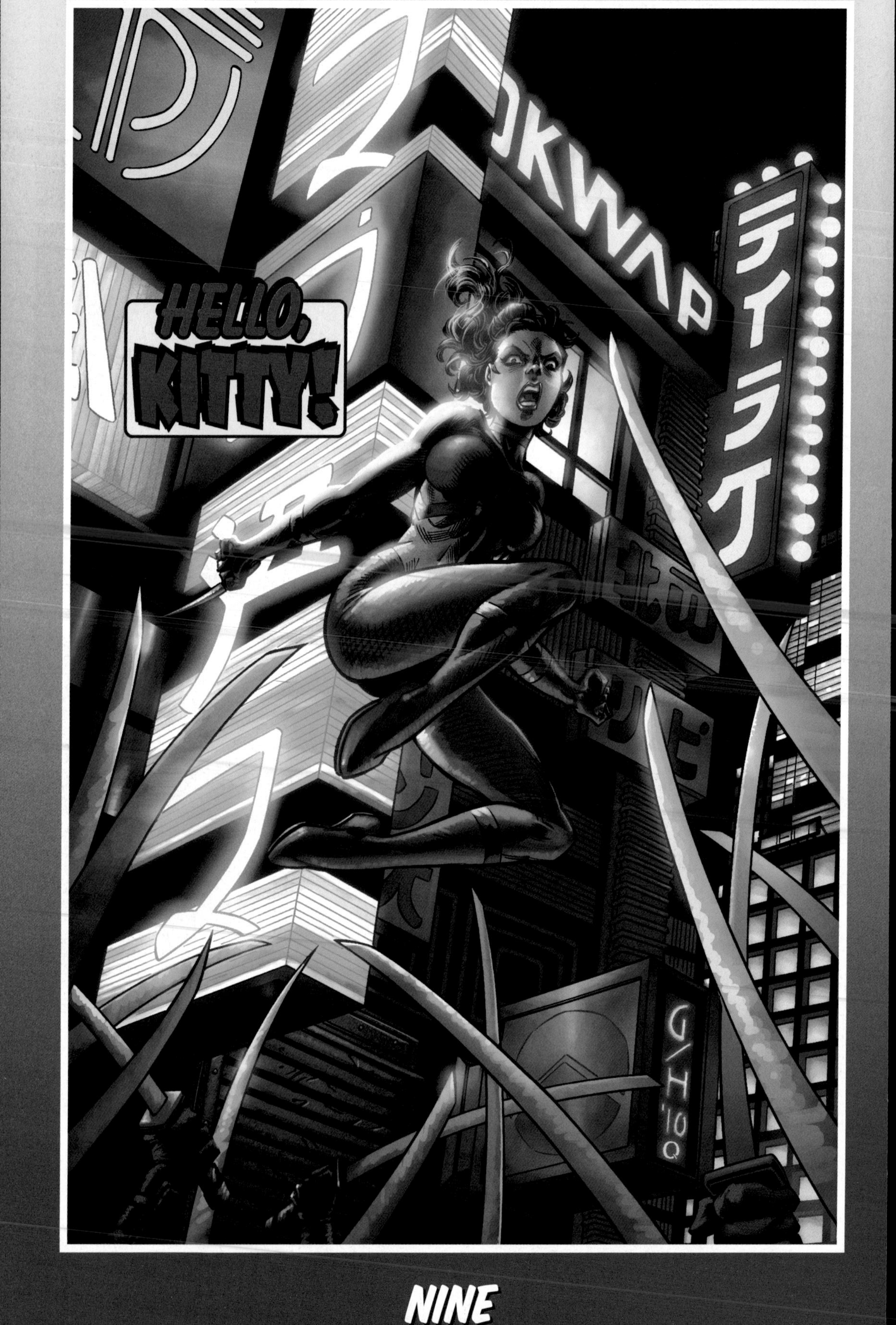
HELLO, KITTY!

NINE

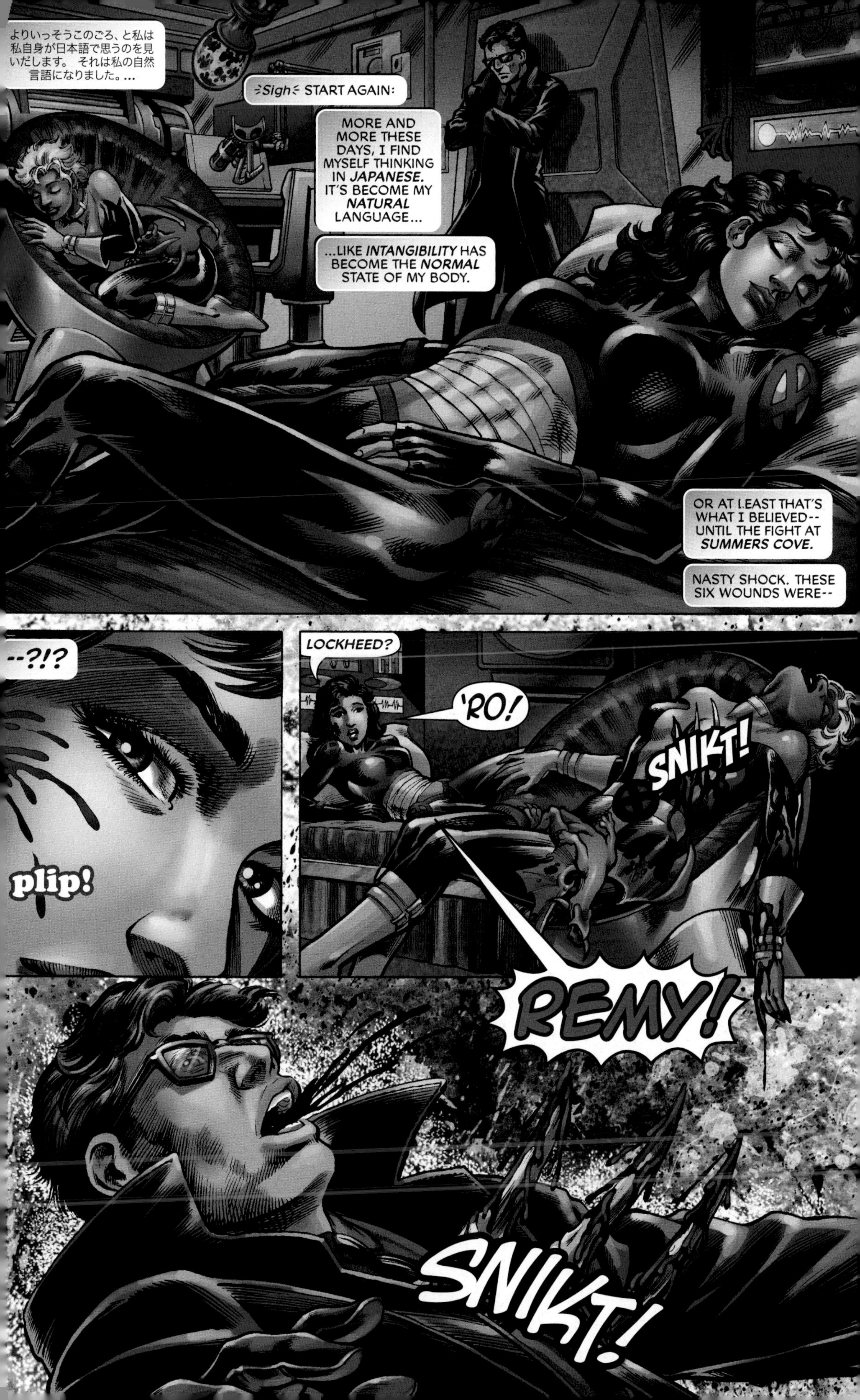

よりいっそうこのごろ、と私は私自身が日本語で思うのを見いだします。 それは私の自然言語になりました。...
Sigh START AGAIN:
MORE AND MORE THESE DAYS, I FIND MYSELF THINKING IN JAPANESE. IT'S BECOME MY NATURAL LANGUAGE...
...LIKE INTANGIBILITY HAS BECOME THE NORMAL STATE OF MY BODY.
OR AT LEAST THAT'S WHAT I BELIEVED-- UNTIL THE FIGHT AT SUMMERS COVE.
NASTY SHOCK. THESE SIX WOUNDS WERE--
--?!?
plip!
LOCKHEED?
'RO!
SNIKT!
REMY!
SNIKT!

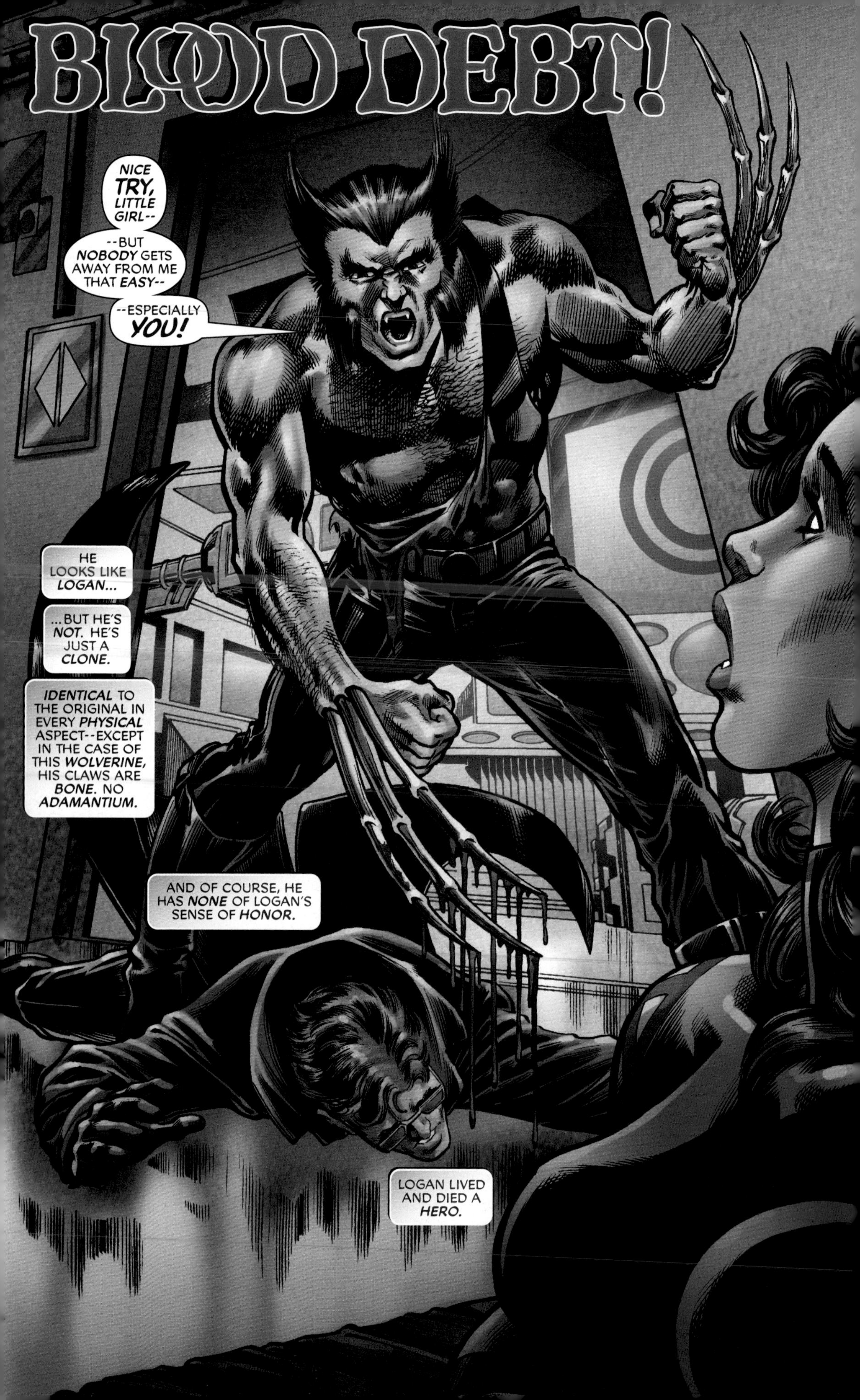
BLOOD DEBT!
NICE TRY, LITTLE GIRL--
--BUT NOBODY GETS AWAY FROM ME THAT EASY--
--ESPECIALLY YOU!
HE LOOKS LIKE LOGAN...
...BUT HE'S NOT. HE'S JUST A CLONE.
IDENTICAL TO THE ORIGINAL IN EVERY PHYSICAL ASPECT--EXCEPT IN THE CASE OF THIS WOLVERINE, HIS CLAWS ARE BONE. NO ADAMANTIUM.
AND OF COURSE, HE HAS NONE OF LOGAN'S SENSE OF HONOR.
LOGAN LIVED AND DIED A HERO.

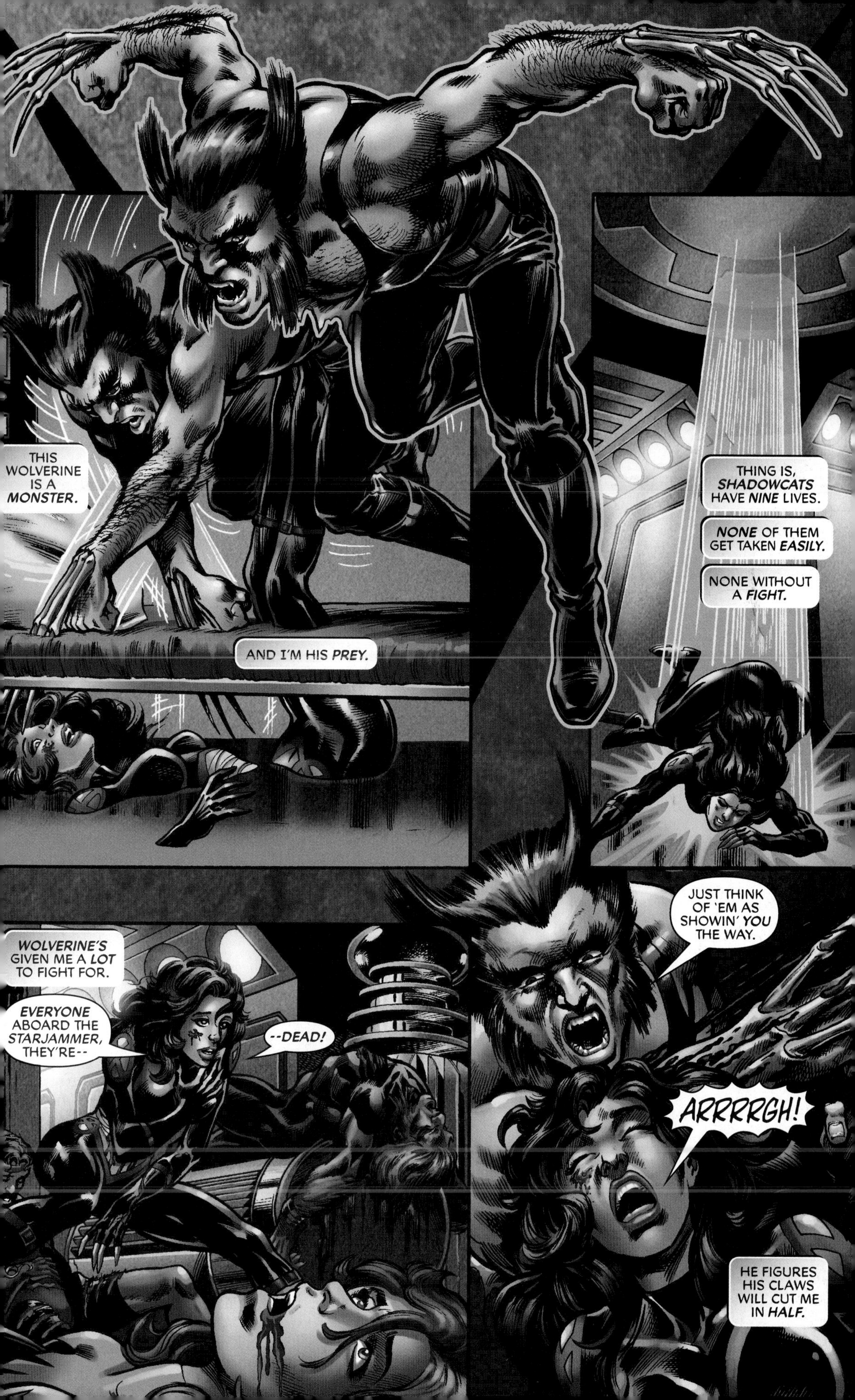

THIS WOLVERINE IS A MONSTER.
AND I'M HIS PREY.
THING IS, SHADOWCATS HAVE NINE LIVES.
NONE OF THEM GET TAKEN EASILY.
NONE WITHOUT A FIGHT.
WOLVERINE'S GIVEN ME A LOT TO FIGHT FOR.
EVERYONE ABOARD THE STARJAMMER, THEY'RE--
--DEAD!
JUST THINK OF 'EM AS SHOWIN' YOU THE WAY.
ARRRRGH!
HE FIGURES HIS CLAWS WILL CUT ME IN HALF.

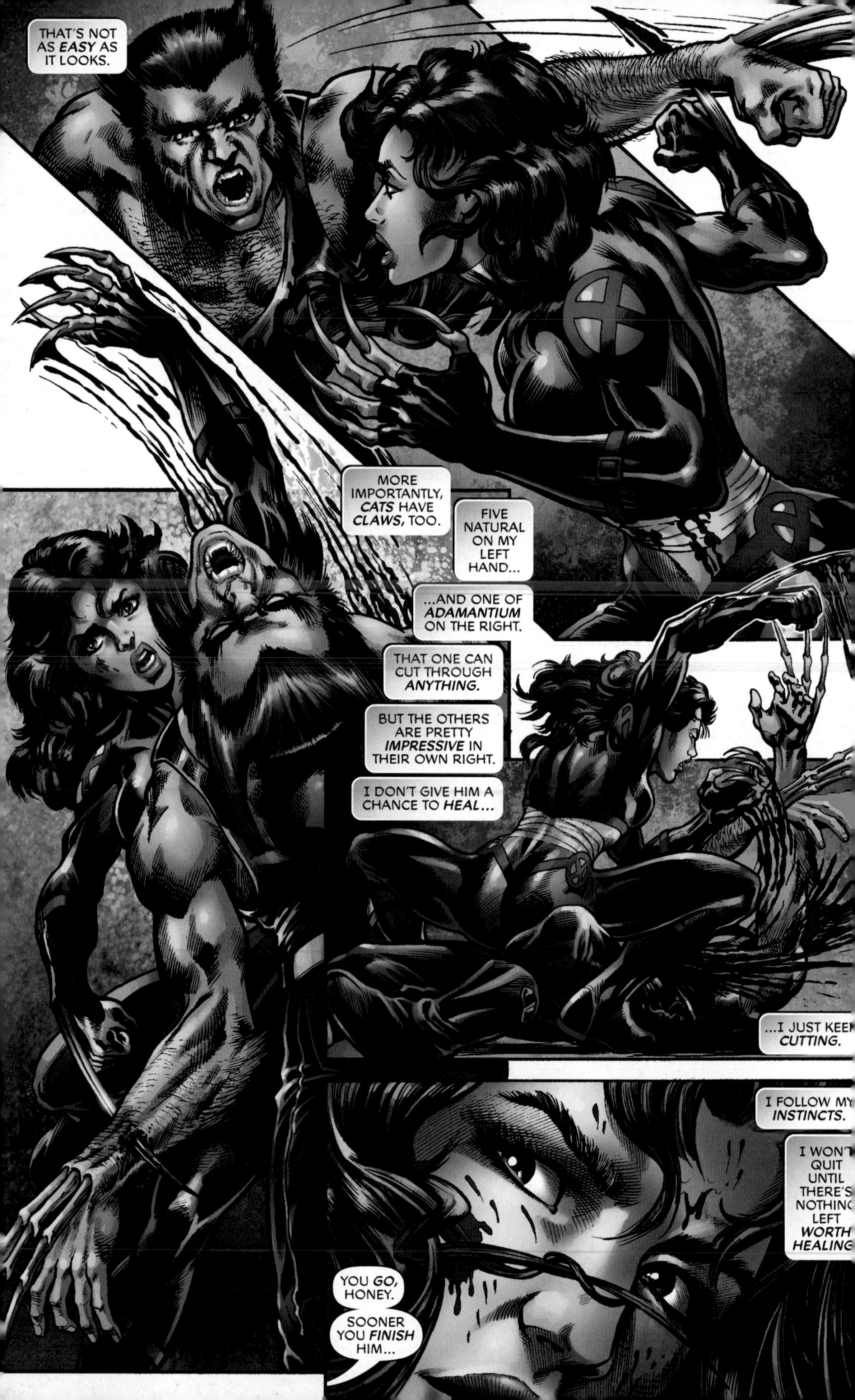
THAT'S NOT AS EASY AS IT LOOKS.
MORE IMPORTANTLY, CATS HAVE CLAWS, TOO.
FIVE NATURAL ON MY LEFT HAND...
...AND ONE OF ADAMANTIUM ON THE RIGHT.
THAT ONE CAN CUT THROUGH ANYTHING.
BUT THE OTHERS ARE PRETTY IMPRESSIVE IN THEIR OWN RIGHT.
I DON'T GIVE HIM A CHANCE TO HEAL...
...I JUST KEEP CUTTING.
I FOLLOW MY INSTINCTS.
I WON'T QUIT UNTIL THERE'S NOTHING LEFT WORTH HEALING.
YOU GO, HONEY.
SOONER YOU FINISH HIM...

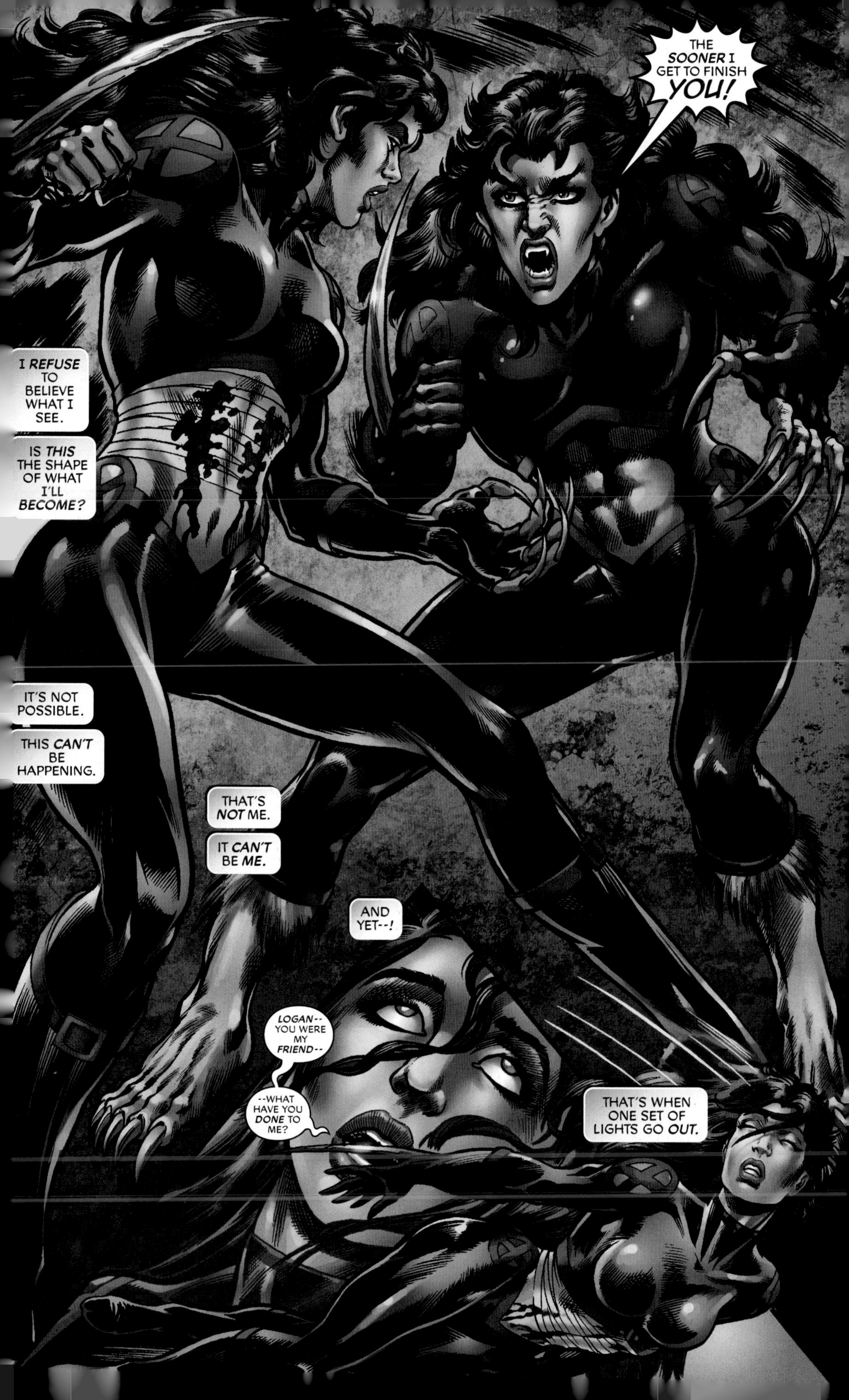
THE SOONER I GET TO FINISH YOU!
I REFUSE TO BELIEVE WHAT I SEE.
IS THIS THE SHAPE OF WHAT I'LL BECOME?
IT'S NOT POSSIBLE.
THIS CAN'T BE HAPPENING.
THAT'S NOT ME.
IT CAN'T BE ME.
AND YET--!
LOGAN-- YOU WERE MY FRIEND--
--WHAT HAVE YOU DONE TO ME?
THAT'S WHEN ONE SET OF LIGHTS GO OUT.

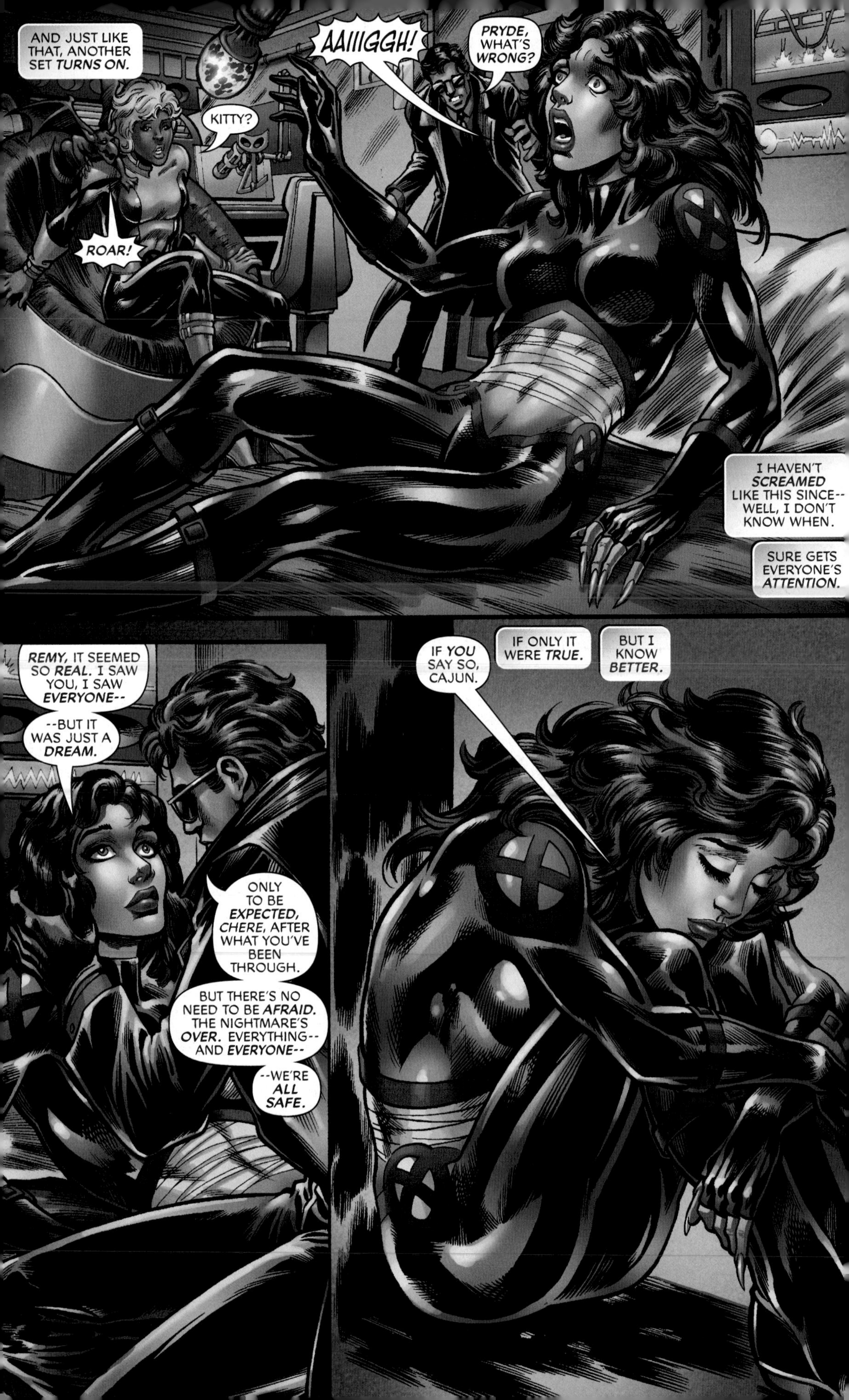
AND JUST LIKE THAT, ANOTHER SET TURNS ON.
AAIIIGGH!
PRYDE, WHAT'S WRONG?
KITTY?
ROAR!
I HAVEN'T SCREAMED LIKE THIS SINCE--WELL, I DON'T KNOW WHEN.
SURE GETS EVERYONE'S ATTENTION.
REMY, IT SEEMED SO REAL. I SAW YOU, I SAW EVERYONE--
--BUT IT WAS JUST A DREAM.
ONLY TO BE EXPECTED, CHERE, AFTER WHAT YOU'VE BEEN THROUGH.
BUT THERE'S NO NEED TO BE AFRAID. THE NIGHTMARE'S OVER. EVERYTHING--AND EVERYONE--
--WE'RE ALL SAFE.
IF YOU SAY SO, CAJUN.
IF ONLY IT WERE TRUE.
BUT I KNOW BETTER.

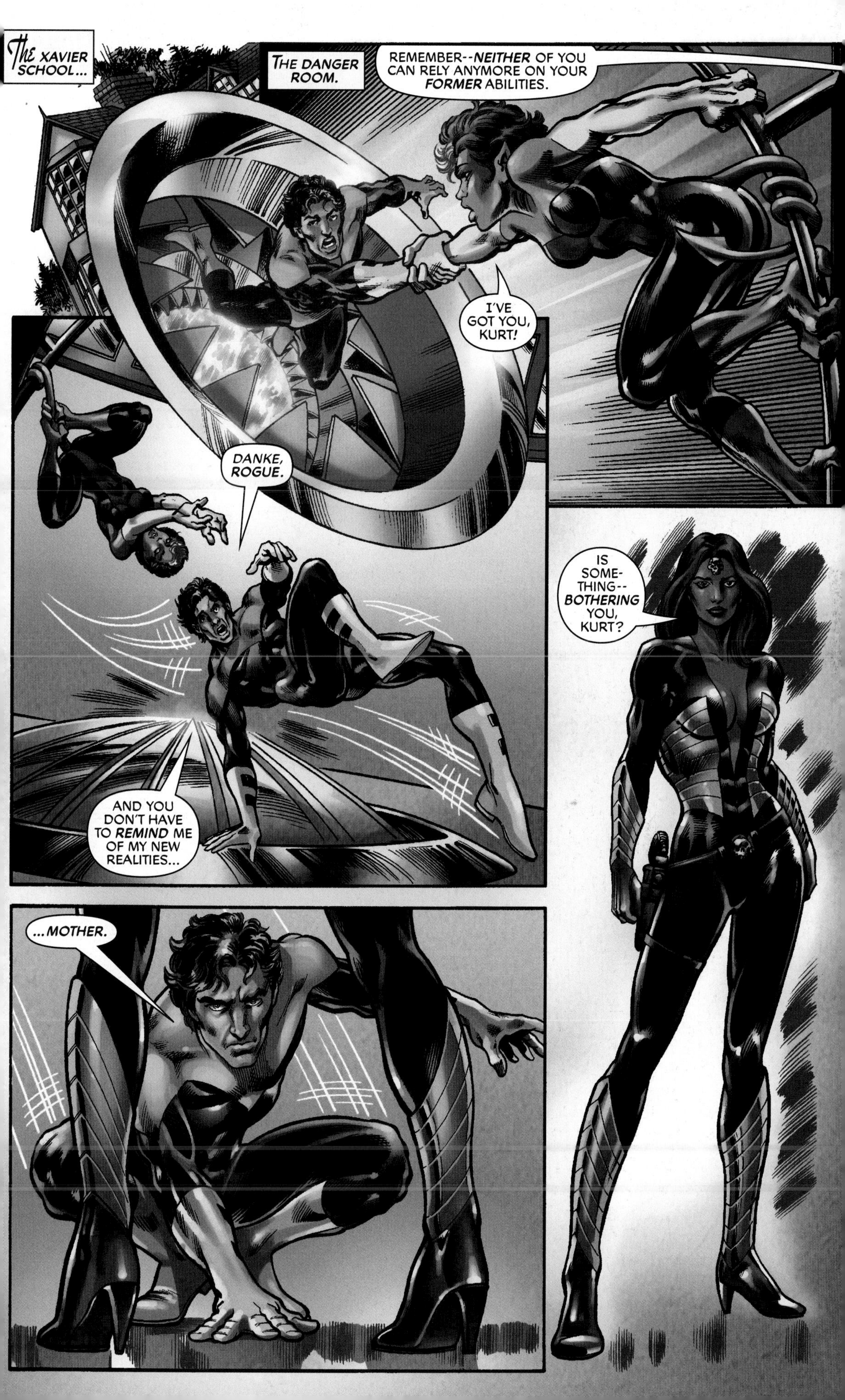
THE XAVIER SCHOOL...
THE DANGER ROOM.
REMEMBER--NEITHER OF YOU CAN RELY ANYMORE ON YOUR FORMER ABILITIES.
I'VE GOT YOU, KURT!
DANKE, ROGUE.
AND YOU DON'T HAVE TO REMIND ME OF MY NEW REALITIES...
IS SOME-THING--BOTHERING YOU, KURT?
...MOTHER.

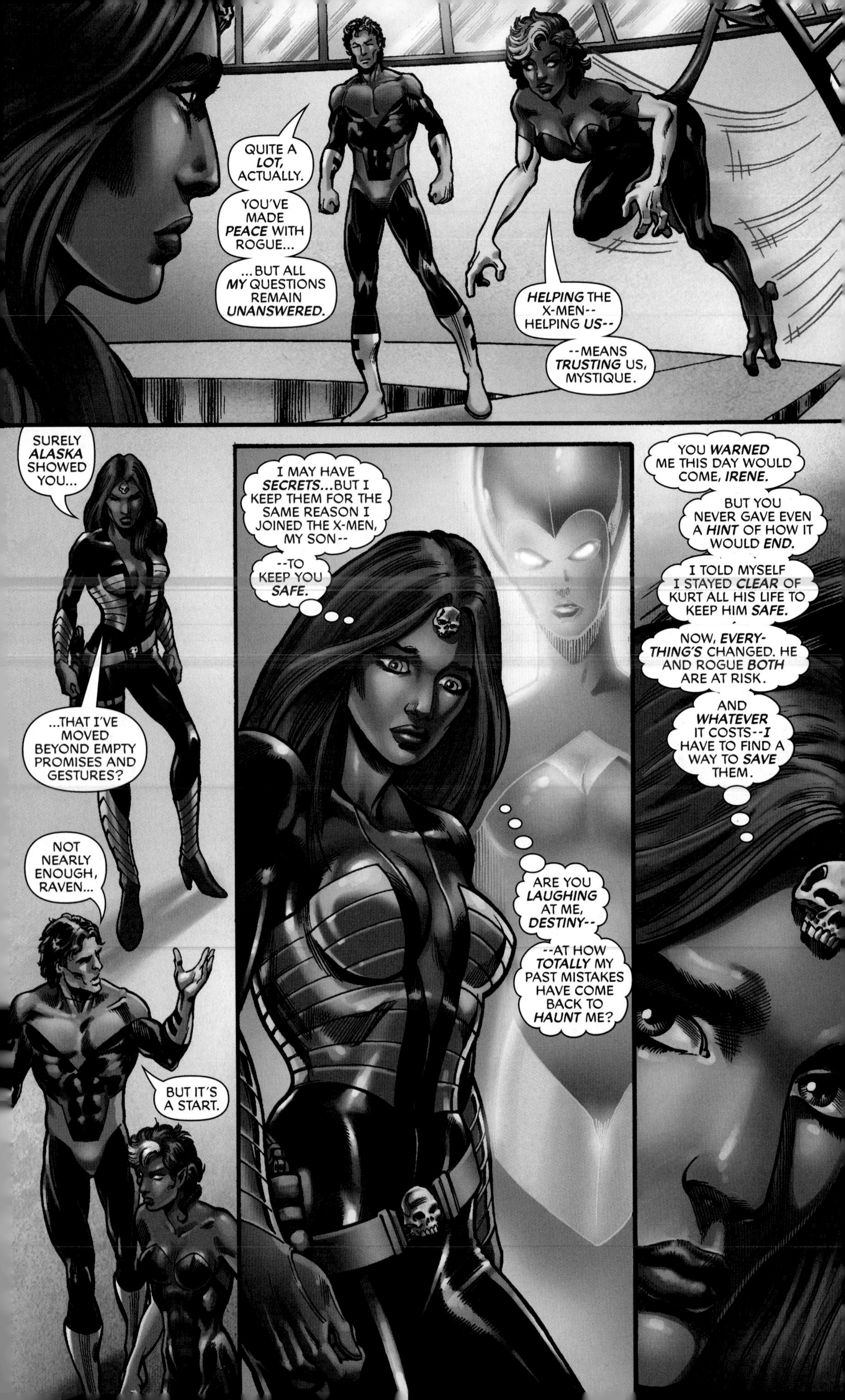
QUITE A LOT, ACTUALLY.
YOU'VE MADE PEACE WITH ROGUE...
...BUT ALL MY QUESTIONS REMAIN UNANSWERED.
HELPING THE X-MEN-- HELPING US--
--MEANS TRUSTING US, MYSTIQUE.
SURELY ALASKA SHOWED YOU...
...THAT I'VE MOVED BEYOND EMPTY PROMISES AND GESTURES?
NOT NEARLY ENOUGH, RAVEN...
BUT IT'S A START.
I MAY HAVE SECRETS...BUT I KEEP THEM FOR THE SAME REASON I JOINED THE X-MEN, MY SON--
--TO KEEP YOU SAFE.
ARE YOU LAUGHING AT ME, DESTINY--
--AT HOW TOTALLY MY PAST MISTAKES HAVE COME BACK TO HAUNT ME?
YOU WARNED ME THIS DAY WOULD COME, IRENE.
BUT YOU NEVER GAVE EVEN A HINT OF HOW IT WOULD END.
I TOLD MYSELF I STAYED CLEAR OF KURT ALL HIS LIFE TO KEEP HIM SAFE.
NOW, EVERYTHING'S CHANGED. HE AND ROGUE BOTH ARE AT RISK.
AND WHATEVER IT COSTS--I HAVE TO FIND A WAY TO SAVE THEM.

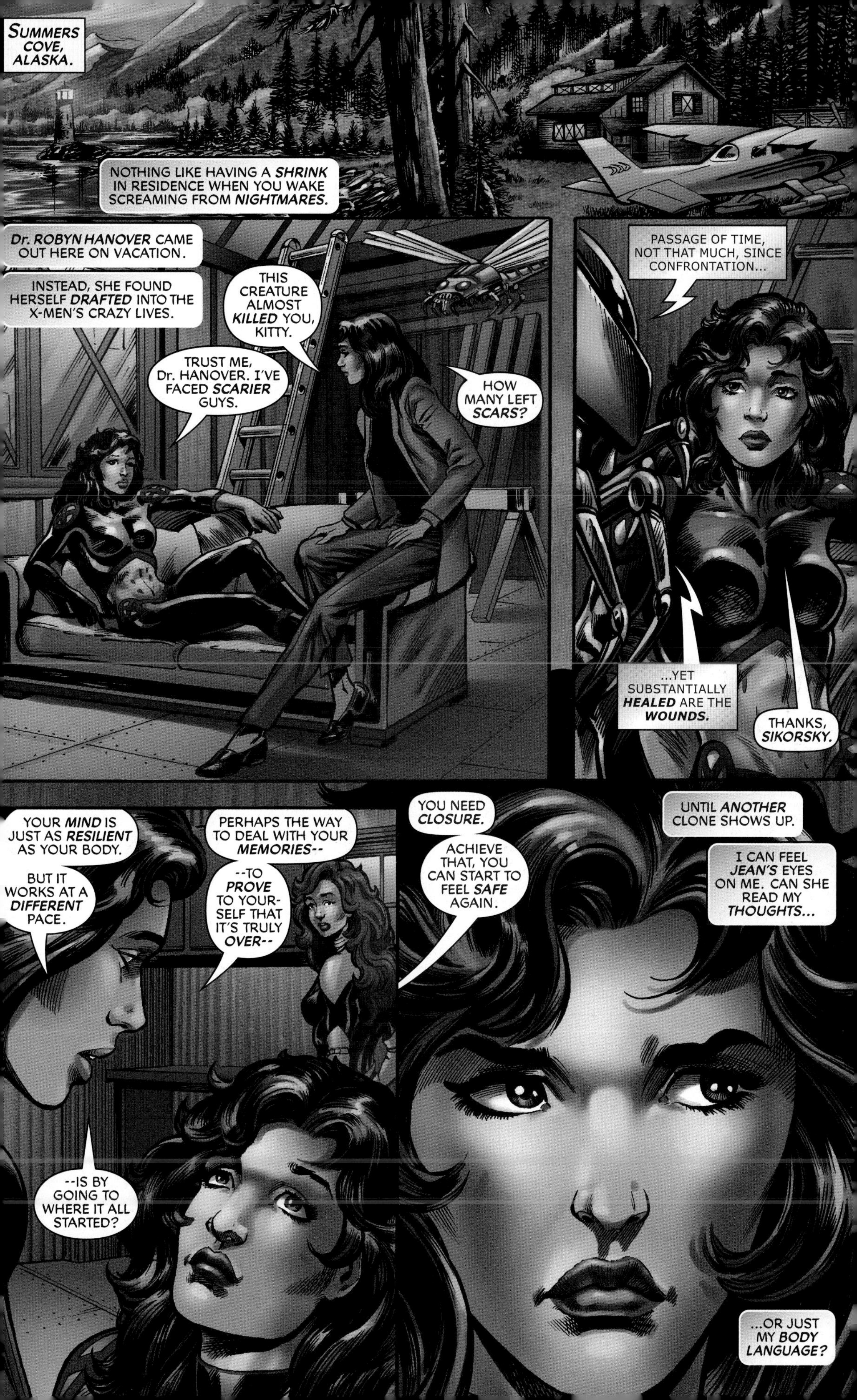
SUMMERS COVE, ALASKA.
NOTHING LIKE HAVING A SHRINK IN RESIDENCE WHEN YOU WAKE SCREAMING FROM NIGHTMARES.
Dr. ROBYN HANOVER CAME OUT HERE ON VACATION.
INSTEAD, SHE FOUND HERSELF DRAFTED INTO THE X-MEN'S CRAZY LIVES.
THIS CREATURE ALMOST KILLED YOU, KITTY.
TRUST ME, Dr. HANOVER. I'VE FACED SCARIER GUYS.
HOW MANY LEFT SCARS?
PASSAGE OF TIME, NOT THAT MUCH, SINCE CONFRONTATION...
...YET SUBSTANTIALLY HEALED ARE THE WOUNDS.
THANKS, SIKORSKY.
YOUR MIND IS JUST AS RESILIENT AS YOUR BODY.
BUT IT WORKS AT A DIFFERENT PACE.
PERHAPS THE WAY TO DEAL WITH YOUR MEMORIES--
--TO PROVE TO YOURSELF THAT IT'S TRULY OVER--
--IS BY GOING TO WHERE IT ALL STARTED?
YOU NEED CLOSURE.
ACHIEVE THAT, YOU CAN START TO FEEL SAFE AGAIN.
UNTIL ANOTHER CLONE SHOWS UP.
I CAN FEEL JEAN'S EYES ON ME. CAN SHE READ MY THOUGHTS...
...OR JUST MY BODY LANGUAGE?

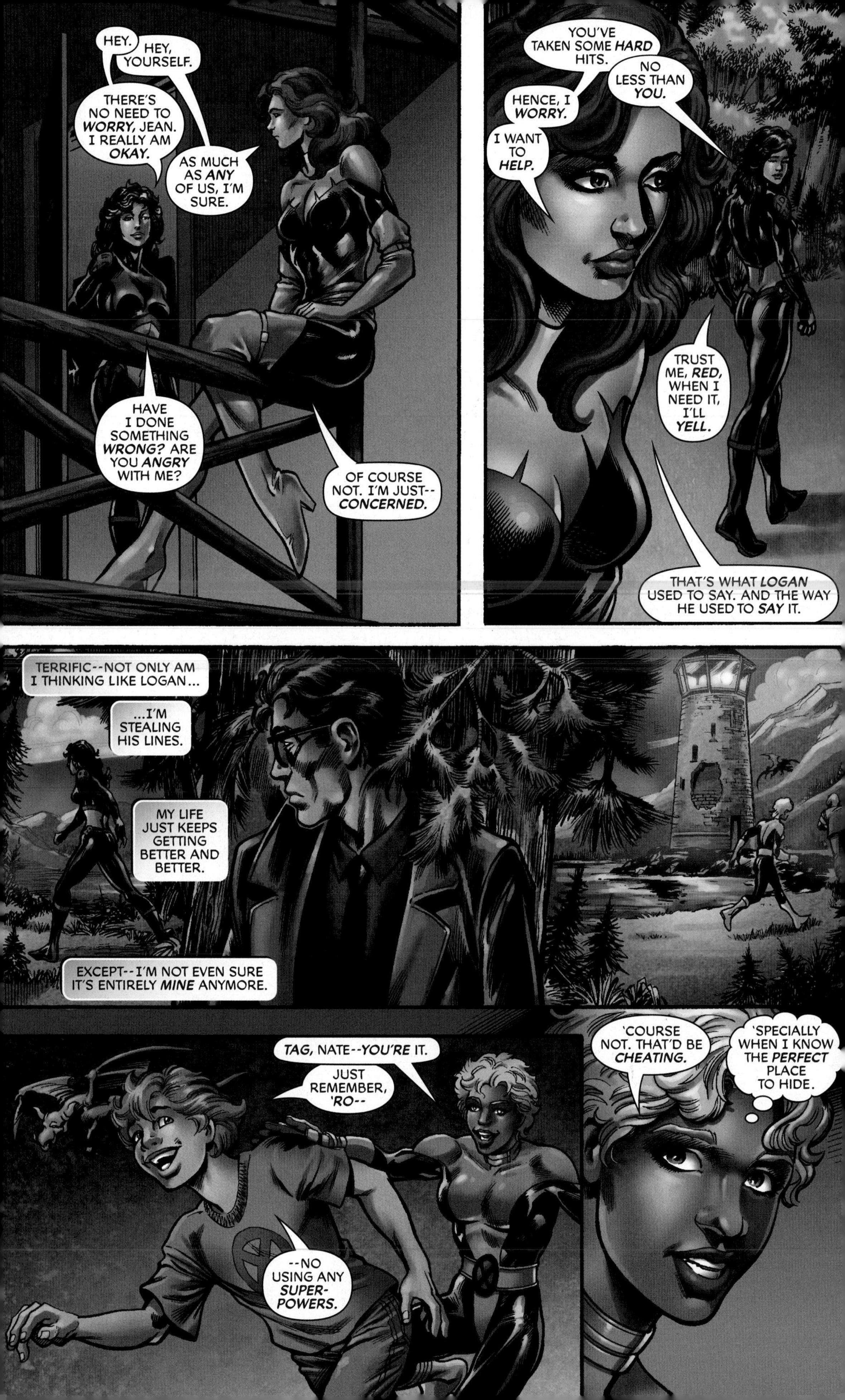
HEY.
HEY, YOURSELF.
THERE'S NO NEED TO WORRY, JEAN. I REALLY AM OKAY.
AS MUCH AS ANY OF US, I'M SURE.
HAVE I DONE SOMETHING WRONG? ARE YOU ANGRY WITH ME?
OF COURSE NOT. I'M JUST--CONCERNED.
YOU'VE TAKEN SOME HARD HITS.
NO LESS THAN YOU.
HENCE, I WORRY.
I WANT TO HELP.
TRUST ME, RED, WHEN I NEED IT, I'LL YELL.
THAT'S WHAT LOGAN USED TO SAY. AND THE WAY HE USED TO SAY IT.
TERRIFIC--NOT ONLY AM I THINKING LIKE LOGAN...
...I'M STEALING HIS LINES.
MY LIFE JUST KEEPS GETTING BETTER AND BETTER.
EXCEPT--I'M NOT EVEN SURE IT'S ENTIRELY MINE ANYMORE.
TAG, NATE--YOU'RE IT.
JUST REMEMBER, 'RO--
--NO USING ANY SUPER-POWERS.
'COURSE NOT. THAT'D BE CHEATING.
'SPECIALLY WHEN I KNOW THE PERFECT PLACE TO HIDE.

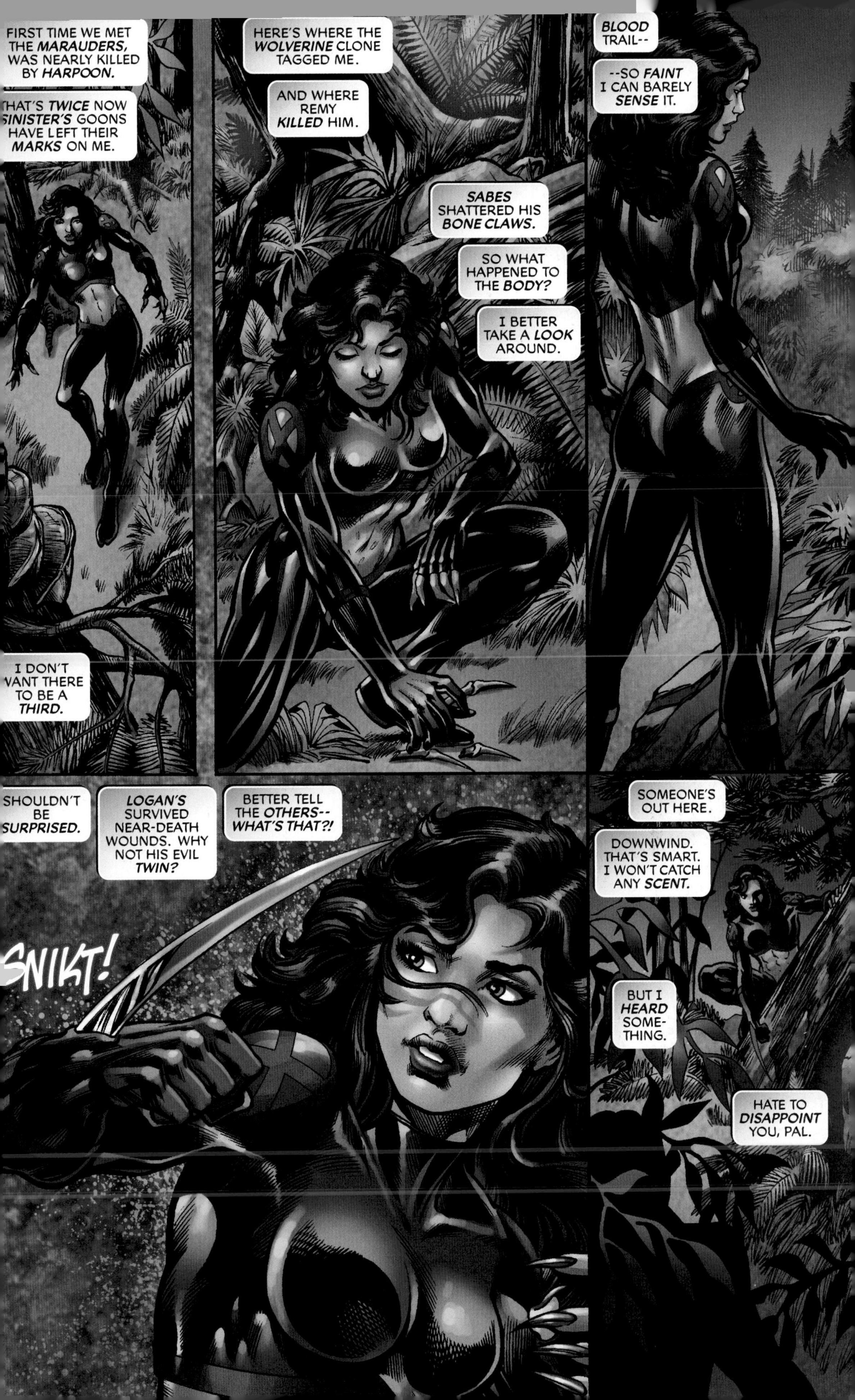
FIRST TIME WE MET THE MARAUDERS, WAS NEARLY KILLED BY HARPOON.
THAT'S TWICE NOW SINISTER'S GOONS HAVE LEFT THEIR MARKS ON ME.
I DON'T WANT THERE TO BE A THIRD.
HERE'S WHERE THE WOLVERINE CLONE TAGGED ME.
AND WHERE REMY KILLED HIM.
SABES SHATTERED HIS BONE CLAWS.
SO WHAT HAPPENED TO THE BODY?
I BETTER TAKE A LOOK AROUND.
BLOOD TRAIL--
--SO FAINT I CAN BARELY SENSE IT.
SHOULDN'T BE SURPRISED.
LOGAN'S SURVIVED NEAR-DEATH WOUNDS. WHY NOT HIS EVIL TWIN?
BETTER TELL THE OTHERS--WHAT'S THAT?!
SNIKT!
SOMEONE'S OUT HERE.
DOWNWIND. THAT'S SMART. I WON'T CATCH ANY SCENT.
BUT I HEARD SOME-THING.
HATE TO DISAPPOINT YOU, PAL.

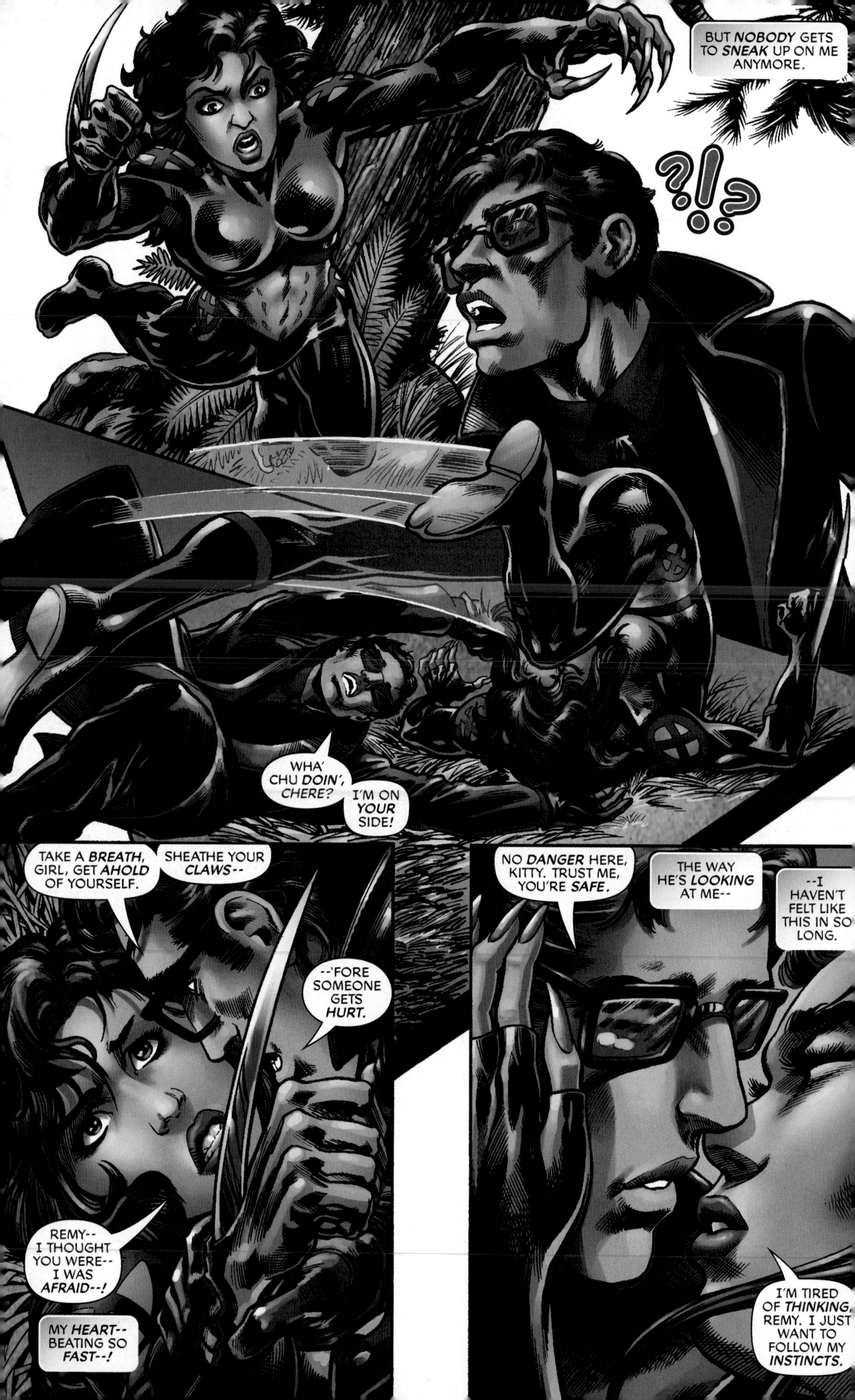
BUT NOBODY GETS TO SNEAK UP ON ME ANYMORE.
?!?
WHA' CHU DOIN', CHERE?
I'M ON YOUR SIDE!
TAKE A BREATH, GIRL, GET AHOLD OF YOURSELF.
SHEATHE YOUR CLAWS--
--'FORE SOMEONE GETS HURT.
REMY-- I THOUGHT YOU WERE-- I WAS AFRAID--!
MY HEART-- BEATING SO FAST--!
NO DANGER HERE, KITTY. TRUST ME, YOU'RE SAFE.
THE WAY HE'S LOOKING AT ME--
--I HAVEN'T FELT LIKE THIS IN SO LONG.
I'M TIRED OF THINKING, REMY. I JUST WANT TO FOLLOW MY INSTINCTS.

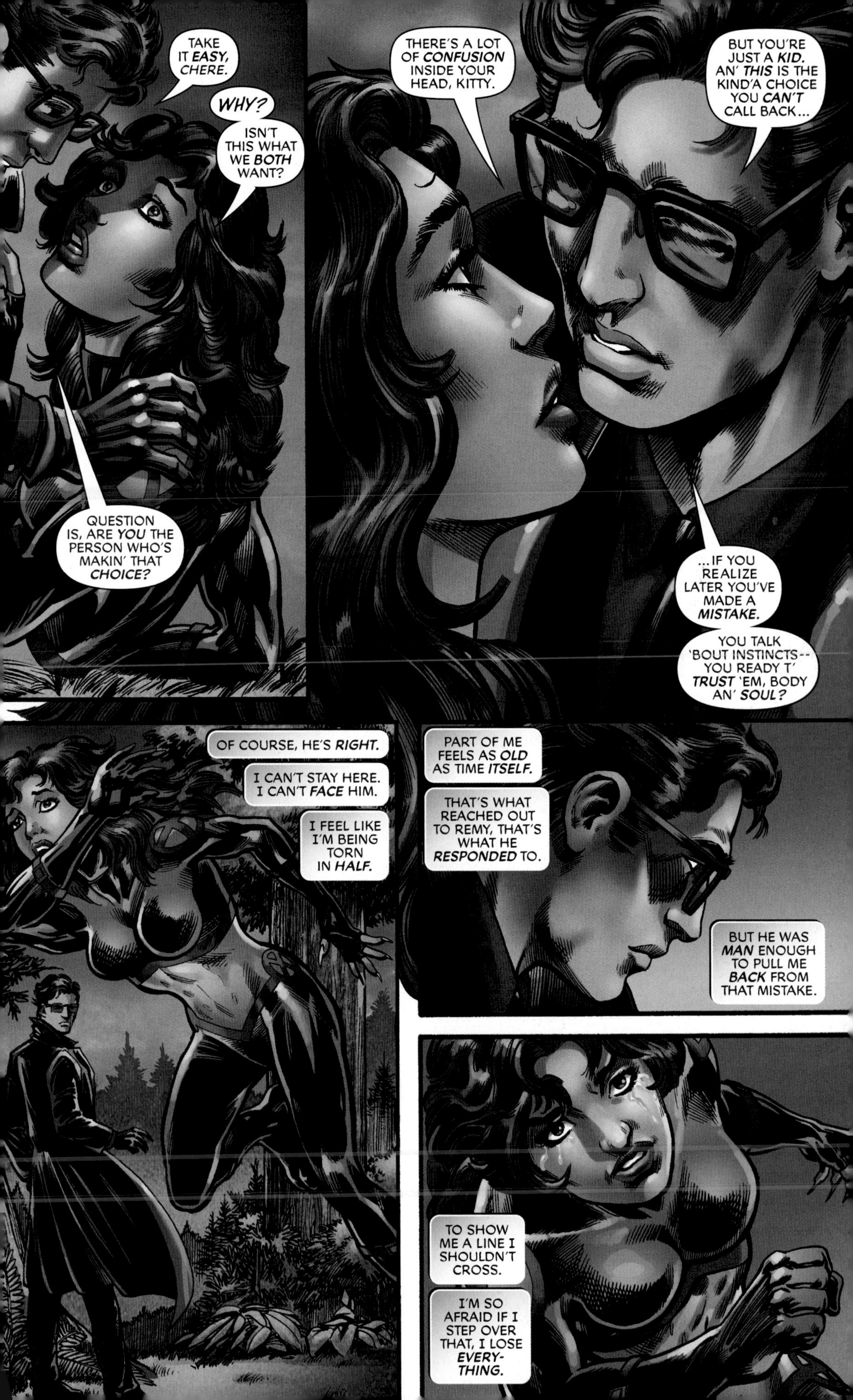
TAKE IT *EASY*, *CHERE.*
WHY?
ISN'T THIS WHAT WE *BOTH* WANT?
QUESTION IS, ARE *YOU* THE PERSON WHO'S MAKIN' THAT *CHOICE?*
THERE'S A LOT OF *CONFUSION* INSIDE YOUR HEAD, KITTY.
BUT YOU'RE JUST A *KID.* AN' *THIS* IS THE KIND'A CHOICE YOU *CAN'T* CALL BACK...
...IF YOU REALIZE LATER YOU'VE MADE A *MISTAKE.*
YOU TALK 'BOUT INSTINCTS-- YOU READY T' *TRUST* 'EM, BODY AN' *SOUL?*
OF COURSE, HE'S *RIGHT.*
I CAN'T STAY HERE. I CAN'T *FACE* HIM.
I FEEL LIKE I'M BEING TORN IN *HALF.*
PART OF ME FEELS AS *OLD* AS TIME *ITSELF.*
THAT'S WHAT REACHED OUT TO REMY, THAT'S WHAT HE *RESPONDED* TO.
BUT HE WAS *MAN* ENOUGH TO PULL ME *BACK* FROM THAT MISTAKE.
TO SHOW ME A LINE I SHOULDN'T CROSS.
I'M SO AFRAID IF I STEP OVER THAT, I LOSE *EVERY-THING.*

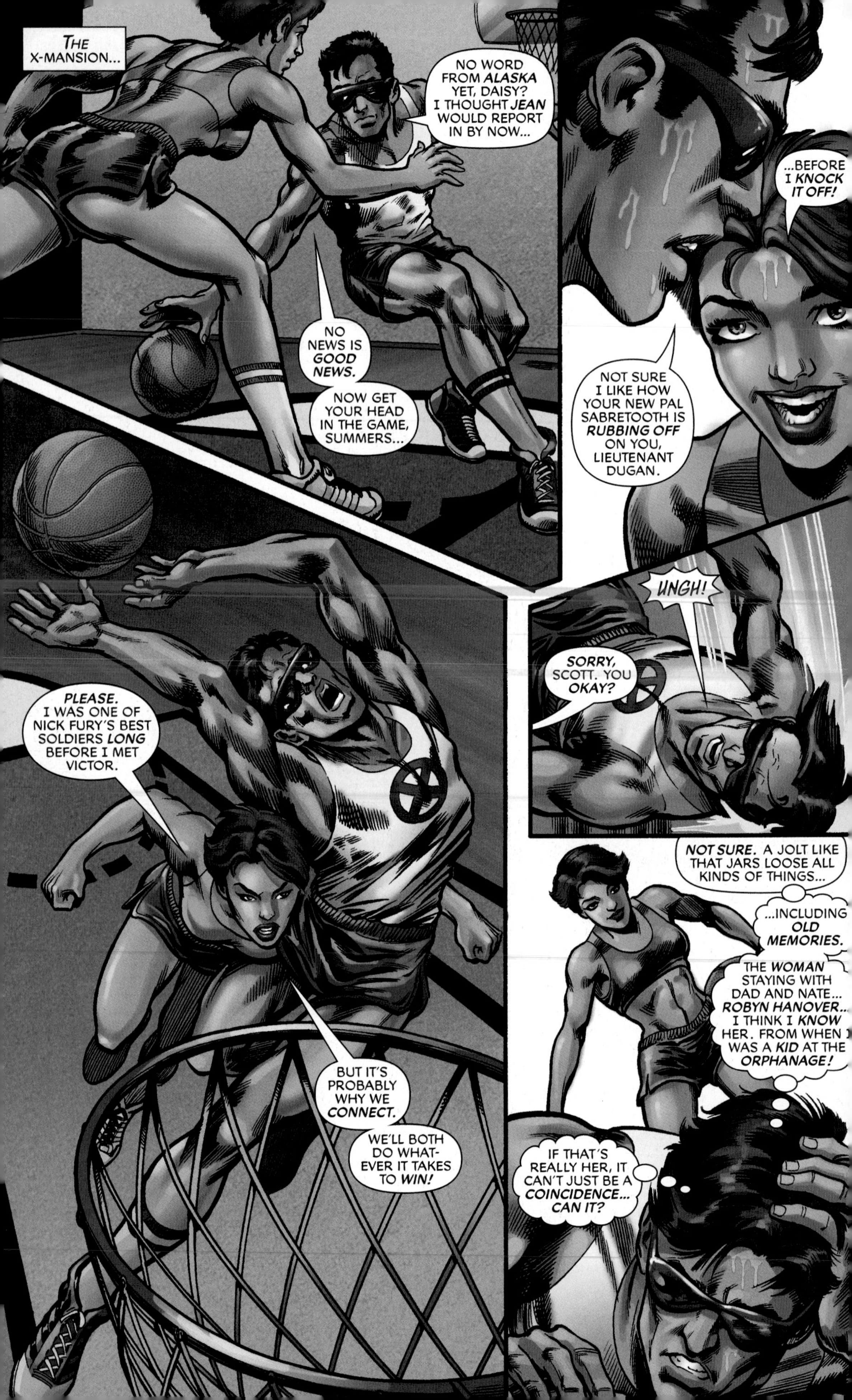
THE X-MANSION...
NO WORD FROM ALASKA YET, DAISY? I THOUGHT JEAN WOULD REPORT IN BY NOW...
NO NEWS IS GOOD NEWS.
NOW GET YOUR HEAD IN THE GAME, SUMMERS...
...BEFORE I KNOCK IT OFF!
NOT SURE I LIKE HOW YOUR NEW PAL SABRETOOTH IS RUBBING OFF ON YOU, LIEUTENANT DUGAN.
PLEASE. I WAS ONE OF NICK FURY'S BEST SOLDIERS LONG BEFORE I MET VICTOR.
BUT IT'S PROBABLY WHY WE CONNECT.
WE'LL BOTH DO WHAT-EVER IT TAKES TO WIN!
UNGH!
SORRY, SCOTT. YOU OKAY?
NOT SURE. A JOLT LIKE THAT JARS LOOSE ALL KINDS OF THINGS...
...INCLUDING OLD MEMORIES.
THE WOMAN STAYING WITH DAD AND NATE... ROBYN HANOVER... I THINK I KNOW HER. FROM WHEN I WAS A KID AT THE ORPHANAGE!
IF THAT'S REALLY HER, IT CAN'T JUST BE A COINCIDENCE... CAN IT?

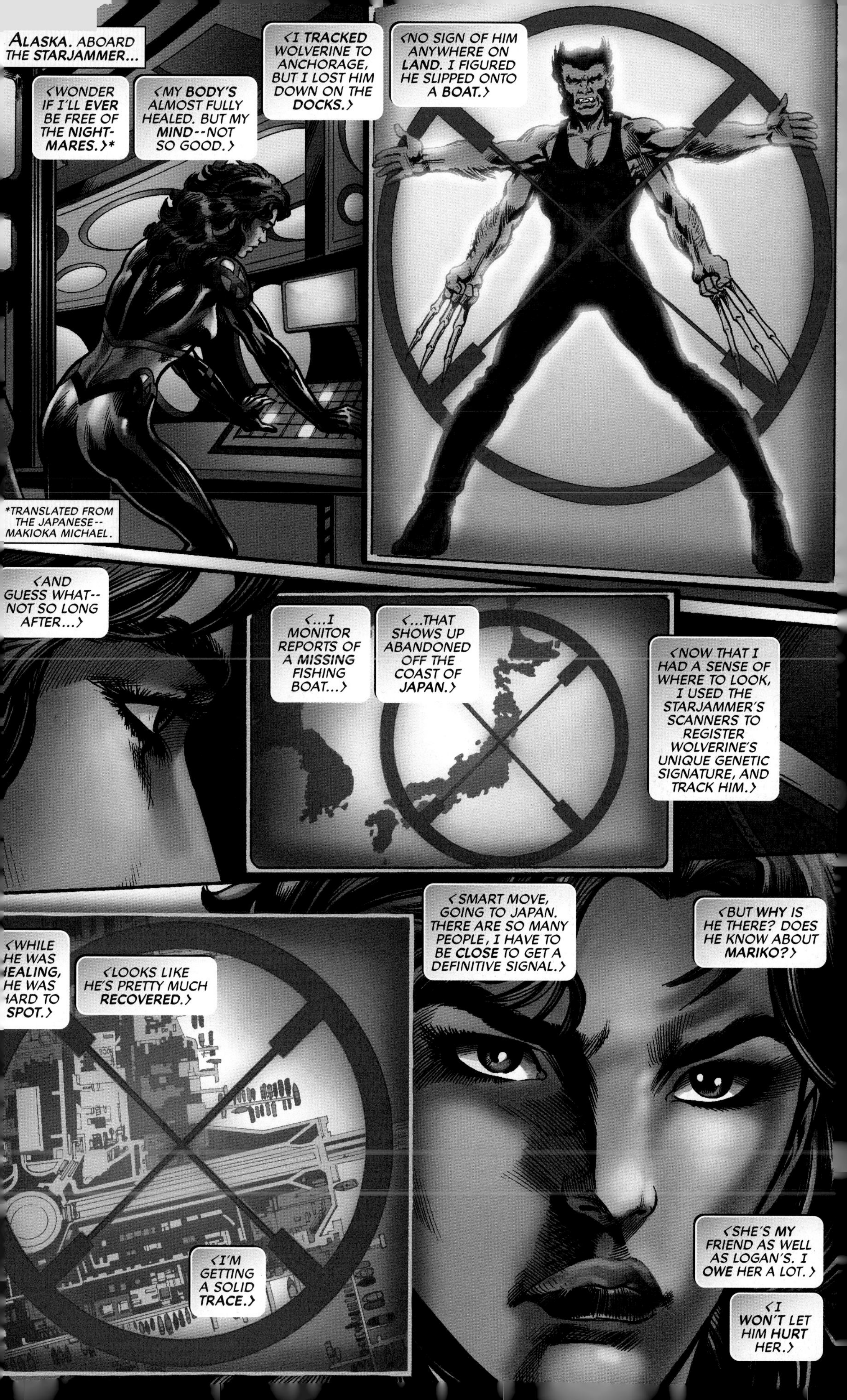

ALASKA. ABOARD THE STARJAMMER...
<WONDER IF I'LL EVER BE FREE OF THE NIGHT-MARES.>*
<MY BODY'S ALMOST FULLY HEALED. BUT MY MIND--NOT SO GOOD.>
*TRANSLATED FROM THE JAPANESE-- MAKIOKA MICHAEL.
<I TRACKED WOLVERINE TO ANCHORAGE, BUT I LOST HIM DOWN ON THE DOCKS.>
<NO SIGN OF HIM ANYWHERE ON LAND. I FIGURED HE SLIPPED ONTO A BOAT.>
<AND GUESS WHAT--NOT SO LONG AFTER...>
<...I MONITOR REPORTS OF A MISSING FISHING BOAT...>
<...THAT SHOWS UP ABANDONED OFF THE COAST OF JAPAN.>
<NOW THAT I HAD A SENSE OF WHERE TO LOOK, I USED THE STARJAMMER'S SCANNERS TO REGISTER WOLVERINE'S UNIQUE GENETIC SIGNATURE, AND TRACK HIM.>
<WHILE HE WAS HEALING, HE WAS HARD TO SPOT.>
<LOOKS LIKE HE'S PRETTY MUCH RECOVERED.>
<I'M GETTING A SOLID TRACE.>
<SMART MOVE, GOING TO JAPAN. THERE ARE SO MANY PEOPLE, I HAVE TO BE CLOSE TO GET A DEFINITIVE SIGNAL.>
<BUT WHY IS HE THERE? DOES HE KNOW ABOUT MARIKO?>
<SHE'S MY FRIEND AS WELL AS LOGAN'S. I OWE HER A LOT.>
<I WON'T LET HIM HURT HER.>

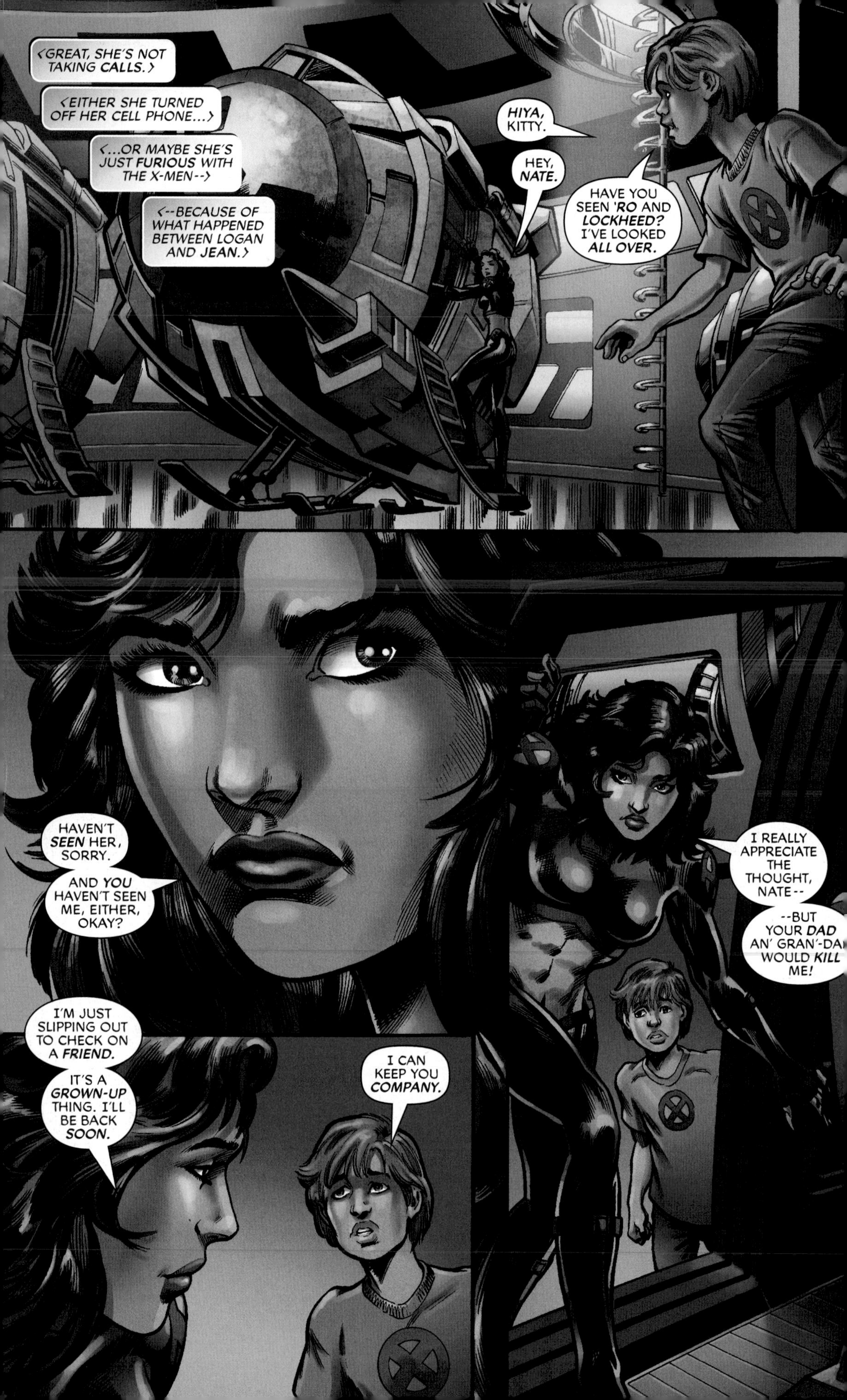
<GREAT, SHE'S NOT TAKING CALLS.>
<EITHER SHE TURNED OFF HER CELL PHONE...>
<...OR MAYBE SHE'S JUST FURIOUS WITH THE X-MEN-->
<--BECAUSE OF WHAT HAPPENED BETWEEN LOGAN AND JEAN.>
HIYA, KITTY.
HEY, NATE.
HAVE YOU SEEN 'RO AND LOCKHEED? I'VE LOOKED ALL OVER.
HAVEN'T SEEN HER, SORRY.
AND YOU HAVEN'T SEEN ME, EITHER, OKAY?
I'M JUST SLIPPING OUT TO CHECK ON A FRIEND.
IT'S A GROWN-UP THING. I'LL BE BACK SOON.
I CAN KEEP YOU COMPANY.
I REALLY APPRECIATE THE THOUGHT, NATE--
--BUT YOUR DAD AN' GRAN'-DA WOULD KILL ME!

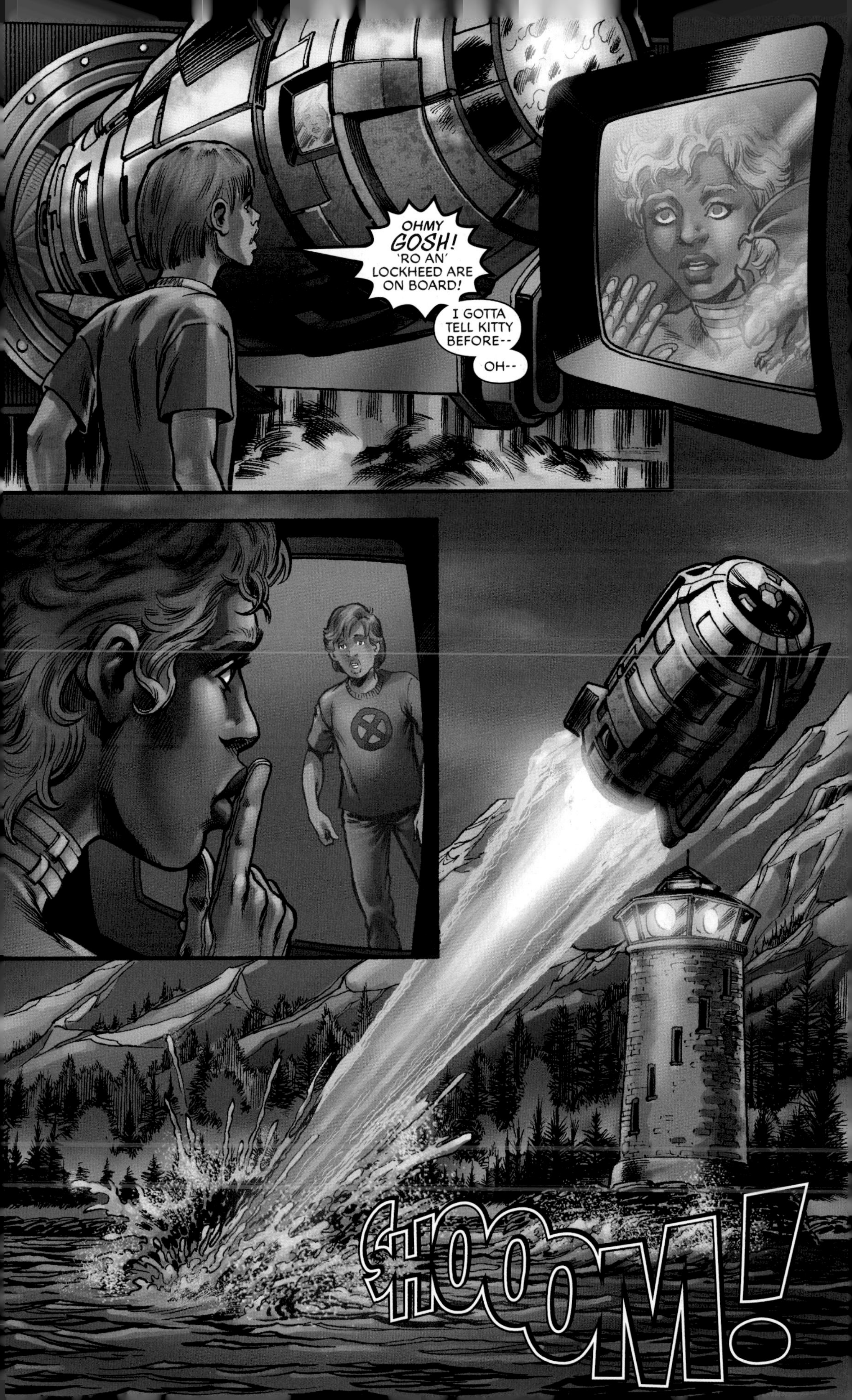
OHMY
GOSH!
'RO AN'
LOCKHEED ARE
ON BOARD!
I GOTTA
TELL KITTY
BEFORE--
OH--
SHOOOOM!

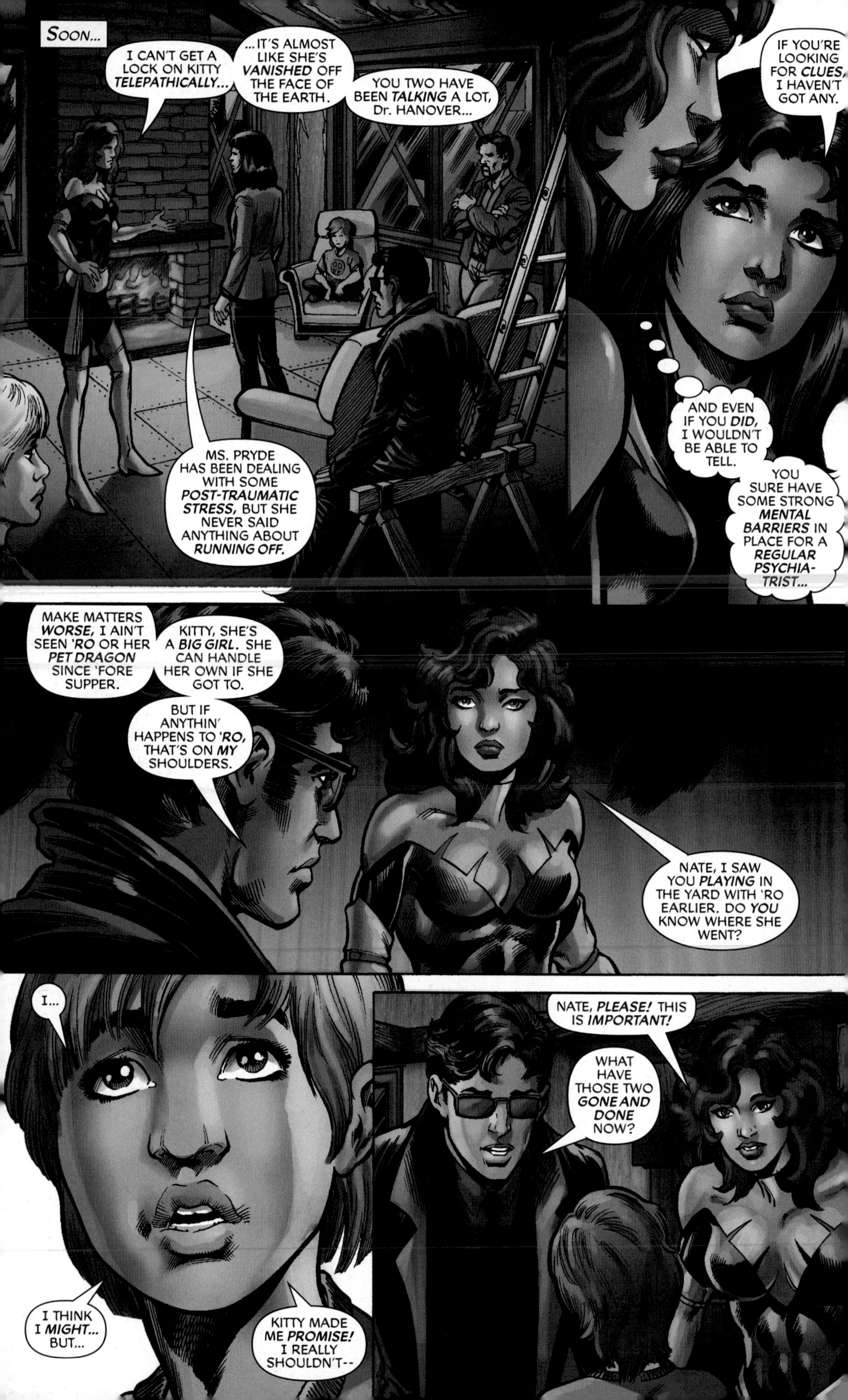
SOON...
I CAN'T GET A LOCK ON KITTY TELEPATHICALLY...
...IT'S ALMOST LIKE SHE'S VANISHED OFF THE FACE OF THE EARTH.
YOU TWO HAVE BEEN TALKING A LOT, Dr. HANOVER...
MS. PRYDE HAS BEEN DEALING WITH SOME POST-TRAUMATIC STRESS, BUT SHE NEVER SAID ANYTHING ABOUT RUNNING OFF.
IF YOU'RE LOOKING FOR CLUES, I HAVEN'T GOT ANY.
AND EVEN IF YOU DID, I WOULDN'T BE ABLE TO TELL.
YOU SURE HAVE SOME STRONG MENTAL BARRIERS IN PLACE FOR A REGULAR PSYCHIA-TRIST...
MAKE MATTERS WORSE, I AIN'T SEEN 'RO OR HER PET DRAGON SINCE 'FORE SUPPER.
KITTY, SHE'S A BIG GIRL. SHE CAN HANDLE HER OWN IF SHE GOT TO.
BUT IF ANYTHIN' HAPPENS TO 'RO, THAT'S ON MY SHOULDERS.
NATE, I SAW YOU PLAYING IN THE YARD WITH 'RO EARLIER. DO YOU KNOW WHERE SHE WENT?
I...
I THINK I MIGHT... BUT...
KITTY MADE ME PROMISE! I REALLY SHOULDN'T--
NATE, PLEASE! THIS IS IMPORTANT!
WHAT HAVE THOSE TWO GONE AND DONE NOW?

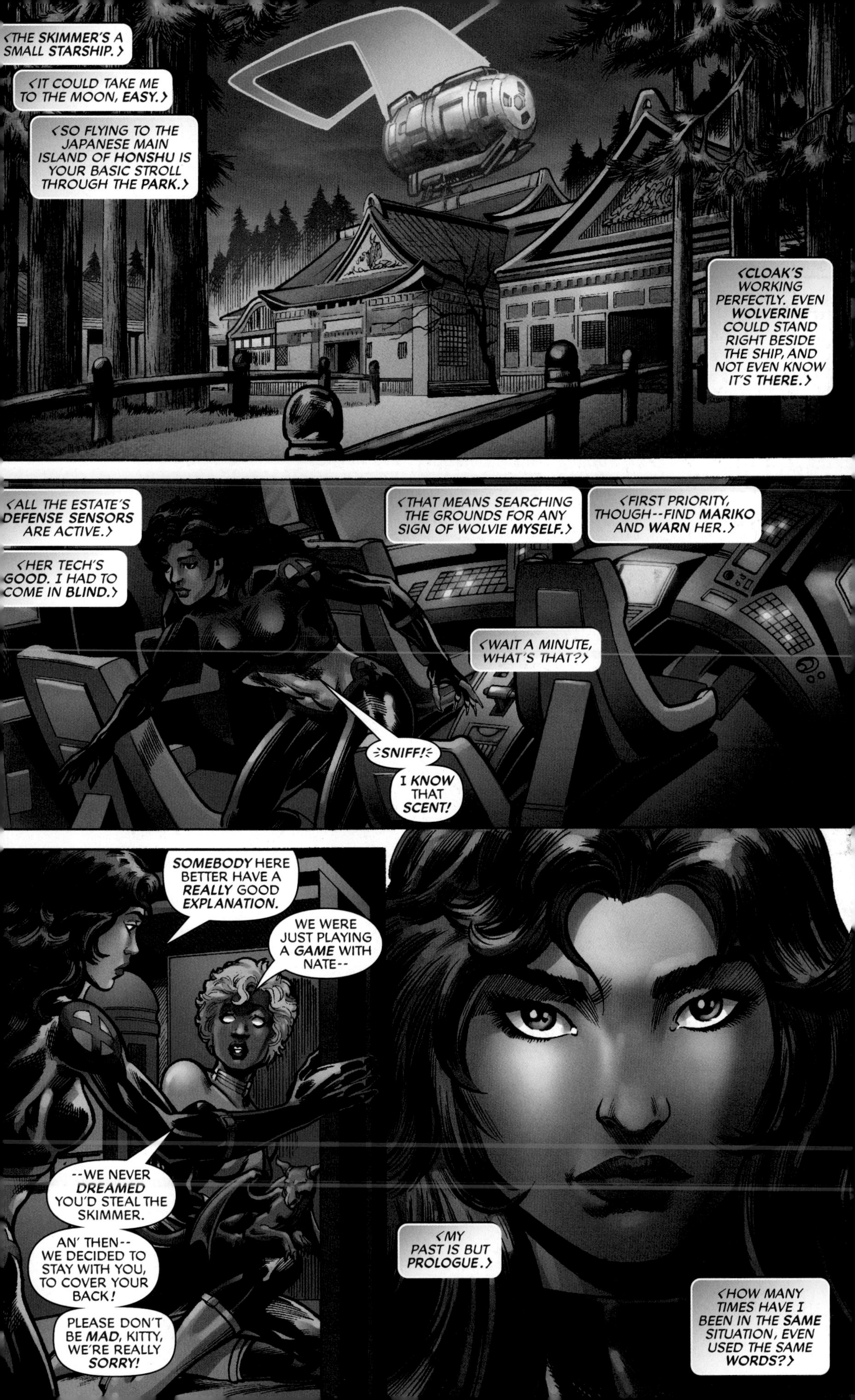

<THE SKIMMER'S A SMALL STARSHIP.>
<IT COULD TAKE ME TO THE MOON, EASY.>
<SO FLYING TO THE JAPANESE MAIN ISLAND OF HONSHU IS YOUR BASIC STROLL THROUGH THE PARK.>
<CLOAK'S WORKING PERFECTLY. EVEN WOLVERINE COULD STAND RIGHT BESIDE THE SHIP, AND NOT EVEN KNOW IT'S THERE.>
<ALL THE ESTATE'S DEFENSE SENSORS ARE ACTIVE.>
<HER TECH'S GOOD. I HAD TO COME IN BLIND.>
<THAT MEANS SEARCHING THE GROUNDS FOR ANY SIGN OF WOLVIE MYSELF.>
<FIRST PRIORITY, THOUGH--FIND MARIKO AND WARN HER.>
<WAIT A MINUTE, WHAT'S THAT?>
SNIFF!
I KNOW THAT SCENT!
SOMEBODY HERE BETTER HAVE A REALLY GOOD EXPLANATION.
WE WERE JUST PLAYING A GAME WITH NATE--
--WE NEVER DREAMED YOU'D STEAL THE SKIMMER.
AN' THEN--WE DECIDED TO STAY WITH YOU, TO COVER YOUR BACK!
PLEASE DON'T BE MAD, KITTY, WE'RE REALLY SORRY!
<MY PAST IS BUT PROLOGUE.>
<HOW MANY TIMES HAVE I BEEN IN THE SAME SITUATION, EVEN USED THE SAME WORDS?>

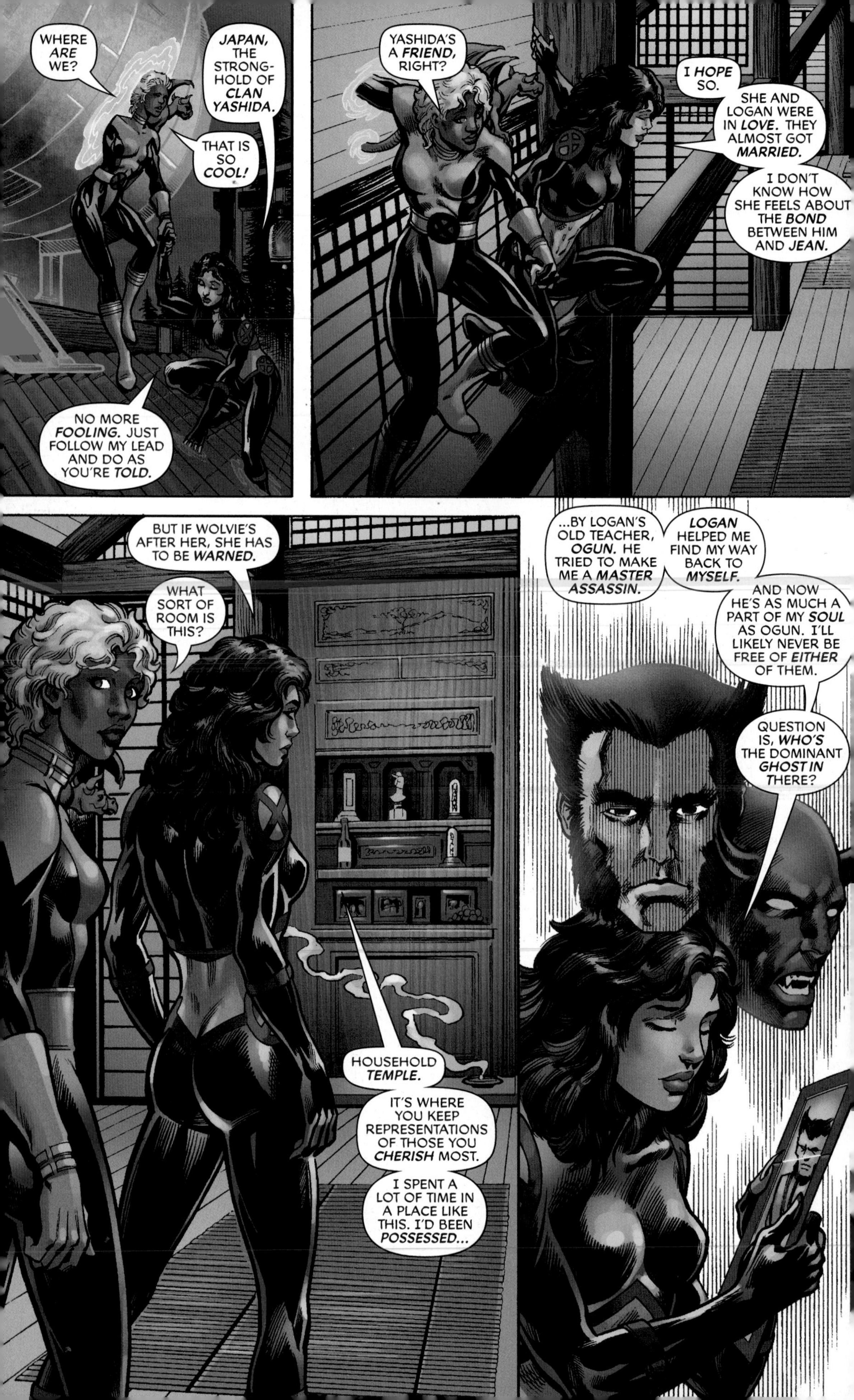
WHERE ARE WE?
JAPAN, THE STRONGHOLD OF CLAN YASHIDA.
THAT IS SO COOL!
NO MORE FOOLING. JUST FOLLOW MY LEAD AND DO AS YOU'RE TOLD.
YASHIDA'S A FRIEND, RIGHT?
I HOPE SO.
SHE AND LOGAN WERE IN LOVE. THEY ALMOST GOT MARRIED.
I DON'T KNOW HOW SHE FEELS ABOUT THE BOND BETWEEN HIM AND JEAN.
BUT IF WOLVIE'S AFTER HER, SHE HAS TO BE WARNED.
WHAT SORT OF ROOM IS THIS?
HOUSEHOLD TEMPLE.
IT'S WHERE YOU KEEP REPRESENTATIONS OF THOSE YOU CHERISH MOST.
I SPENT A LOT OF TIME IN A PLACE LIKE THIS. I'D BEEN POSSESSED...
...BY LOGAN'S OLD TEACHER, OGUN. HE TRIED TO MAKE ME A MASTER ASSASSIN.
LOGAN HELPED ME FIND MY WAY BACK TO MYSELF.
AND NOW HE'S AS MUCH A PART OF MY SOUL AS OGUN. I'LL LIKELY NEVER BE FREE OF EITHER OF THEM.
QUESTION IS, WHO'S THE DOMINANT GHOST IN THERE?

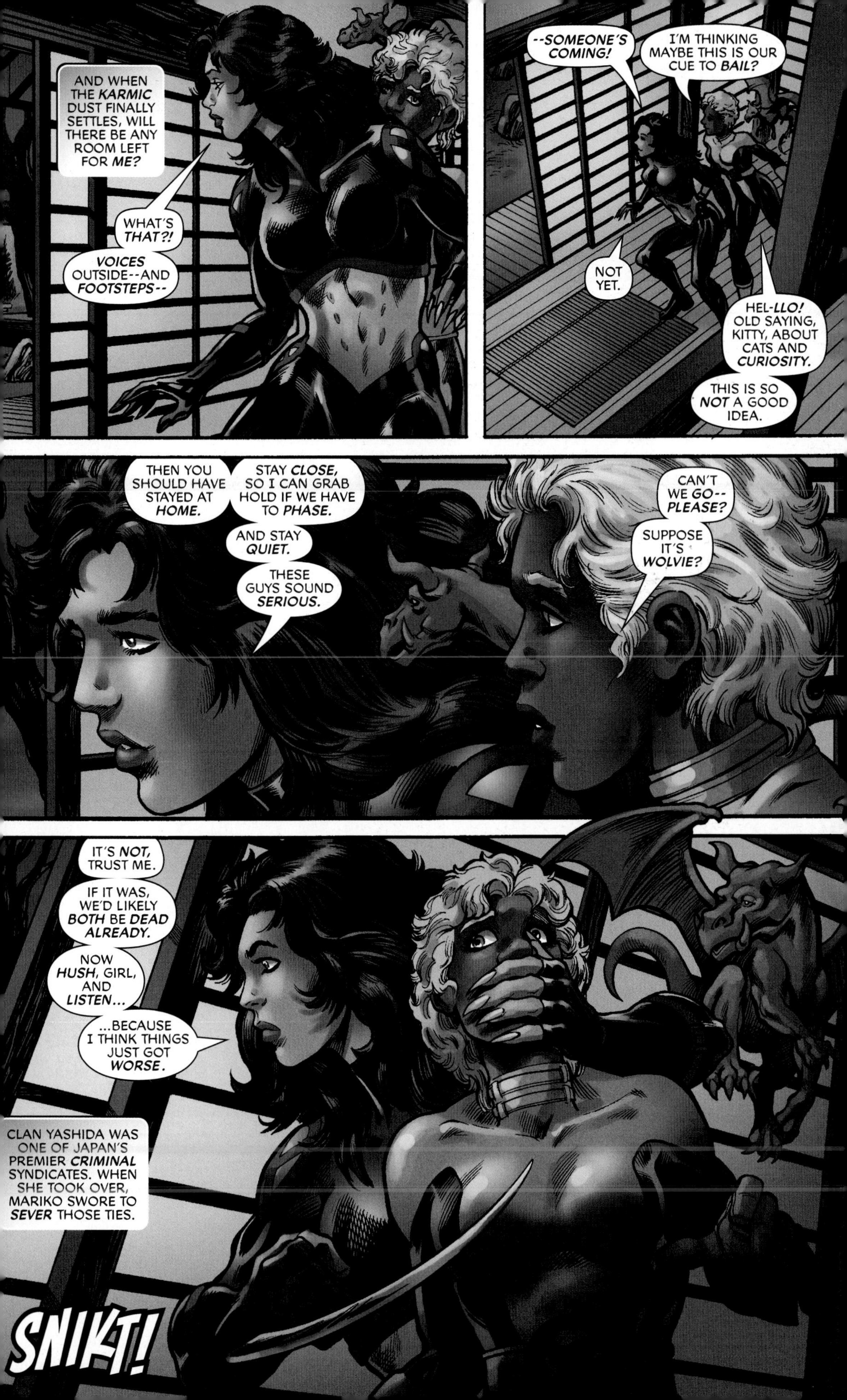
AND WHEN THE KARMIC DUST FINALLY SETTLES, WILL THERE BE ANY ROOM LEFT FOR ME?
WHAT'S THAT?!
VOICES OUTSIDE--AND FOOTSTEPS--
--SOMEONE'S COMING!
I'M THINKING MAYBE THIS IS OUR CUE TO BAIL?
NOT YET.
HEL-LLO! OLD SAYING, KITTY, ABOUT CATS AND CURIOSITY.
THIS IS SO NOT A GOOD IDEA.
THEN YOU SHOULD HAVE STAYED AT HOME.
STAY CLOSE, SO I CAN GRAB HOLD IF WE HAVE TO PHASE.
AND STAY QUIET.
THESE GUYS SOUND SERIOUS.
CAN'T WE GO--PLEASE?
SUPPOSE IT'S WOLVIE?
IT'S NOT, TRUST ME.
IF IT WAS, WE'D LIKELY BOTH BE DEAD ALREADY.
NOW HUSH, GIRL, AND LISTEN...
...BECAUSE I THINK THINGS JUST GOT WORSE.
CLAN YASHIDA WAS ONE OF JAPAN'S PREMIER CRIMINAL SYNDICATES. WHEN SHE TOOK OVER, MARIKO SWORE TO SEVER THOSE TIES.
SNIKT!

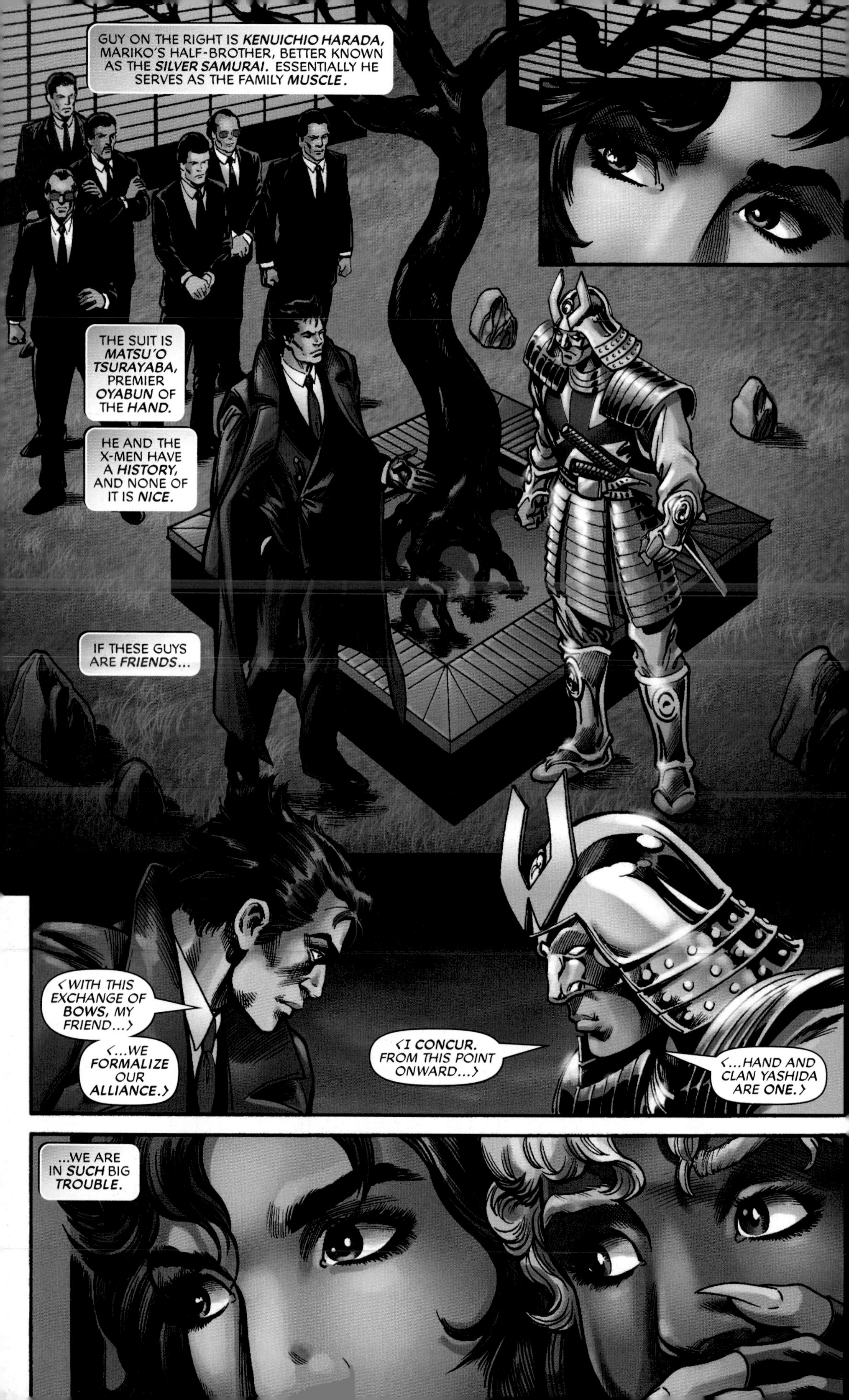
GUY ON THE RIGHT IS *KENUICHIO HARADA,* MARIKO'S HALF-BROTHER, BETTER KNOWN AS THE *SILVER SAMURAI.* ESSENTIALLY HE SERVES AS THE FAMILY *MUSCLE.*
THE SUIT IS *MATSU'O TSURAYABA,* PREMIER *OYABUN* OF THE *HAND.*
HE AND THE X-MEN HAVE A *HISTORY,* AND NONE OF IT IS *NICE.*
IF THESE GUYS ARE *FRIENDS...*
‹WITH THIS EXCHANGE OF *BOWS,* MY FRIEND...›
‹...WE *FORMALIZE* OUR *ALLIANCE.*›
‹I CONCUR. FROM THIS POINT ONWARD...›
‹...HAND AND CLAN YASHIDA ARE ONE.›
...WE ARE IN *SUCH* BIG *TROUBLE.*

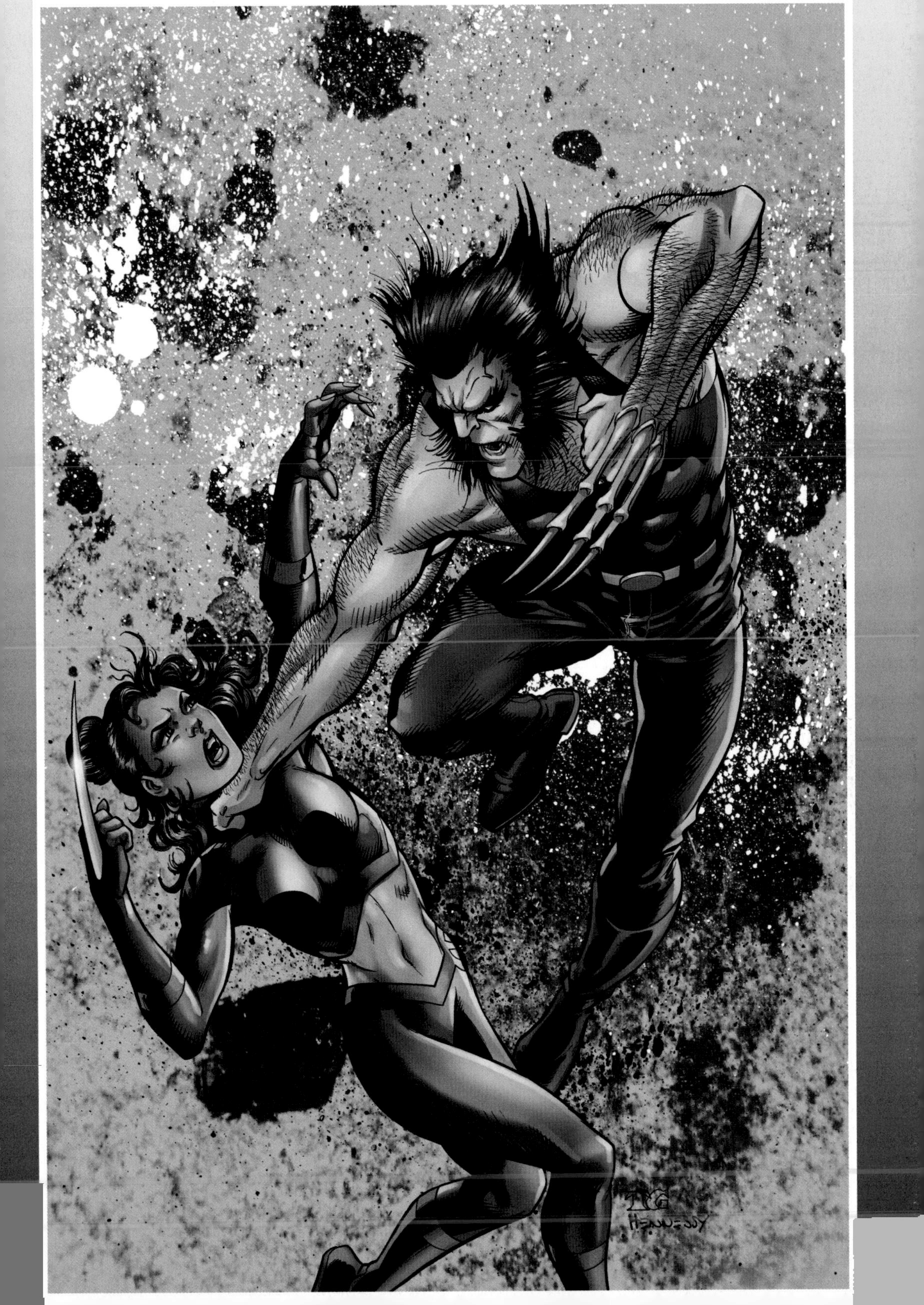

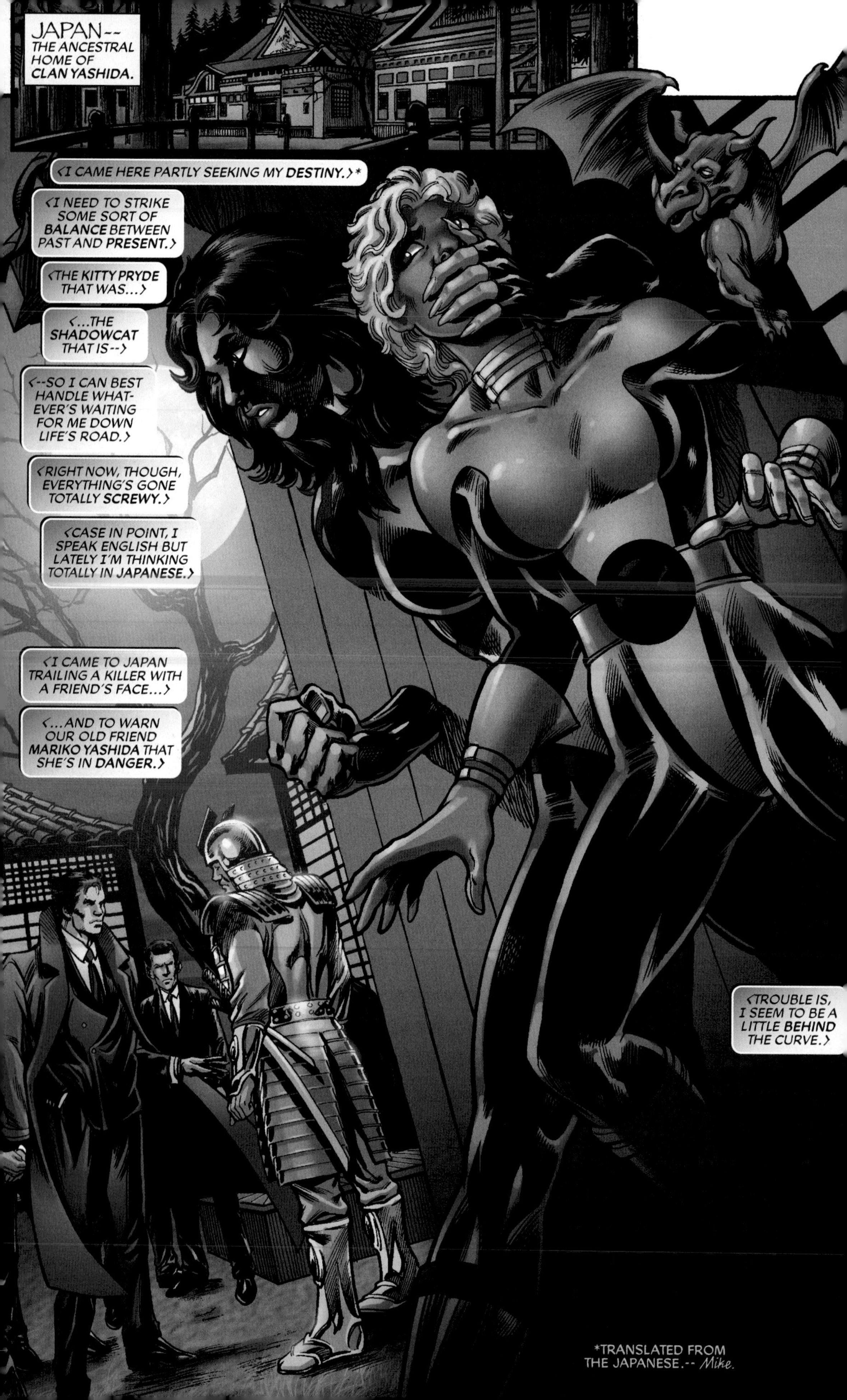
JAPAN-- THE ANCESTRAL HOME OF CLAN YASHIDA.
<I CAME HERE PARTLY SEEKING MY DESTINY.>*
<I NEED TO STRIKE SOME SORT OF BALANCE BETWEEN PAST AND PRESENT.>
<THE KITTY PRYDE THAT WAS...>
<...THE SHADOWCAT THAT IS-->
<--SO I CAN BEST HANDLE WHAT-EVER'S WAITING FOR ME DOWN LIFE'S ROAD.>
<RIGHT NOW, THOUGH, EVERYTHING'S GONE TOTALLY SCREWY.>
<CASE IN POINT, I SPEAK ENGLISH BUT LATELY I'M THINKING TOTALLY IN JAPANESE.>
<I CAME TO JAPAN TRAILING A KILLER WITH A FRIEND'S FACE...>
<...AND TO WARN OUR OLD FRIEND MARIKO YASHIDA THAT SHE'S IN DANGER.>
<TROUBLE IS, I SEEM TO BE A LITTLE BEHIND THE CURVE.>
*TRANSLATED FROM THE JAPANESE.-- Mike.

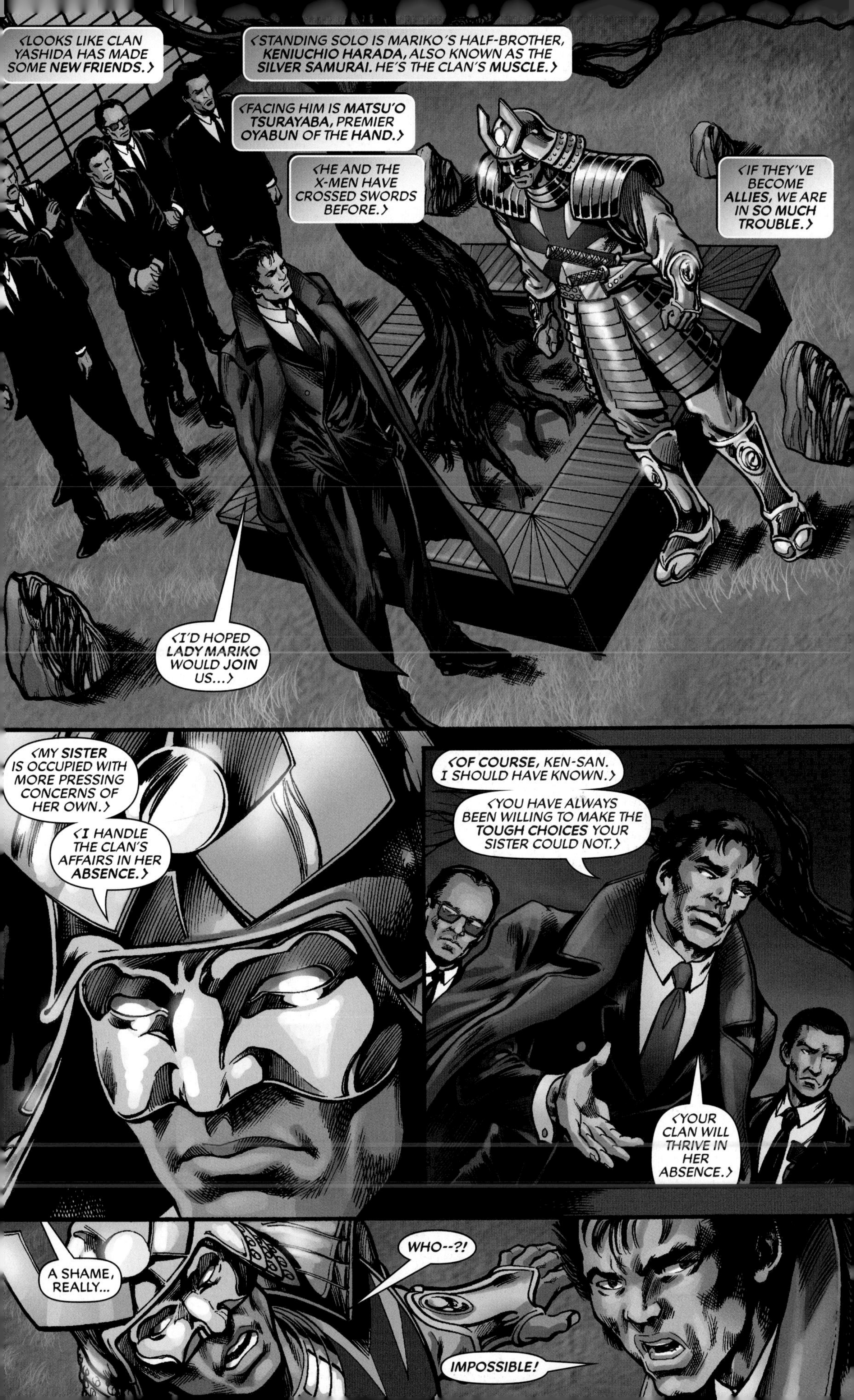

‹LOOKS LIKE CLAN YASHIDA HAS MADE SOME NEW FRIENDS.›
‹STANDING SOLO IS MARIKO'S HALF-BROTHER, KENIUCHIO HARADA, ALSO KNOWN AS THE SILVER SAMURAI. HE'S THE CLAN'S MUSCLE.›
‹FACING HIM IS MATSU'O TSURAYABA, PREMIER OYABUN OF THE HAND.›
‹HE AND THE X-MEN HAVE CROSSED SWORDS BEFORE.›
‹IF THEY'VE BECOME ALLIES, WE ARE IN SO MUCH TROUBLE.›
‹I'D HOPED LADY MARIKO WOULD JOIN US...›
‹MY SISTER IS OCCUPIED WITH MORE PRESSING CONCERNS OF HER OWN.›
‹I HANDLE THE CLAN'S AFFAIRS IN HER ABSENCE.›
‹OF COURSE, KEN-SAN. I SHOULD HAVE KNOWN.›
‹YOU HAVE ALWAYS BEEN WILLING TO MAKE THE TOUGH CHOICES YOUR SISTER COULD NOT.›
‹YOUR CLAN WILL THRIVE IN HER ABSENCE.›
A SHAME, REALLY...
WHO--?!
IMPOSSIBLE!

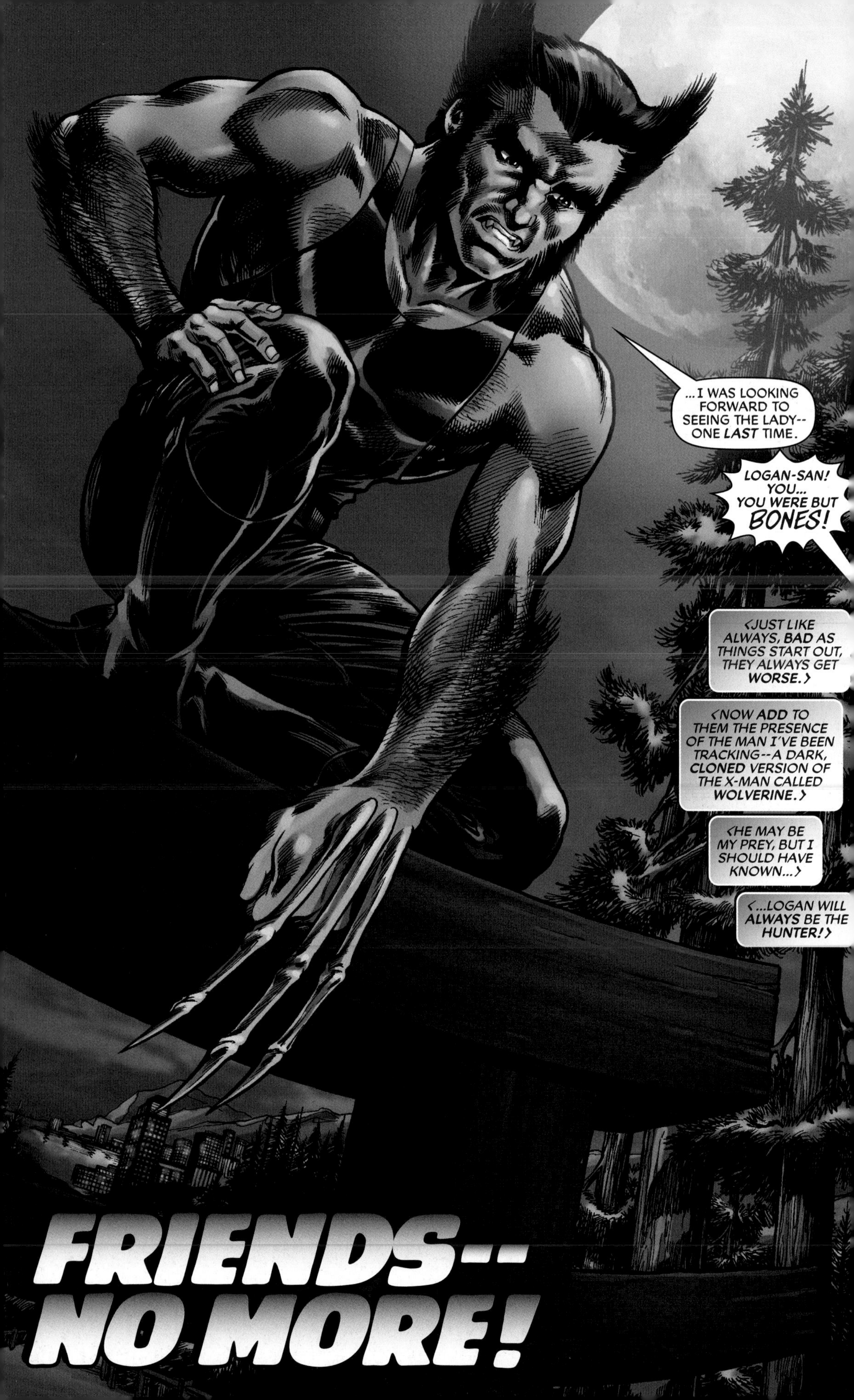
...I WAS LOOKING FORWARD TO SEEING THE LADY-- ONE LAST TIME.
LOGAN-SAN! YOU... YOU WERE BUT BONES!
<JUST LIKE ALWAYS, BAD AS THINGS START OUT, THEY ALWAYS GET WORSE.>
<NOW ADD TO THEM THE PRESENCE OF THE MAN I'VE BEEN TRACKING--A DARK, CLONED VERSION OF THE X-MAN CALLED WOLVERINE.>
<HE MAY BE MY PREY, BUT I SHOULD HAVE KNOWN...>
<...LOGAN WILL ALWAYS BE THE HUNTER!>
FRIENDS-- NO MORE!

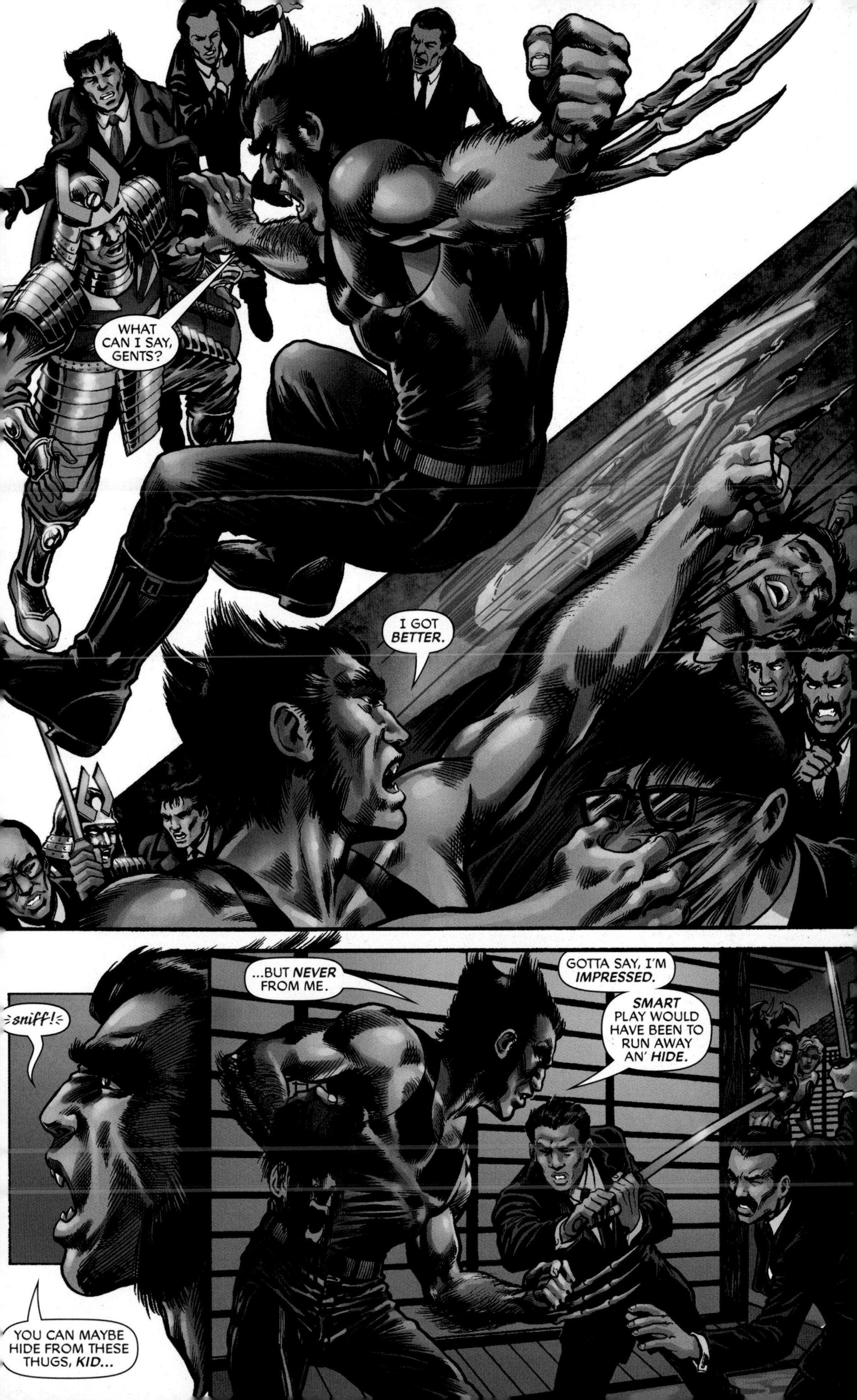
WHAT CAN I SAY, GENTS?
I GOT *BETTER.*
sniff!
YOU CAN MAYBE HIDE FROM THESE THUGS, *KID...*
...BUT *NEVER* FROM ME.
GOTTA SAY, I'M *IMPRESSED.*
SMART PLAY WOULD HAVE BEEN TO RUN AWAY AN' *HIDE.*

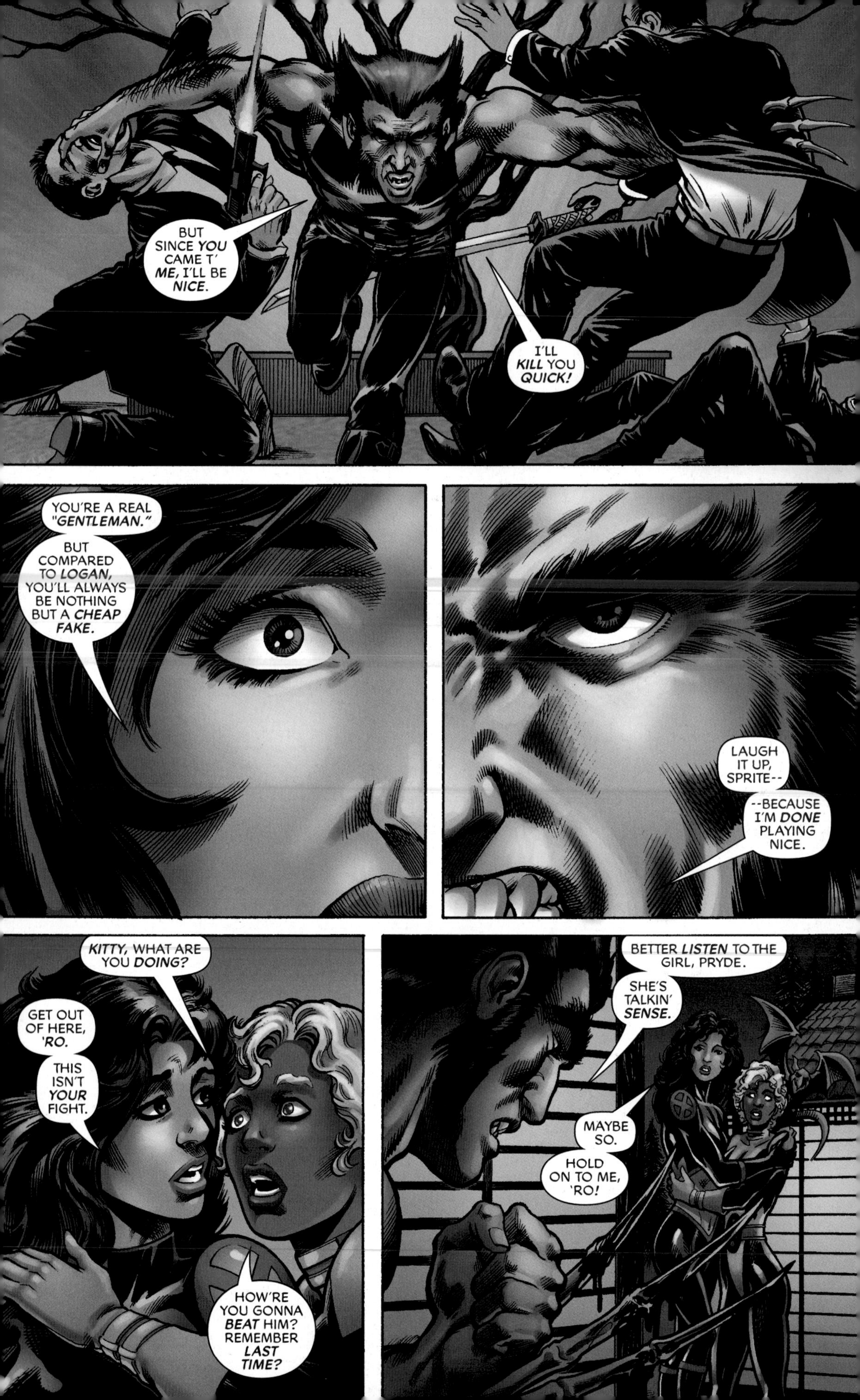
BUT SINCE *YOU* CAME T' *ME,* I'LL BE *NICE*.
I'LL *KILL* YOU *QUICK!*
YOU'RE A REAL *"GENTLEMAN."*
BUT COMPARED TO *LOGAN,* YOU'LL ALWAYS BE NOTHING BUT A *CHEAP FAKE.*
LAUGH IT UP, SPRITE--
--BECAUSE I'M *DONE* PLAYING NICE.
KITTY, WHAT ARE YOU *DOING?*
GET OUT OF HERE, *'RO.*
THIS ISN'T *YOUR* FIGHT.
HOW'RE YOU GONNA *BEAT* HIM? REMEMBER *LAST TIME?*
BETTER *LISTEN* TO THE GIRL, PRYDE.
SHE'S TALKIN' *SENSE.*
MAYBE SO.
HOLD ON TO ME, 'RO*!*

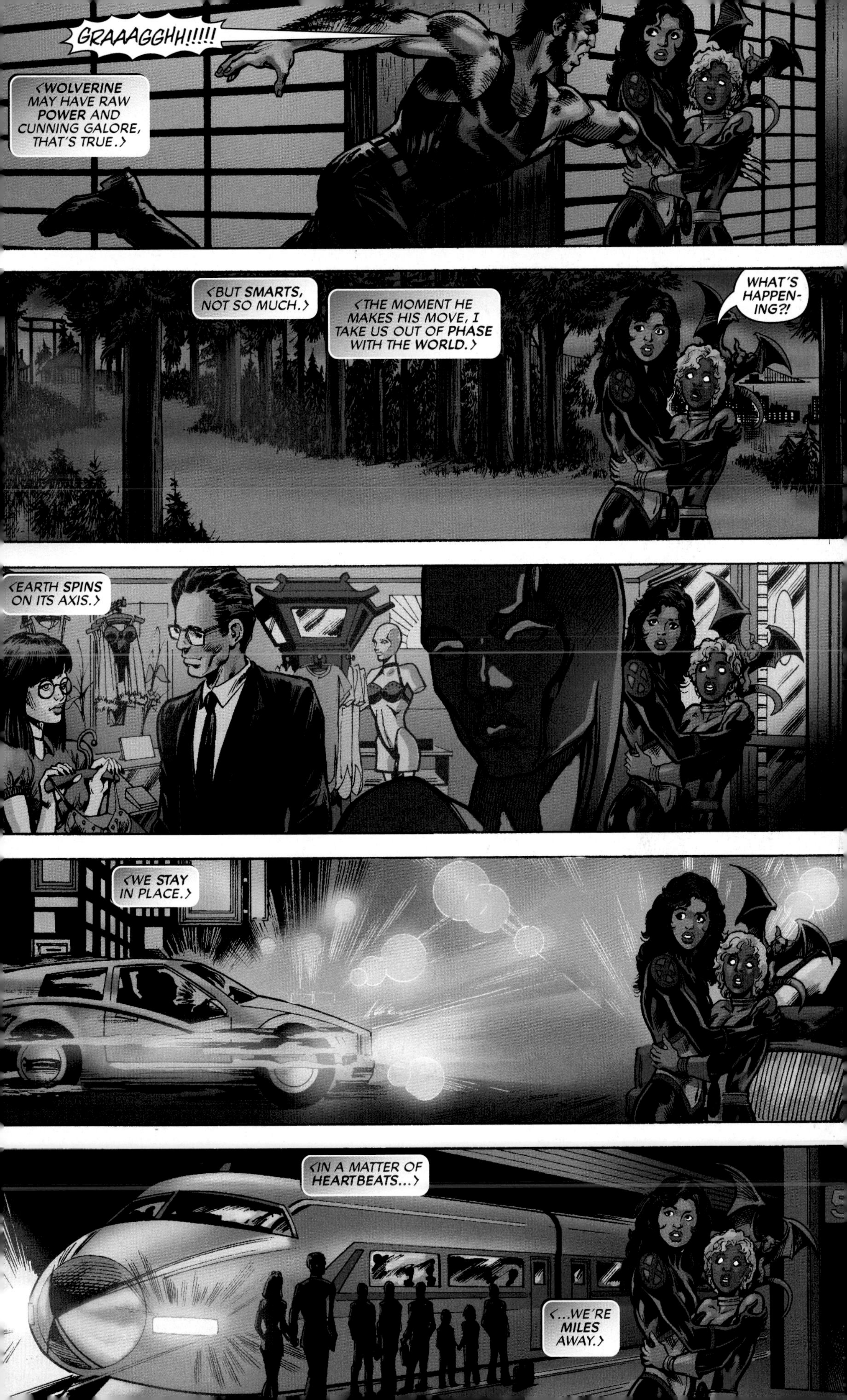
GRAAAGGHH!!!!!
<WOLVERINE MAY HAVE RAW POWER AND CUNNING GALORE, THAT'S TRUE.>
<BUT SMARTS, NOT SO MUCH.>
<THE MOMENT HE MAKES HIS MOVE, I TAKE US OUT OF PHASE WITH THE WORLD.>
WHAT'S HAPPEN-ING?!
<EARTH SPINS ON ITS AXIS.>
<WE STAY IN PLACE.>
<IN A MATTER OF HEARTBEATS...>
<...WE'RE MILES AWAY.>

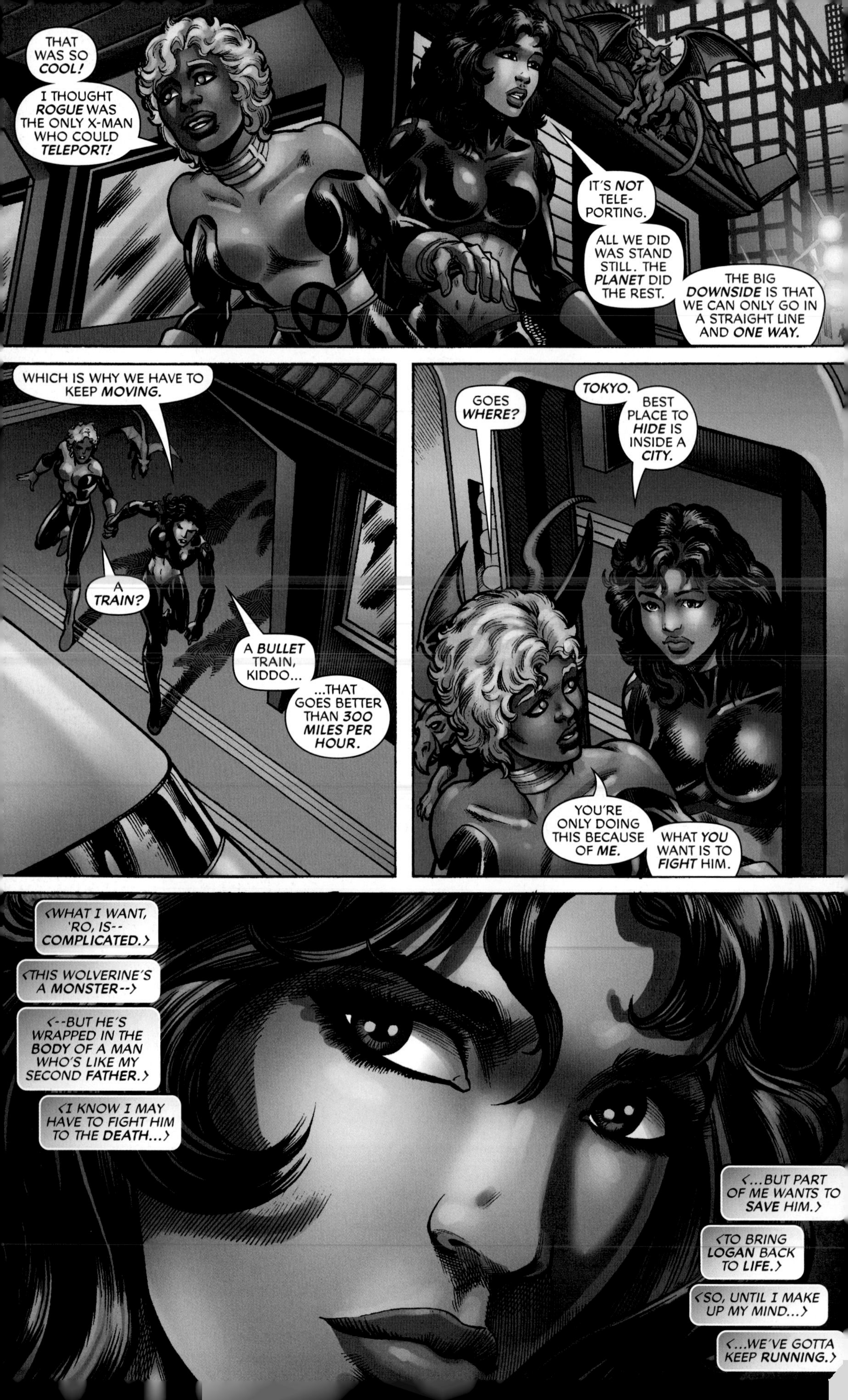
THAT WAS SO COOL!
I THOUGHT ROGUE WAS THE ONLY X-MAN WHO COULD TELEPORT!
IT'S NOT TELE-PORTING.
ALL WE DID WAS STAND STILL. THE PLANET DID THE REST.
THE BIG DOWNSIDE IS THAT WE CAN ONLY GO IN A STRAIGHT LINE AND ONE WAY.
WHICH IS WHY WE HAVE TO KEEP MOVING.
A TRAIN?
A BULLET TRAIN, KIDDO...
...THAT GOES BETTER THAN 300 MILES PER HOUR.
GOES WHERE?
TOKYO.
BEST PLACE TO HIDE IS INSIDE A CITY.
YOU'RE ONLY DOING THIS BECAUSE OF ME.
WHAT YOU WANT IS TO FIGHT HIM.
‹WHAT I WANT, 'RO, IS-- COMPLICATED.›
‹THIS WOLVERINE'S A MONSTER--›
‹--BUT HE'S WRAPPED IN THE BODY OF A MAN WHO'S LIKE MY SECOND FATHER.›
‹I KNOW I MAY HAVE TO FIGHT HIM TO THE DEATH...›
‹...BUT PART OF ME WANTS TO SAVE HIM.›
‹TO BRING LOGAN BACK TO LIFE.›
‹SO, UNTIL I MAKE UP MY MIND...›
‹...WE'VE GOTTA KEEP RUNNING.›

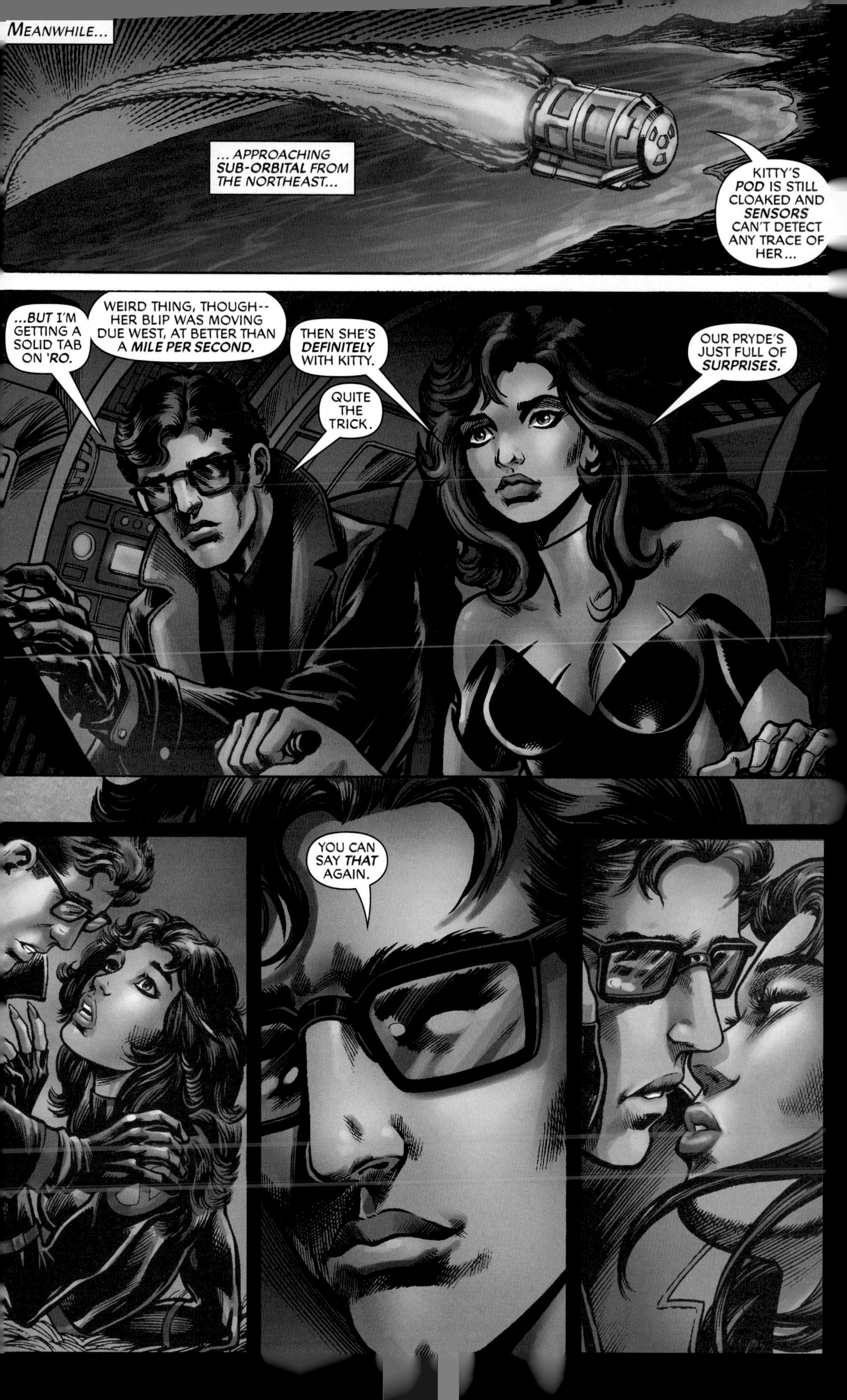
MEANWHILE...
... APPROACHING SUB-ORBITAL FROM THE NORTHEAST...
KITTY'S POD IS STILL CLOAKED AND SENSORS CAN'T DETECT ANY TRACE OF HER...
...BUT I'M GETTING A SOLID TAB ON 'RO.
WEIRD THING, THOUGH-- HER BLIP WAS MOVING DUE WEST, AT BETTER THAN A MILE PER SECOND.
THEN SHE'S DEFINITELY WITH KITTY.
QUITE THE TRICK.
OUR PRYDE'S JUST FULL OF SURPRISES.
YOU CAN SAY THAT AGAIN.

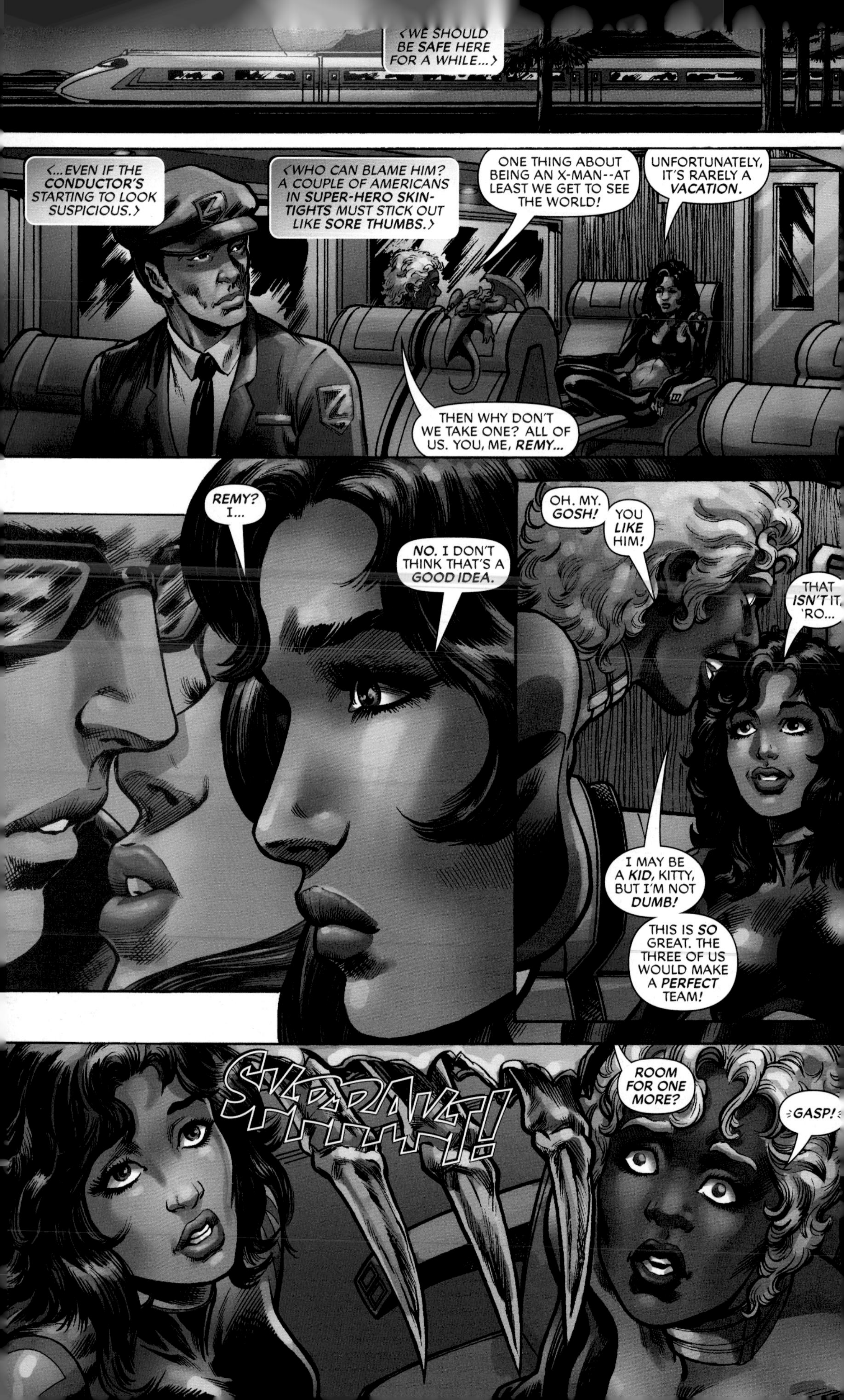

<WE SHOULD BE SAFE HERE FOR A WHILE...>
<...EVEN IF THE CONDUCTOR'S STARTING TO LOOK SUSPICIOUS.>
<WHO CAN BLAME HIM? A COUPLE OF AMERICANS IN SUPER-HERO SKIN-TIGHTS MUST STICK OUT LIKE SORE THUMBS.>
ONE THING ABOUT BEING AN X-MAN--AT LEAST WE GET TO SEE THE WORLD!
UNFORTUNATELY, IT'S RARELY A VACATION.
THEN WHY DON'T WE TAKE ONE? ALL OF US. YOU, ME, REMY...
REMY? I...
NO. I DON'T THINK THAT'S A GOOD IDEA.
OH. MY. GOSH!
YOU LIKE HIM!
THAT ISN'T IT, 'RO...
I MAY BE A KID, KITTY, BUT I'M NOT DUMB!
THIS IS SO GREAT. THE THREE OF US WOULD MAKE A PERFECT TEAM!
SKRAKT!
ROOM FOR ONE MORE?
GASP!

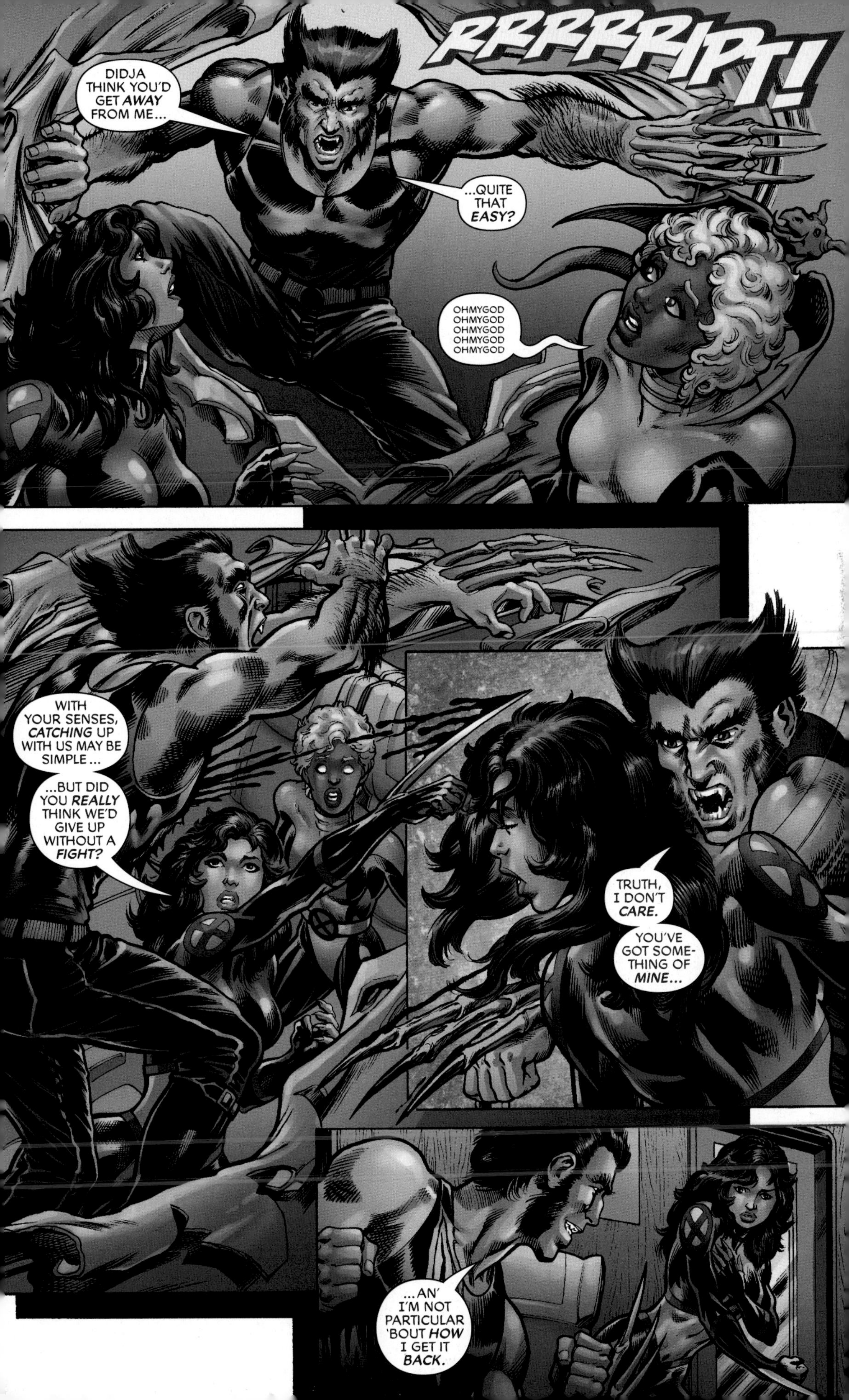
RRRRRIPT!
DIDJA THINK YOU'D GET AWAY FROM ME...
...QUITE THAT EASY?
OHMYGOD OHMYGOD OHMYGOD OHMYGOD OHMYGOD
WITH YOUR SENSES, CATCHING UP WITH US MAY BE SIMPLE...
...BUT DID YOU REALLY THINK WE'D GIVE UP WITHOUT A FIGHT?
TRUTH, I DON'T CARE.
YOU'VE GOT SOME-THING OF MINE...
...AN' I'M NOT PARTICULAR 'BOUT HOW I GET IT BACK.

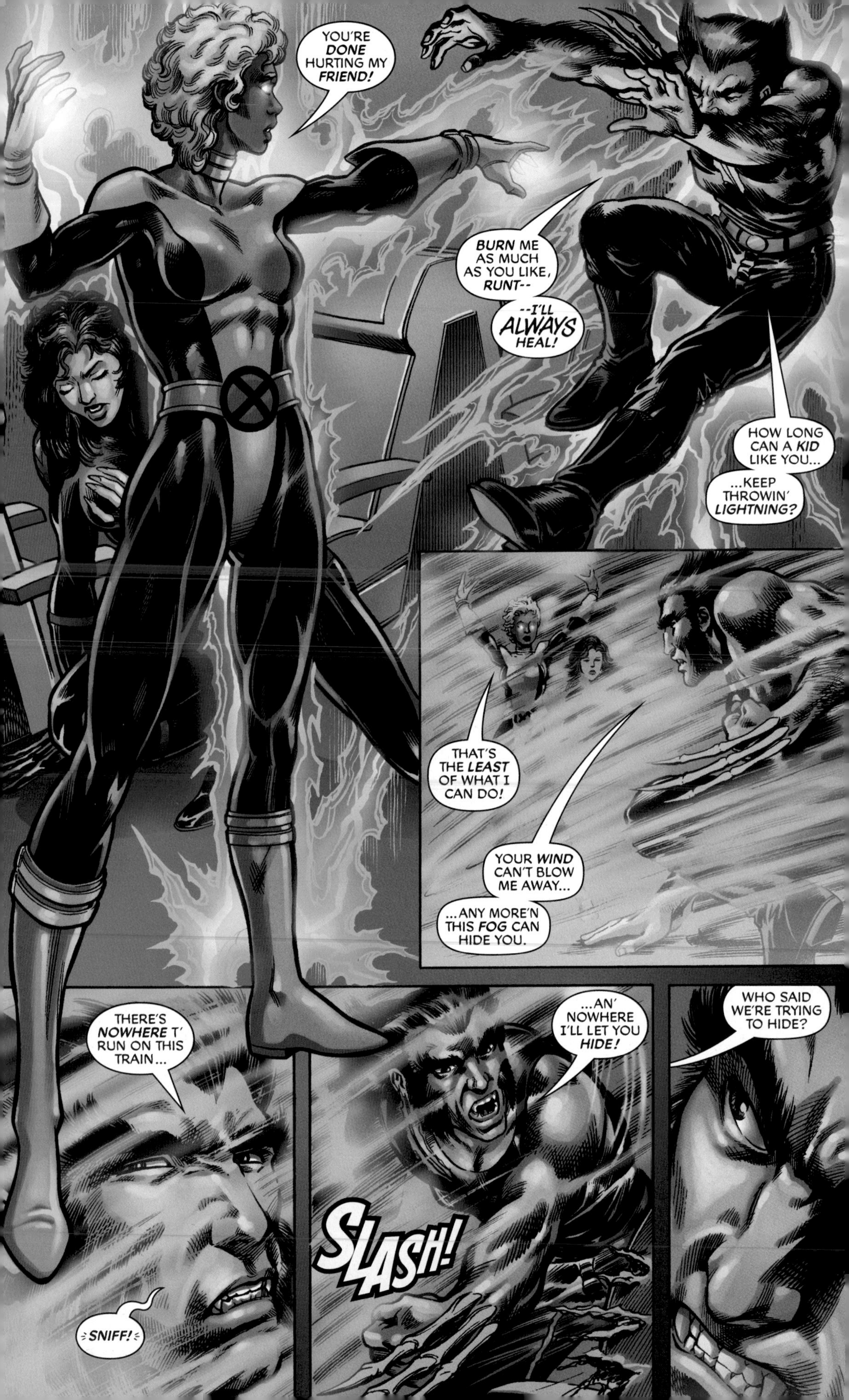

YOU'RE DONE HURTING MY FRIEND!
BURN ME AS MUCH AS YOU LIKE, RUNT--
--I'LL ALWAYS HEAL!
HOW LONG CAN A KID LIKE YOU...
...KEEP THROWIN' LIGHTNING?
THAT'S THE LEAST OF WHAT I CAN DO!
YOUR WIND CAN'T BLOW ME AWAY...
...ANY MORE'N THIS FOG CAN HIDE YOU.
THERE'S NOWHERE T' RUN ON THIS TRAIN...
SNIFF!
...AN' NOWHERE I'LL LET YOU HIDE!
SLASH!
WHO SAID WE'RE TRYING TO HIDE?

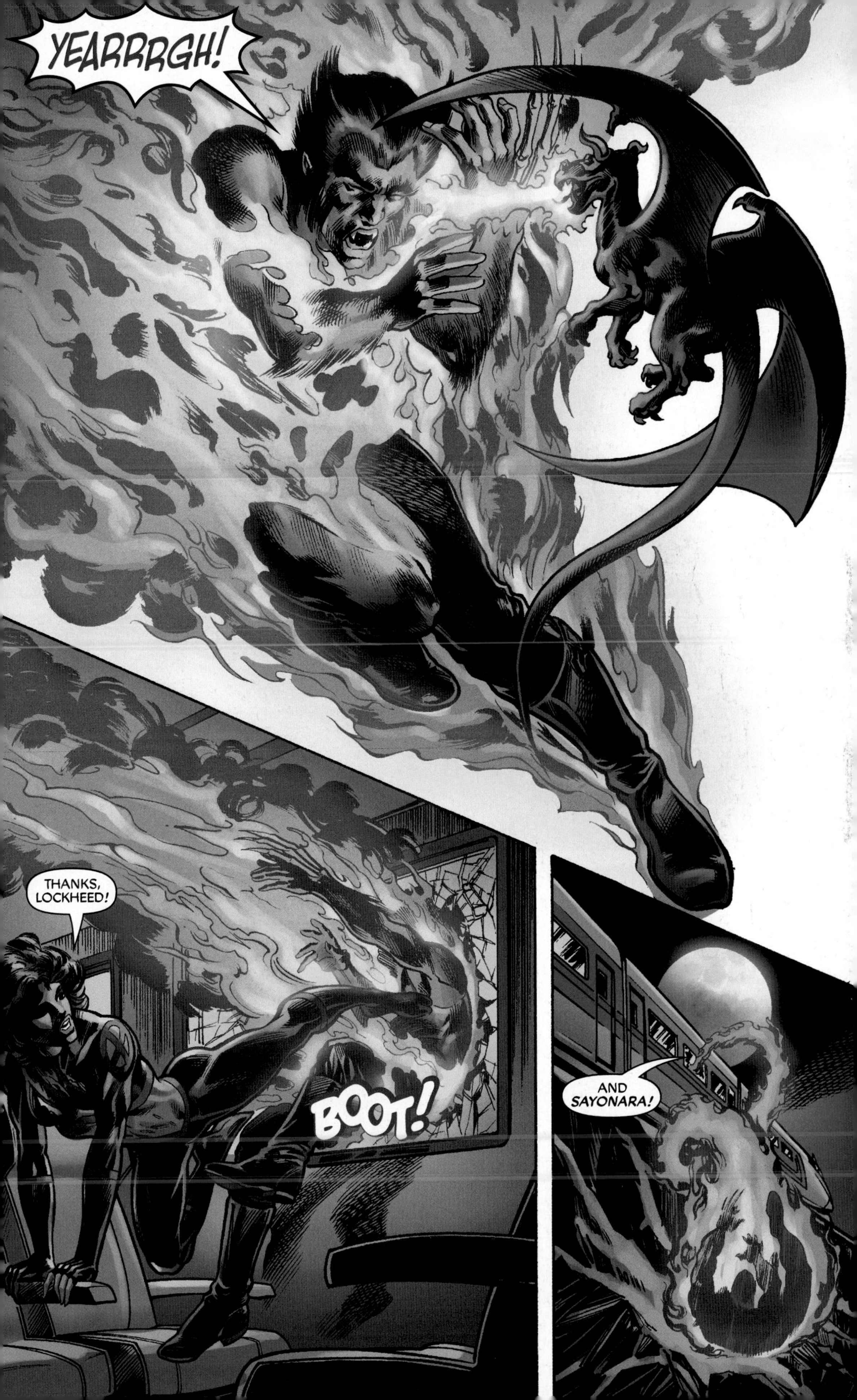
YEARRRGH!
THANKS, LOCKHEED!
BOOT!
AND SAYONARA!

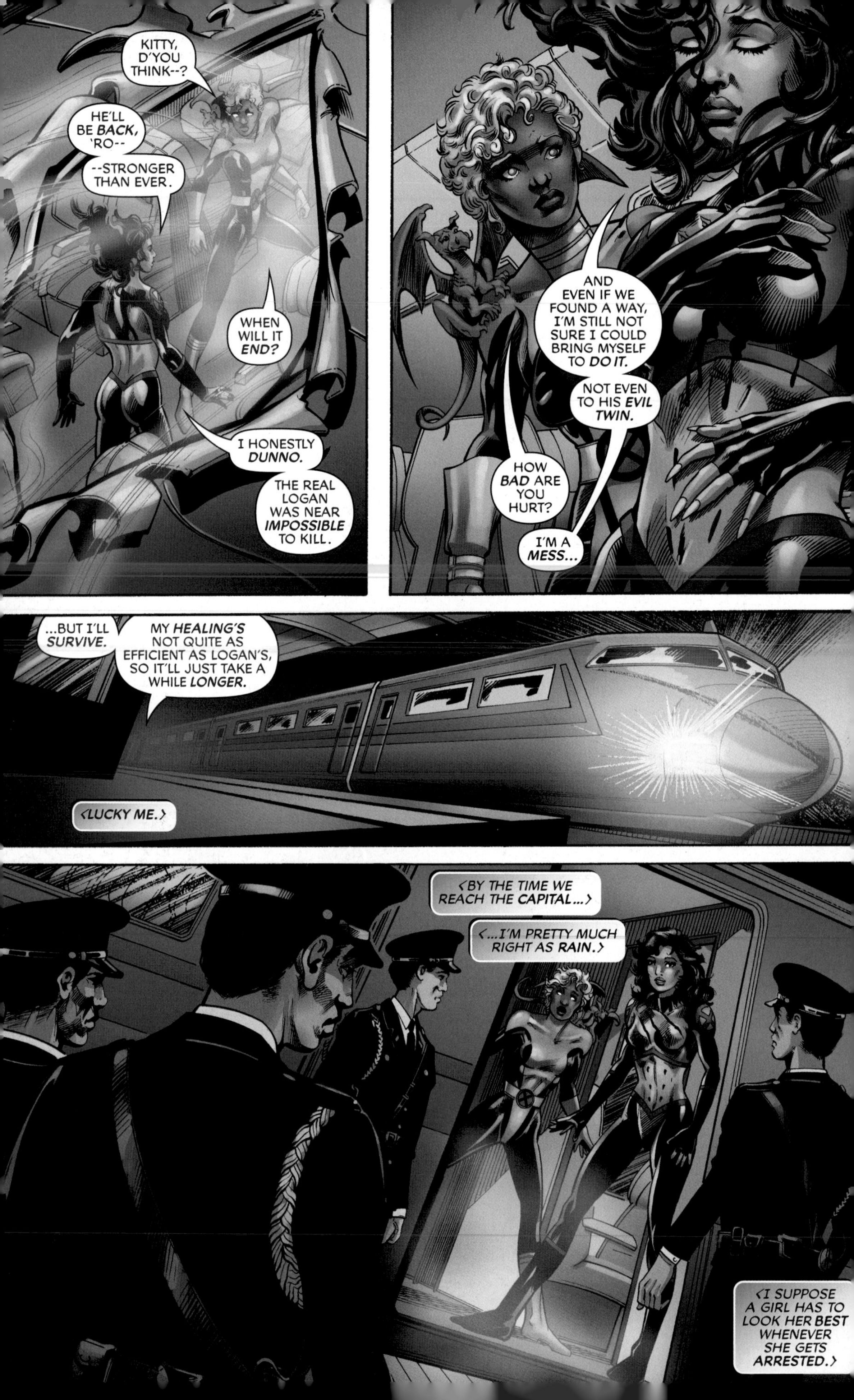
KITTY, D'YOU THINK--?
HE'LL BE BACK, 'RO--
--STRONGER THAN EVER.
WHEN WILL IT END?
I HONESTLY DUNNO.
THE REAL LOGAN WAS NEAR IMPOSSIBLE TO KILL.
AND EVEN IF WE FOUND A WAY, I'M STILL NOT SURE I COULD BRING MYSELF TO DO IT.
NOT EVEN TO HIS EVIL TWIN.
HOW BAD ARE YOU HURT?
I'M A MESS...
...BUT I'LL SURVIVE.
MY HEALING'S NOT QUITE AS EFFICIENT AS LOGAN'S, SO IT'LL JUST TAKE A WHILE LONGER.
‹LUCKY ME.›
‹BY THE TIME WE REACH THE CAPITAL...›
‹...I'M PRETTY MUCH RIGHT AS RAIN.›
‹I SUPPOSE A GIRL HAS TO LOOK HER BEST WHENEVER SHE GETS ARRESTED.›

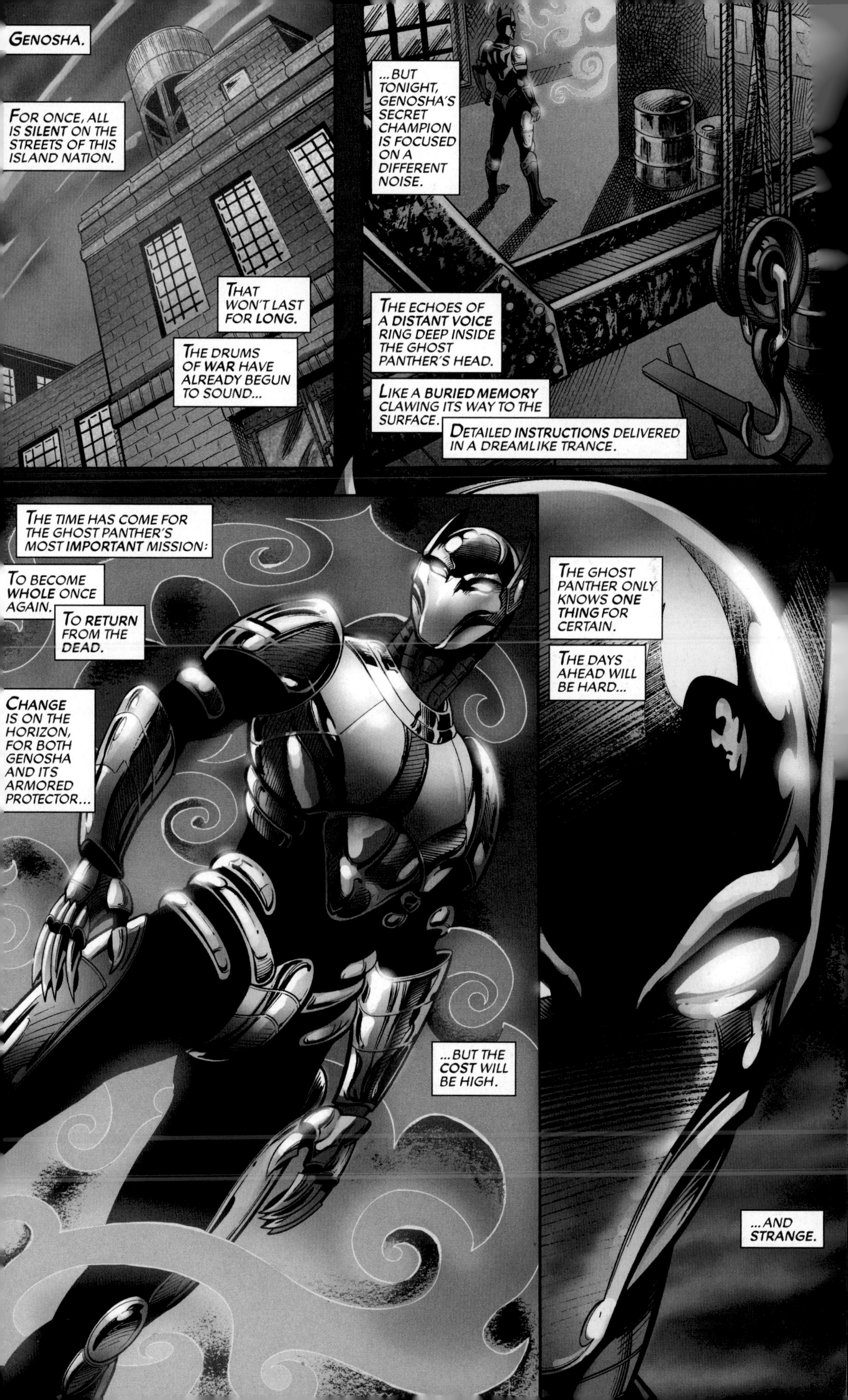
GENOSHA.
FOR ONCE, ALL IS SILENT ON THE STREETS OF THIS ISLAND NATION.
THAT WON'T LAST FOR LONG.
THE DRUMS OF WAR HAVE ALREADY BEGUN TO SOUND...
...BUT TONIGHT, GENOSHA'S SECRET CHAMPION IS FOCUSED ON A DIFFERENT NOISE.
THE ECHOES OF A DISTANT VOICE RING DEEP INSIDE THE GHOST PANTHER'S HEAD.
LIKE A BURIED MEMORY CLAWING ITS WAY TO THE SURFACE.
DETAILED INSTRUCTIONS DELIVERED IN A DREAMLIKE TRANCE.
THE TIME HAS COME FOR THE GHOST PANTHER'S MOST IMPORTANT MISSION:
TO BECOME WHOLE ONCE AGAIN.
TO RETURN FROM THE DEAD.
CHANGE IS ON THE HORIZON, FOR BOTH GENOSHA AND ITS ARMORED PROTECTOR...
...BUT THE COST WILL BE HIGH.
THE GHOST PANTHER ONLY KNOWS ONE THING FOR CERTAIN.
THE DAYS AHEAD WILL BE HARD...
...AND STRANGE.

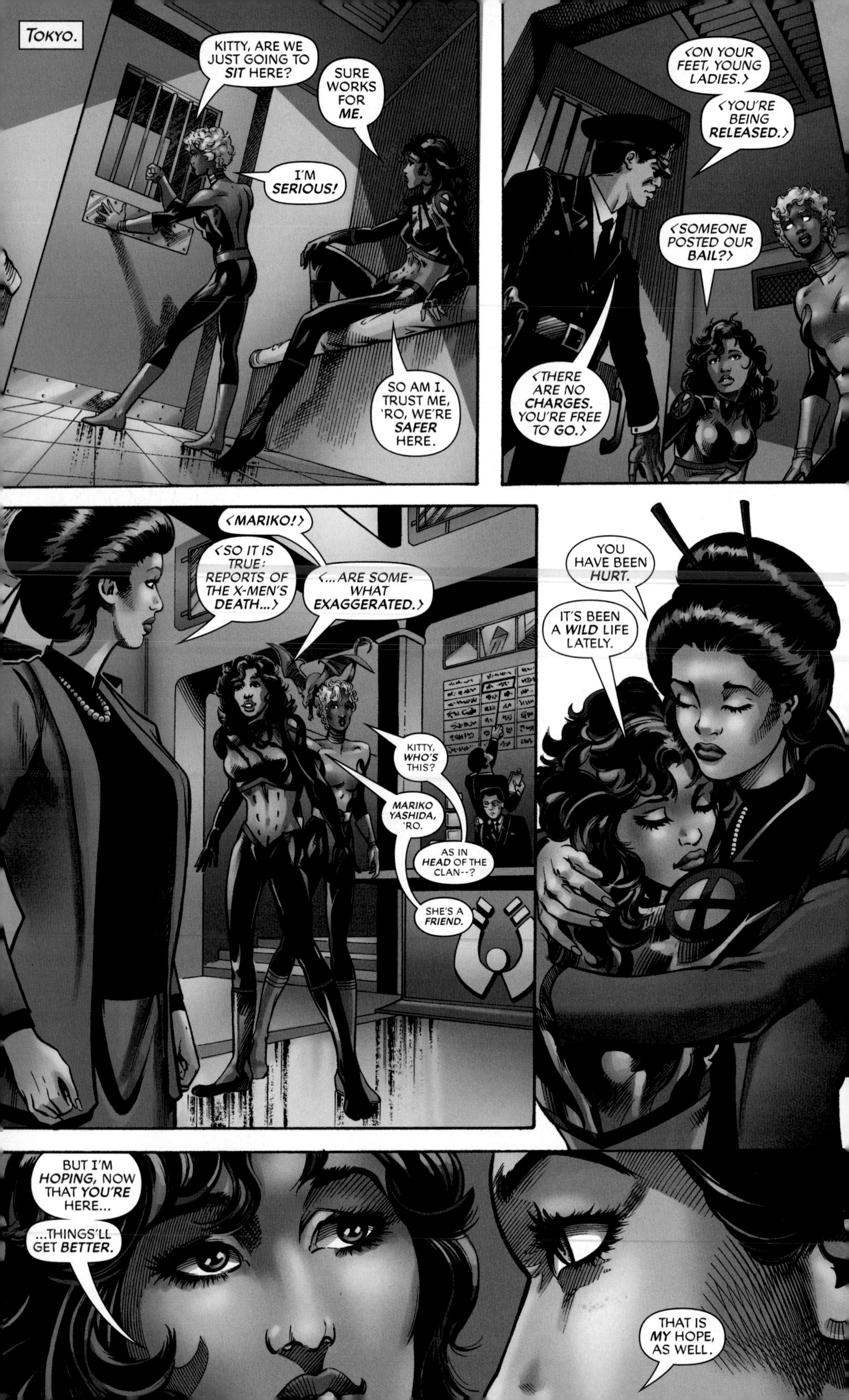
TOKYO.
KITTY, ARE WE JUST GOING TO SIT HERE?
SURE WORKS FOR ME.
I'M SERIOUS!
SO AM I. TRUST ME, 'RO, WE'RE SAFER HERE.
<ON YOUR FEET, YOUNG LADIES.>
<YOU'RE BEING RELEASED.>
<SOMEONE POSTED OUR BAIL?>
<THERE ARE NO CHARGES. YOU'RE FREE TO GO.>
<MARIKO!>
<SO IT IS TRUE: REPORTS OF THE X-MEN'S DEATH...>
<...ARE SOME-WHAT EXAGGERATED.>
KITTY, WHO'S THIS?
MARIKO YASHIDA, 'RO.
AS IN HEAD OF THE CLAN--?
SHE'S A FRIEND.
YOU HAVE BEEN HURT.
IT'S BEEN A WILD LIFE LATELY.
BUT I'M HOPING, NOW THAT YOU'RE HERE...
...THINGS'LL GET BETTER.
THAT IS MY HOPE, AS WELL.

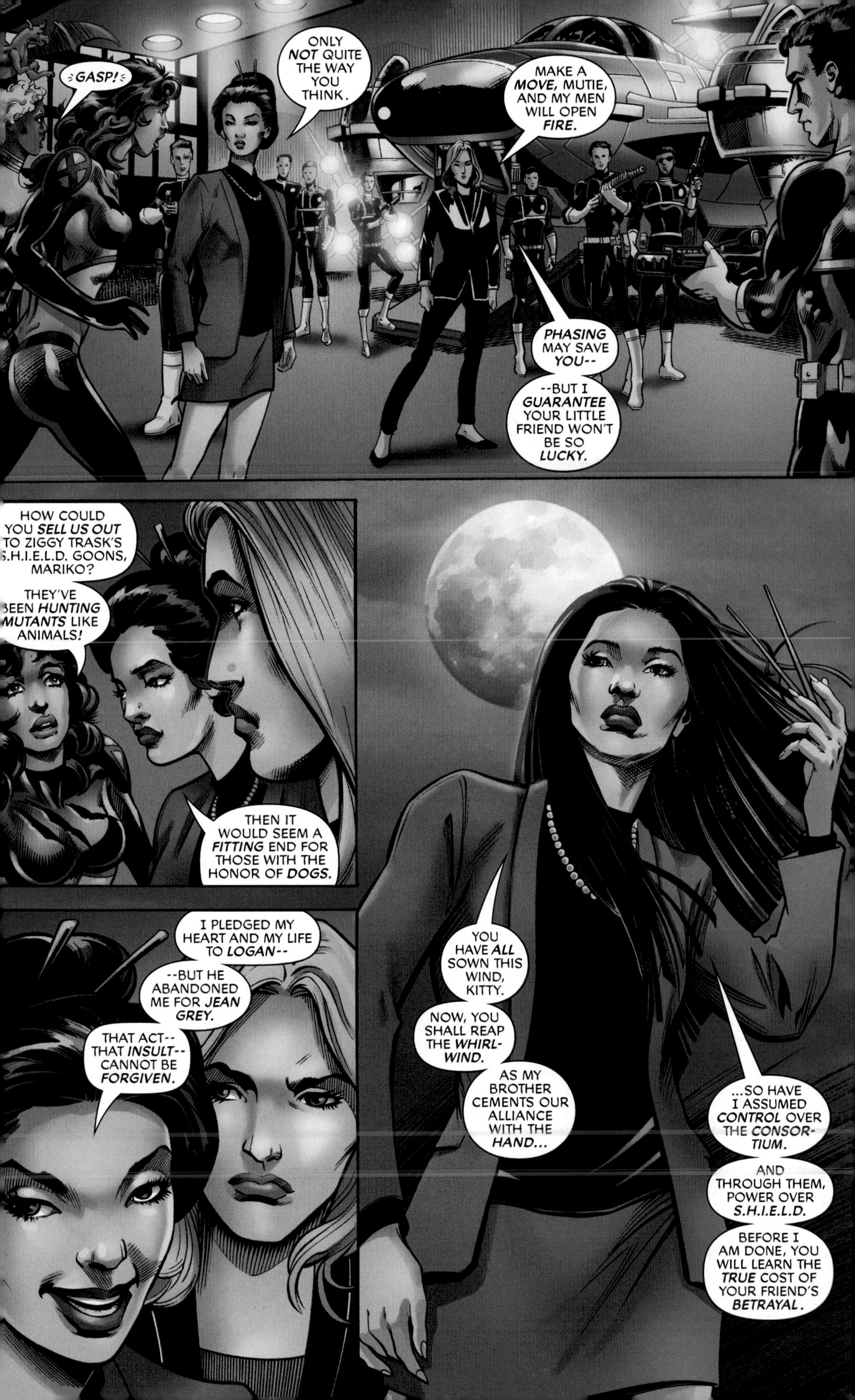
GASP!
ONLY NOT QUITE THE WAY YOU THINK.
MAKE A MOVE, MUTIE, AND MY MEN WILL OPEN FIRE.
PHASING MAY SAVE YOU--
--BUT I GUARANTEE YOUR LITTLE FRIEND WON'T BE SO LUCKY.
HOW COULD YOU SELL US OUT TO ZIGGY TRASK'S S.H.I.E.L.D. GOONS, MARIKO?
THEY'VE BEEN HUNTING MUTANTS LIKE ANIMALS!
THEN IT WOULD SEEM A FITTING END FOR THOSE WITH THE HONOR OF DOGS.
I PLEDGED MY HEART AND MY LIFE TO LOGAN--
--BUT HE ABANDONED ME FOR JEAN GREY.
THAT ACT--THAT INSULT--CANNOT BE FORGIVEN.
YOU HAVE ALL SOWN THIS WIND, KITTY.
NOW, YOU SHALL REAP THE WHIRLWIND.
AS MY BROTHER CEMENTS OUR ALLIANCE WITH THE HAND...
...SO HAVE I ASSUMED CONTROL OVER THE CONSORTIUM.
AND THROUGH THEM, POWER OVER S.H.I.E.L.D.
BEFORE I AM DONE, YOU WILL LEARN THE TRUE COST OF YOUR FRIEND'S BETRAYAL.

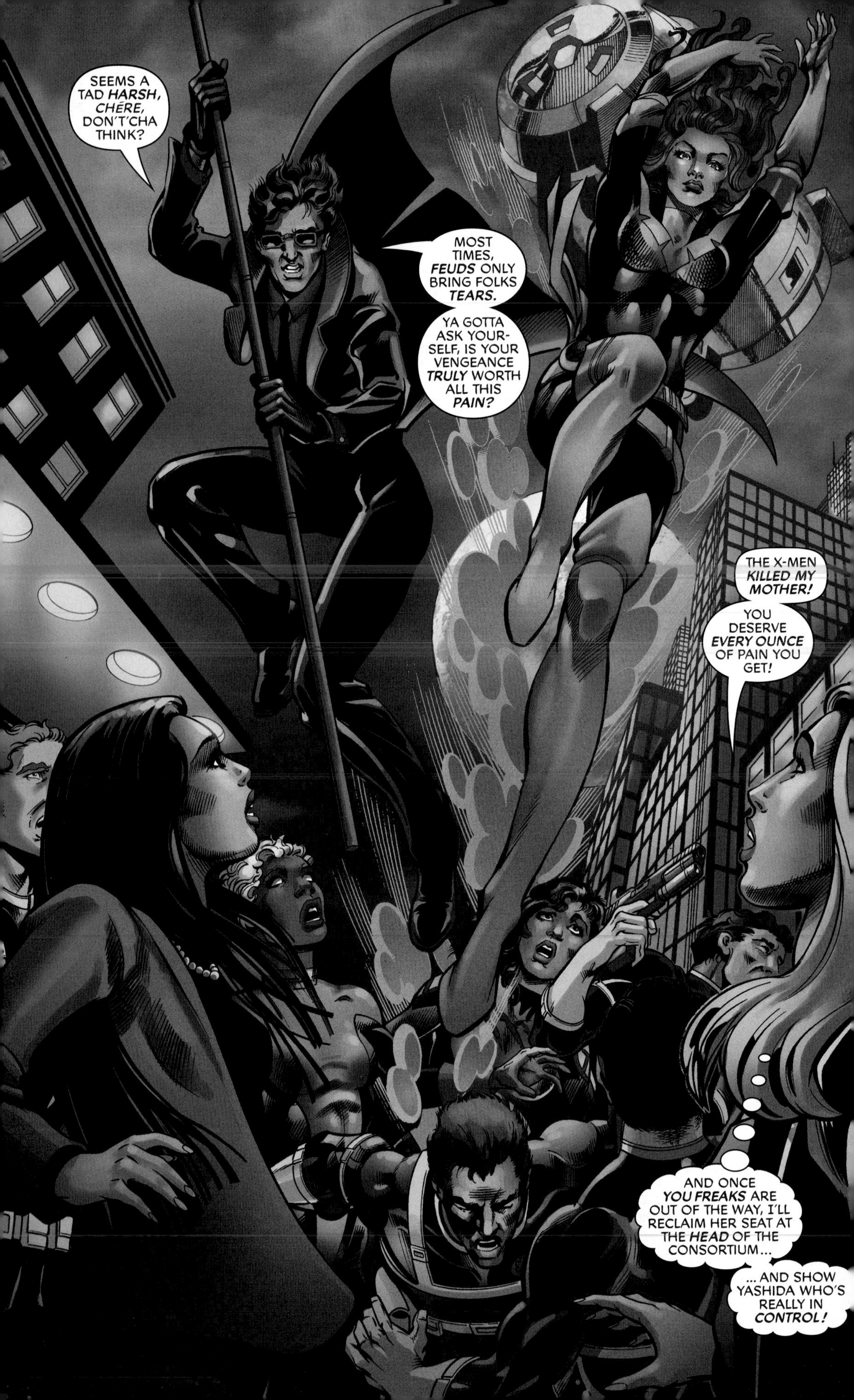
SEEMS A TAD HARSH, CHÈRE, DON'T'CHA THINK?
MOST TIMES, FEUDS ONLY BRING FOLKS TEARS.
YA GOTTA ASK YOURSELF, IS YOUR VENGEANCE TRULY WORTH ALL THIS PAIN?
THE X-MEN KILLED MY MOTHER!
YOU DESERVE EVERY OUNCE OF PAIN YOU GET!
AND ONCE YOU FREAKS ARE OUT OF THE WAY, I'LL RECLAIM HER SEAT AT THE HEAD OF THE CONSORTIUM...
...AND SHOW YASHIDA WHO'S REALLY IN CONTROL!

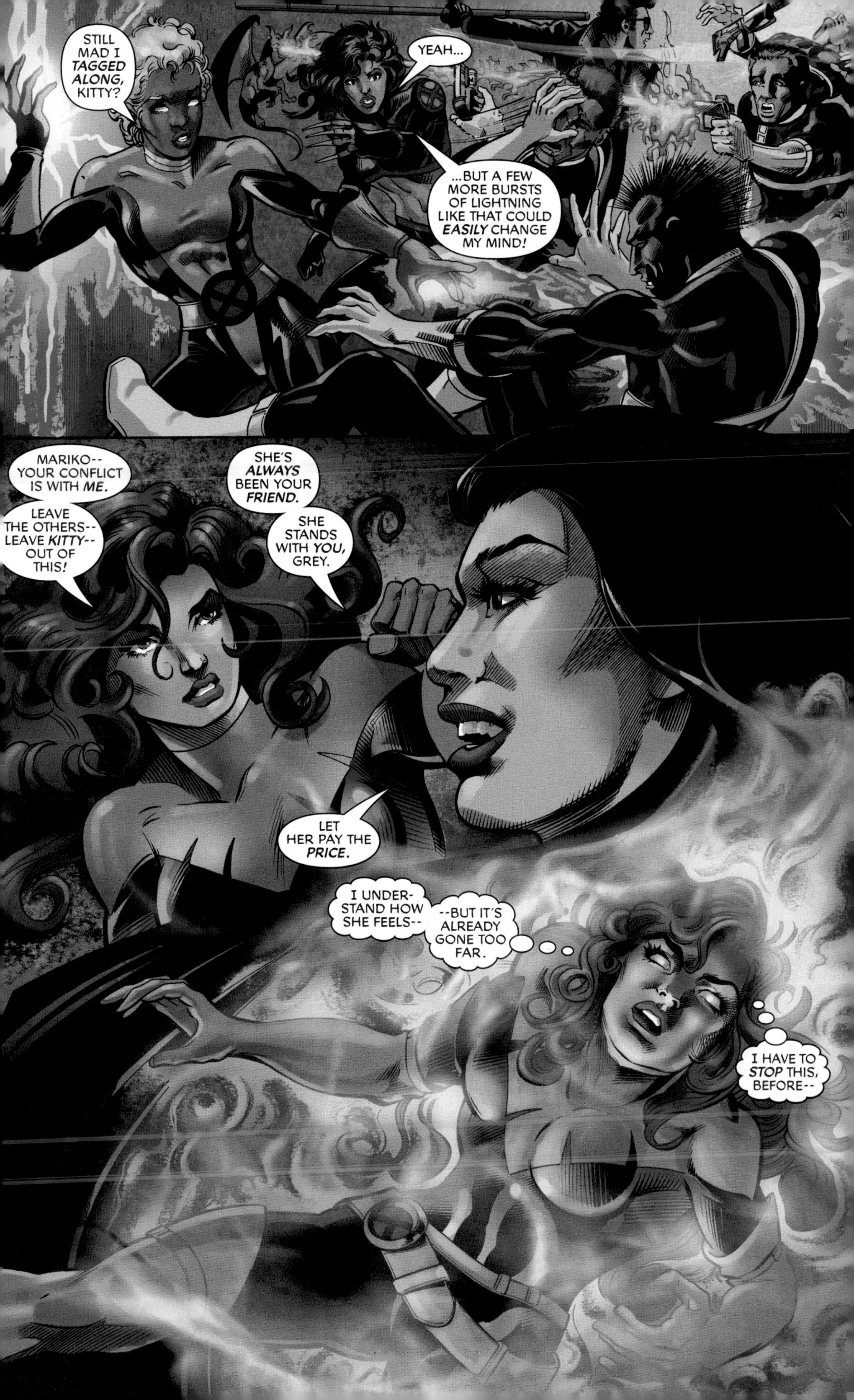
STILL MAD I *TAGGED ALONG,* KITTY?
YEAH...
...BUT A FEW MORE BURSTS OF LIGHTNING LIKE THAT COULD *EASILY* CHANGE MY MIND!
MARIKO-- YOUR CONFLICT IS WITH *ME.*
LEAVE THE OTHERS-- LEAVE *KITTY*-- OUT OF THIS!
SHE'S *ALWAYS* BEEN YOUR *FRIEND.*
SHE STANDS WITH *YOU,* GREY.
LET HER PAY THE *PRICE.*
I UNDER-STAND HOW SHE FEELS--
--BUT IT'S ALREADY GONE TOO FAR.
I HAVE TO *STOP* THIS, BEFORE--

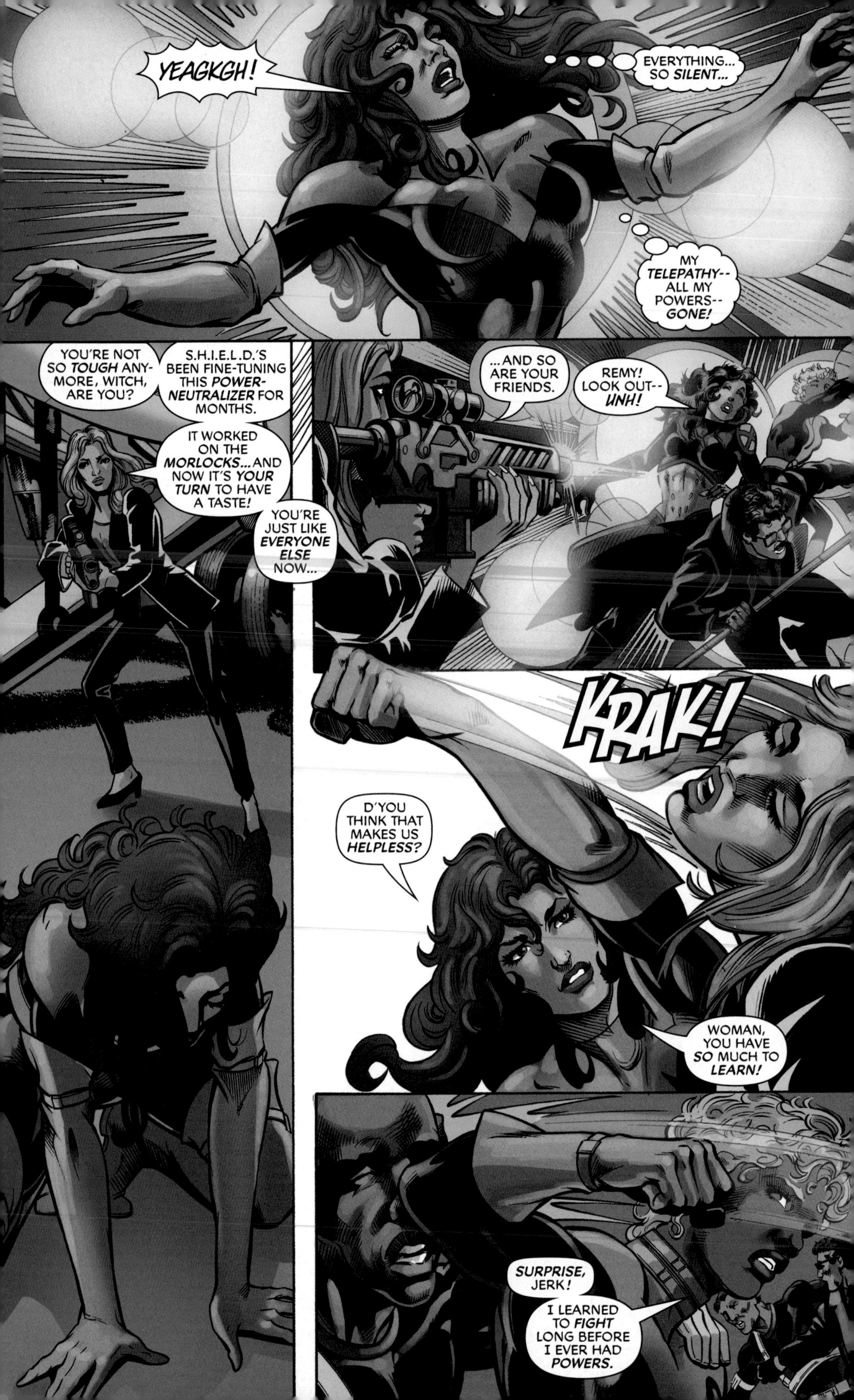
YEAGKGH!
EVERYTHING... SO SILENT...
MY TELEPATHY-- ALL MY POWERS-- GONE!
YOU'RE NOT SO TOUGH ANY-MORE, WITCH, ARE YOU?
S.H.I.E.L.D.'S BEEN FINE-TUNING THIS POWER-NEUTRALIZER FOR MONTHS.
IT WORKED ON THE MORLOCKS...AND NOW IT'S YOUR TURN TO HAVE A TASTE!
YOU'RE JUST LIKE EVERYONE ELSE NOW...
...AND SO ARE YOUR FRIENDS.
REMY! LOOK OUT-- UNH!
KRAK!
D'YOU THINK THAT MAKES US HELPLESS?
WOMAN, YOU HAVE SO MUCH TO LEARN!
SURPRISE, JERK!
I LEARNED TO FIGHT LONG BEFORE I EVER HAD POWERS.

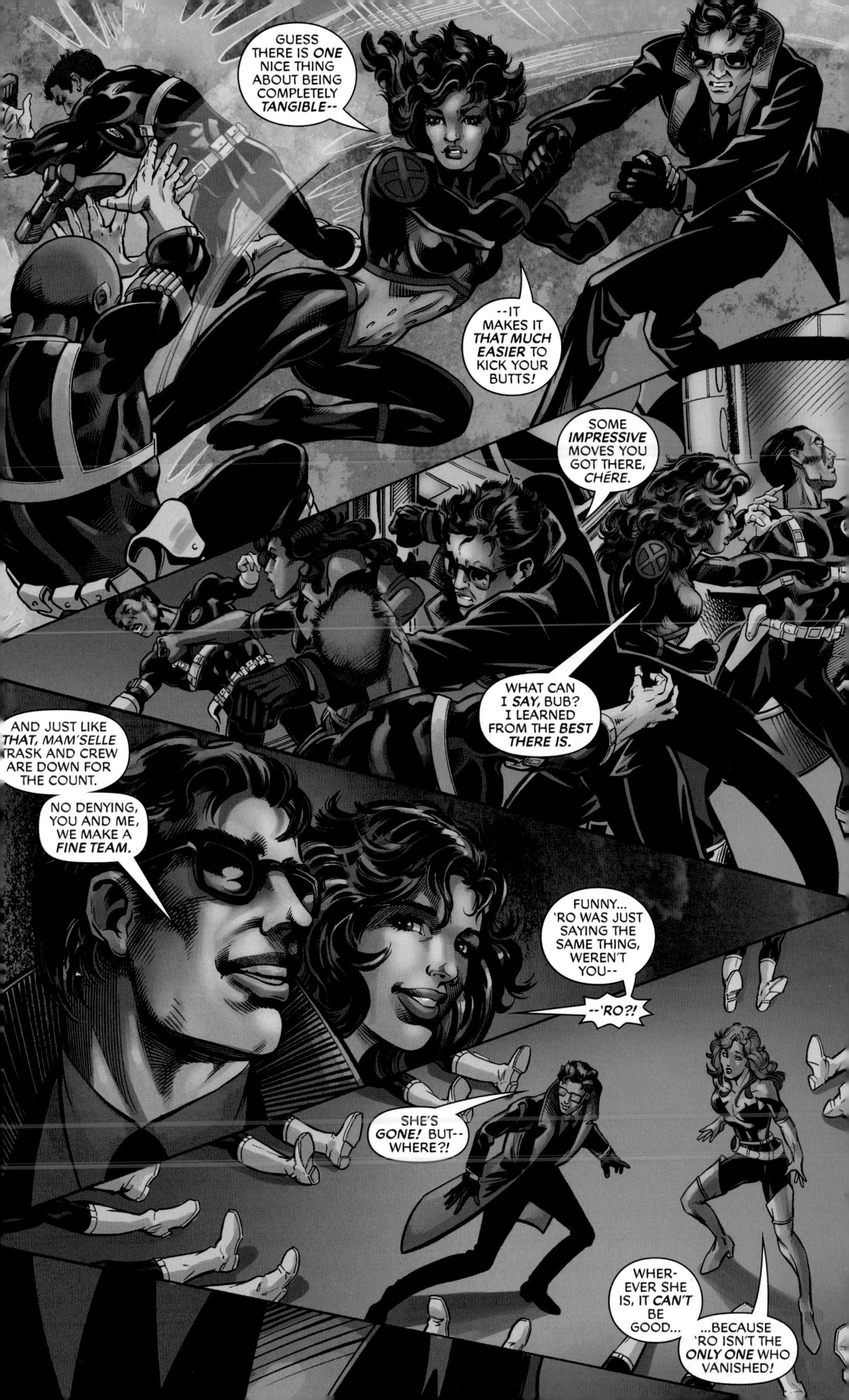
GUESS THERE IS ONE NICE THING ABOUT BEING COMPLETELY TANGIBLE--
--IT MAKES IT THAT MUCH EASIER TO KICK YOUR BUTTS!
SOME IMPRESSIVE MOVES YOU GOT THERE, CHÉRE.
WHAT CAN I SAY, BUB? I LEARNED FROM THE BEST THERE IS.
AND JUST LIKE THAT, MAM'SELLE TRASK AND CREW ARE DOWN FOR THE COUNT.
NO DENYING, YOU AND ME, WE MAKE A FINE TEAM.
FUNNY... 'RO WAS JUST SAYING THE SAME THING, WEREN'T YOU--
--'RO?!
SHE'S GONE! BUT-- WHERE?!
WHER-EVER SHE IS, IT CAN'T BE GOOD...
...BECAUSE 'RO ISN'T THE ONLY ONE WHO VANISHED!

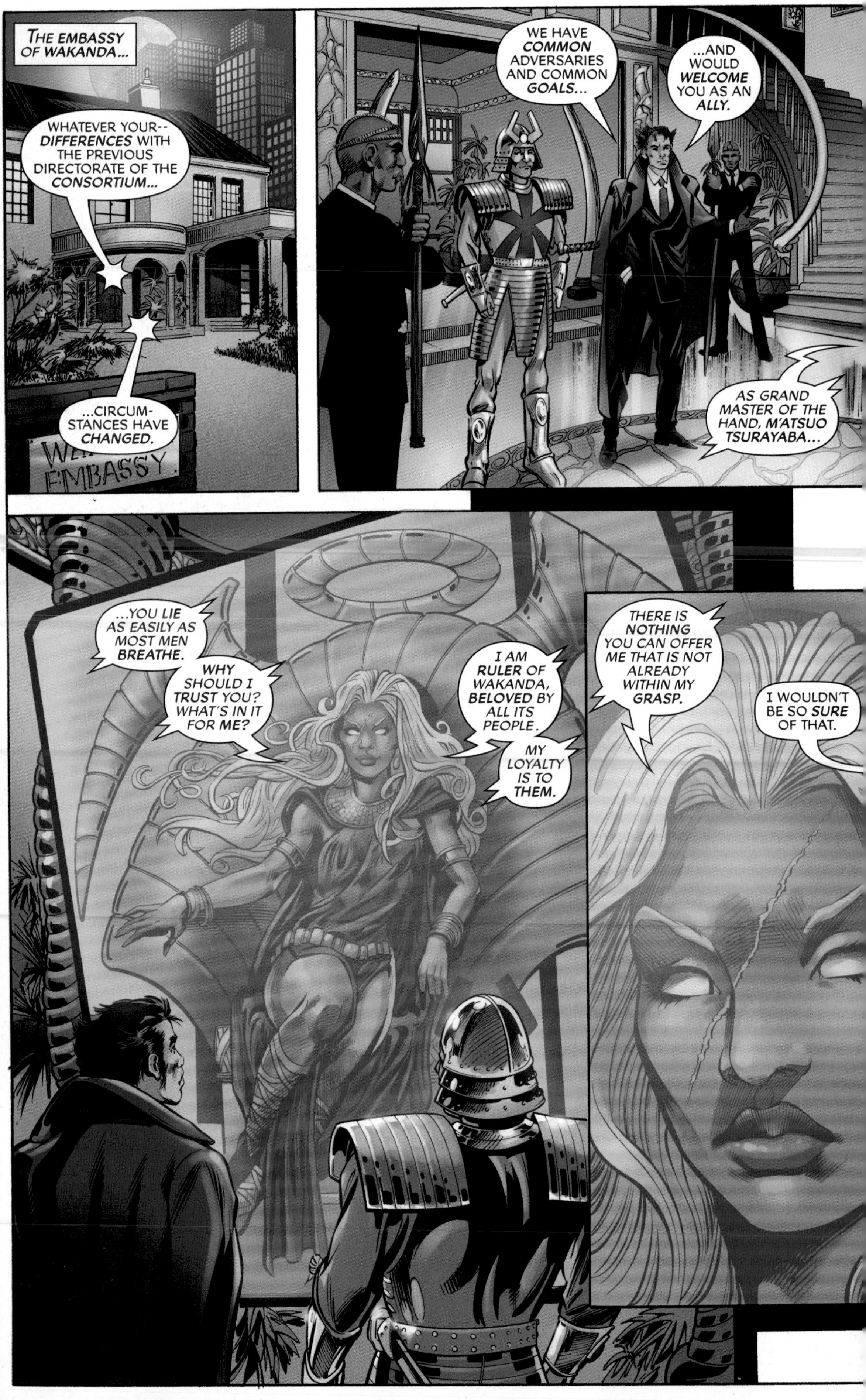
THE EMBASSY OF WAKANDA...
WHATEVER YOUR-- DIFFERENCES WITH THE PREVIOUS DIRECTORATE OF THE CONSORTIUM...
...CIRCUM-STANCES HAVE CHANGED.
EMBASSY
WE HAVE COMMON ADVERSARIES AND COMMON GOALS...
...AND WOULD WELCOME YOU AS AN ALLY.
AS GRAND MASTER OF THE HAND, M'ATSUO TSURAYABA...
...YOU LIE AS EASILY AS MOST MEN BREATHE.
WHY SHOULD I TRUST YOU? WHAT'S IN IT FOR ME?
I AM RULER OF WAKANDA, BELOVED BY ALL ITS PEOPLE.
MY LOYALTY IS TO THEM.
THERE IS NOTHING YOU CAN OFFER ME THAT IS NOT ALREADY WITHIN MY GRASP.
I WOULDN'T BE SO SURE OF THAT.

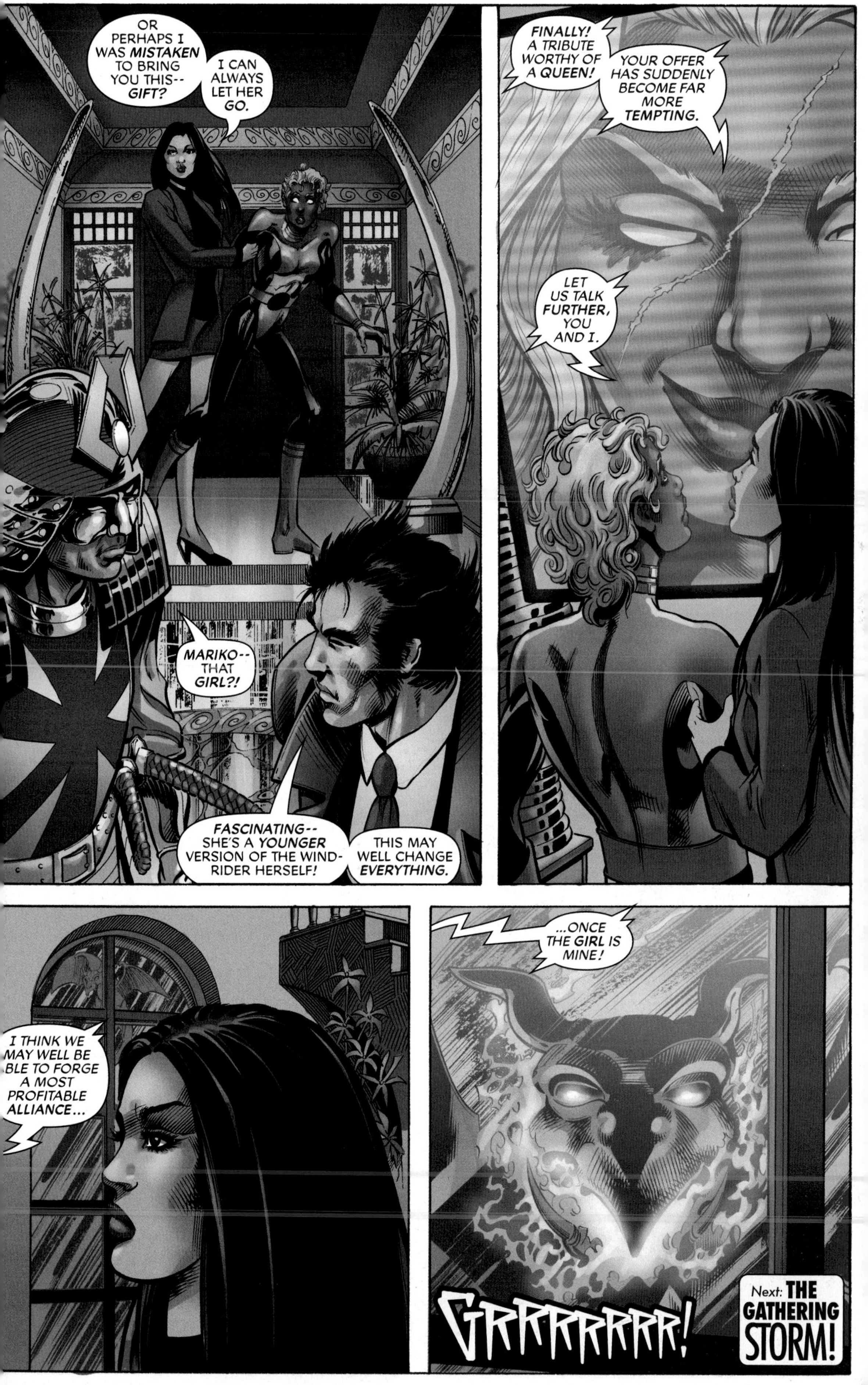
OR PERHAPS I WAS MISTAKEN TO BRING YOU THIS-- GIFT?
I CAN ALWAYS LET HER GO.
MARIKO-- THAT GIRL?!
FASCINATING-- SHE'S A YOUNGER VERSION OF THE WIND-RIDER HERSELF!
THIS MAY WELL CHANGE EVERYTHING.
FINALLY! A TRIBUTE WORTHY OF A QUEEN!
YOUR OFFER HAS SUDDENLY BECOME FAR MORE TEMPTING.
LET US TALK FURTHER, YOU AND I.
I THINK WE MAY WELL BE BLE TO FORGE A MOST PROFITABLE ALLIANCE...
...ONCE THE GIRL IS MINE!
GRRRRRRRR!
Next: THE GATHERING STORM!